A PLUME BOOK

THE ELDER WISDOM CIRCLE™
GUIDE FOR A MEANINGFUL LIFE

DOUG MECKELSON climbed the corporate ladder for seventeen years within the financial services industry. A lifelong affinity for senior citizens has also found Doug active in numerous nonprofit and volunteer activities to benefit seniors. He is on the board of a San Francisco senior housing complex and is active with Meals on Wheels. In 2001, he founded the Elder Wisdom Circle, of which he is president. Leaving corporate life in the summer of 2005, Doug now devotes all his energies to the ever-expanding Elder Wisdom Circle.

DIANE HAITHMAN is a veteran staff writer for the *Los Angeles Times*, covering the fine arts. She has served as Writer-in-Residence at the Annenberg School of Communication at the University of Southern California. Prior to joining the *Times* she was West Coast Bureau Chief and Hollywood columnist for the *Detroit Free Press*, based in Los Angeles. She has contributed to *ArtNEWS*, *Opera News*, and *AdWeek* magazines, as well as other publications.

THE ELDER WISDOM CIRCLE™
GUIDE

—— FOR A ——

MEANINGFUL LIFE

*Seniors Across America Offer
Advice to the Next Generations*

DOUG MECKELSON
AND DIANE HAITHMAN

A PLUME BOOK

PLUME
Published by Penguin Group
Penguin Group (USA) Inc., 375 Hudson Street, New York, New York 10014, U.S.A. • Penguin Group (Canada), 90 Eglinton Avenue East, Suite 700, Toronto, Ontario, Canada M4P 2Y3 (a division of Pearson Penguin Canada Inc.) • Penguin Books Ltd., 80 Strand, London WC2R ORL, England • Penguin Ireland, 25 St. Stephen's Green, Dublin 2, Ireland (a division of Penguin Books Ltd.) • Penguin Group (Australia), 250 Camberwell Road, Camberwell, Victoria 3124, Australia (a division of Pearson Australia Group Pty. Ltd.) • Penguin Books India Pvt. Ltd., 11 Community Centre, Panchsheel Park, New Delhi – 110 017, India • Penguin Group (NZ), 67 Apollo Drive, Rosedale, North Shore 0745, Auckland, New Zealand (a division of Pearson New Zealand Ltd.) • Penguin Books (South Africa) (Pty.) Ltd., 24 Sturdee Avenue, Rosebank, Johannesburg 2196, South Africa

Penguin Books Ltd., Registered Offices: 80 Strand, London WC2R ORL, England

First published by Plume, a member of Penguin Group (USA) Inc.

First Printing, November 2007
10 9 8 7 6 5 4 3 2 1

 REGISTERED TRADEMARK—MARCA REGISTRADA

LIBRARY OF CONGRESS CATALOGING-IN-PUBLICATION DATA
Meckelson, Doug.
  Elder wisdom circle guide for a meaningful life : seniors across America offer advice to the next generations / Doug Meckelson and Diane Haithman.
    p. cm. — (A plume book)
  ISBN 978-0-452-28881-2 (trade pbk.)
1. Intergenerational communication. 2. Wisdom. 3. Self-actualization (Psychology) I. Haithman, Diane. II. Title.
  HM726.M43 2007
  305.2—dc22   2007004567

Printed in the United States of America
Set in Goudy
Designed by Eve L. Kirch

CONTENTS

ACKNOWLEDGMENTS

We would like to thank the following Elders, Elder Groups, and Facilitators for contributing to this project:

Jean Barnard, Frances Bay, Barbara Bernstein, Susan Bistline, Helen Blanks, Donna Brown, Frank J. Brown, Jr., Paul and Barbara Brown, Judith Burkhardt, Linda Burrell, Nancy Carsten, Carol Chapman, Karin Johnson Cobb, Jeanine Dalzell, Bill Driedger, Jack Driedger, Pamela Erdmann, Pauline Everitt, Dena Nisenfeld Forster, Ursula T. Gibson, J insui Giehl, Melinda Goff, Lewis W. Goshorn, Peter Zilahy Ingerman, Linda Johnson, Sylvia Kirkwood, Jim Kowalczyk, Trish Mayyasi, Renee Mazon, Elizabeth McCommon, Tina McHugh, Mary McManemin, Letta Meinen, Danna Merritt, Sharon Morrison, Loren Morrison, Ellen Nemhauser, Karen Rothe Osband, Ethel Otchis, Lester Pazol, Mort Perlmutter, Mollie Pier, Tom Pontac, Karen Purves, Carl Richter, Barbara Flinker Ruttenberg, Dixie Sauvain, Kenneth Saylor, Lucille Smith, Anita R. Somers, Amory Sommaripa, Toni Stuessy, Victoria Thomason, Michelle Walsh, Patricia White, Jack Wilson, Patricia Wood, and Laura Woodruff.

Asbury Friends: Trish Mayyasi, Facilitator; Chelsea Elders: Kathryn Richards, Facilitator; Garden Villa Elders: Bennett Meier, Facilitator; Gold and Wise: Mary Ellen Quinlan, Facilitator; Heavensviewsages: Mark Deskin, Facilitator; Rockymountain Owls: Mark Deskin, Facilitator; WebWisdom: Ruth Widman, Facilitator; Wizeones: Renee Mazon, Facilitator; Your Grandparents: Vicki Vasconi, Facilitator.

The authors would like to extend a special acknowledgment to our insightful volunteer research assistant, Karen Haley of Woodstock, Georgia ("approximately twenty-five miles north of the Big Chicken," she says, offering no further explanation), for poring through thousands of letters to the Elder Wisdom Circle to help find the most universal and provocative questions, for connecting with Elders through personal interviews, and for providing unflagging energy and a finely tuned sense of humor throughout the research process.

We would also like to thank the following people at Plume: Trena Keating, former editor in chief of Plume, for having the vision to see a wonderful book in the Elder Wisdom Circle, and to Cherise Davis, the current editor in chief, for guiding the project to completion; our smart and savvy editor, Allison Dickens, for her compassionate recognition of the value of our Elders' words and her invaluable guidance in shaping that wisdom into compelling chapters; Abigail Powers in managing editorial; Marie Coolman and her able publicity staff; Eve Kirch in interior design; and Melissa Jacoby and Lucy Kim of the art department for making us look so good.

The authors also thank our agent, the boundlessly enthusiastic Jeff Kleinman of Folio Literary Management, for his dedication, perseverance, and belief in this project.

Doug Meckelson would like to thank his parents, Jerry and Mary Lynn Meckelson, for their encouragement and belief in this project, and his grandmother, Revay Meckelson, for the inspiration to create the Elder Wisdom Circle.

Diane Haithman would like to thank her husband, Alan Feldstein, for being there in every sense of the word, and her parents, Charlotte (1919–2003) and Charles Haithman (1918–2006), for being wiser than they ever knew.

The Elder Wisdom Circle would like to thank Google and Verizon corporations for their generous support of the EWC program. We would also like to thank S. Cameron and Mary Jo Ferguson for their financial contributions.

In addition to our Elders, the Elder Wisdom Circle would not be able to operate without a group of dedicated, hardworking volunteers. We would like to acknowledge just a few of them: Greta Boesel, Kendra Brewster, Elana Churchill, Dana Criss, Krishna Govindarajan, Dean Lipsitz, Ajay Ravindranathan, Robert Ross, and Lori Voth.

Several volunteer committees work within the EWC to accomplish numerous operational tasks and we would like to acknowledge their efforts: Content Review, Elder Buddies, Membership, and Quality Control.

Those interested in supporting the Elder Wisdom Circle may contact us at www.ElderWisdomCircle.org.

INTRODUCTION

The Circle Begins

It started with a letter.

"Dear Grandma . . ."

My paternal grandmother's real name was Blanche, but she hated the name, so everybody called her by her middle name, Revay.

Everyone around me viewed my affinity for "old people" as odd. Instead of being bored or annoyed by their stories, I marveled at their comfort with themselves, at the people they had become with the passing of time. I know, the phrase "pearls of wisdom" is a cliché, but that's what I found in what they had to say—real pearls.

Revay was a schoolteacher her entire working career—and, well, let's just say she kept on freelancing in her chosen field long after she retired. Grandma always corrected my manners, my grammar, and sometimes even my opinions, but for some reason I never minded. In fact, I looked forward to hearing what she had to say.

Grandma and I formed a strong bond early on and she became my number one ally in the world. In Grandma's eyes I could do anything I set my sights on—and, if given enough time, I could surely change the world. Looking back now I realize that she gave me total and unconditional love, the biggest gift anyone can give. My parents used to say that in Grandma's book, I gave Jesus a run for his money.

Grandma was deeply saddened by the loss of dignity so many adults experience as they age into their golden years. She also felt that American society treated our seniors with a lack of respect once they were unable to live independently. Grandma was not afraid of death or the actual aging process, but she was afraid of becoming "surplus" in the eyes of society.

Grandma would tell me that she was sure I had the ability to make a change in the way society viewed our seniors. To have Grandma place such confidence in me left a huge impression.

In May of my twenty-sixth year, Grandma was eighty-one. I was working in Walla Walla, Washington, about 150 miles from her home. I felt a very strong pull to sit down and put my appreciation for Grandma in writing. My letter spoke of the confidence she had helped build, the love I had for her and the fun times we had.

After the letter was written I could not find my address book, but felt a sense of urgency to mail the letter right then. My parents lived near her apartment, so I sent the letter to Grandma in care of them.

In a few days, the letter arrived. My dad tried several times to phone to tell her that they would be delivering a very special letter; mail from me was always a treat. But there was no answer. Finally, late that afternoon my parents decided to drive over to her house, since it was odd she had not answered the phone. She did not answer the doorbell, either, so they used their key to enter.

Clutching my letter in his hand, Dad found Grandma snug in her bed—very peaceful, but very dead; she simply went to sleep and never woke up. Grandma would never have to realize her greatest fear: to know what it was like to feel surplus in our society because she was old.

Later that night, my dad called with the news. He told me that my letter was what brought them to her. Even though she never got the chance to read it, I know that Grandma knew what was in that letter.

Of course, I wished I'd mailed that letter a day earlier. Sitting at my desk in front of my computer screen, I had to laugh through my tears: If Grandma had e-mail, she'd have gotten my letter in time. And, probably, corrected my grammar.

While I did not immediately act on Grandma's wishes that I influence society and its view of seniors, her words and our bond traveled with me.

By early 2001 I was feeling burned out and disillusioned. And to top it all off the unthinkable had happened—the stock market where I had stashed all my future hopes and dreams had suffered a monumental meltdown. While I never worked in Silicon Valley, I'd invested in the high tech industry, and, to put it simply, lost my shorts. Now my future plan was in serious question. But instead of giving up, I decided this was a great opportunity to step back and evaluate what was really important.

I switched to a part-time schedule at work and set about involving myself in nonprofit activities serving seniors. I noticed how many of the seniors felt disconnected from much of society. I also noticed how few opportunities existed for them to share their hard-earned knowledge and wisdom. When I asked an older person for his opinion or assistance, the gleam from his eye was almost blinding. In my mind the Elder Wisdom Circle was starting to take shape.

The Circle Grows

I knew that older people had a lot to offer, but I also realized that knowledge wasn't worth much unless I could figure out how to connect that wisdom with a younger generation.

Considering today's fragmented families, it seemed that most people under forty had been denied the ability to turn to a grandparent for advice and support, the way I had always turned to Grandma Revay. This is the "online" generation, and when its members need an answer to almost any question, they turn to the Web.

I was also beginning to realize through my volunteer work that a surprisingly large number of seniors were turning to computers to keep them connected to the world. Cyberspace was fast becoming a lifeline for those isolated by retirement, health problems, or widowhood. It just seemed to click: provide the means for younger folks to write a "letter to Grandma," seeking advice via the Internet.

I created the first Elder Wisdom Circle Web site in 2001, and put out the call for volunteer Elders through VolunteerMatch, a national online system linking volunteers with nonprofit organizations in their area. Within the first couple of months, we'd racked up a grand total of five members—two of whom, Elder Arianne and Elder Treefrog, are still active members, and you'll find some of their best advice in these pages.

It took a lot of effort for the idea to become reality. At first, we had advice to give—but no advice seekers. I devoted hours to posting information about the group to online message boards and chat rooms.

My efforts were met with skepticism; many wrote off the Elder Wisdom Circle as being one of two things: scam or spam. I even walked all over San Francisco putting up postcards explaining who we were and inviting advice seekers to use this innovative service. Finally, the media began to take notice, and the skeptics began to see that our desire to share wisdom wasn't a scam. It came from the heart.

We grew slowly; by 2003, we were answering about four hundred letters a month and had become a nonprofit association. Then a pivotal moment came for us in February 2006, when National Public Radio made the Elder Wisdom Circle the story of the day on its popular *Morning Edition* program.

Since then, the Elder Wisdom Circle has toured the country and the world, so to speak. Our group has been featured on all the major TV networks, as well as in national publications including *USA Today* and *Time* magazine. We've been on the radio as far away as New Zealand and Japan. We distribute an advice column to newspapers across the country.

We have become a vital organization with more than six hundred Elders across North America and even a few in the United Kingdom. We have answered more than 100,000 letters on subjects ranging from sex to foot odor to teenage angst; from nonflowering begonias to in-law hassles. Almost daily I receive warm notes of thanks from the Elders and advice seekers praising the Elder Wisdom Circle.

My very modest goal is for the EWC to become the largest provider of practical personalized advice in the world. As founder of the EWC, all of my proceeds from this book will be donated to support and expand the Elder Wisdom Circle. I hope that the people who are reading the Web site—or this book—will wish our Elders were their grandparents. In a way, they are.

It started with a letter to a grandmother. Now, we have thousands. I think Grandma would have liked that.

The Circle Becomes a Book

Along with burgeoning media interest came inquiries from the publishing world. We thought an Elder Wisdom Circle book was a terrific idea—but in order to make such an effort worthwhile, we knew we had to ask our Elders to provide something more than they were able to do through the Elder Wisdom Circle Web site.

Visitors to ElderWisdomCircle.org may request anonymous, personalized advice on any topic except those that call for a professional opinion: that is, medical, tax, investment, or legal advice. The service offers a reply to every request.

Once your letter is received, it will be answered as soon as possible, usually within a few days, by the most suitable "cyber-grandparent" available. Though most people are only looking for one opinion, the Web site offers a "get two opinions" option. If the advice seeker takes this action, two different Elders will offer their advice and the requester will receive two e-mails in response.

For this book, we changed the rules.

At the beginning of what would be a six-month project, we sent out a "cattle call" to the EWC members, asking for volunteers to help us with the book. We sent out another call about halfway through the process. We ended up with about sixty individual members and nine groups from across North America, all eager to offer their advice in another sort of forum.

With the invaluable assistance of our volunteer researcher, Karen Haley of Woodstock, Georgia, we selected about ninety of the most universal and provocative letters that the Elder Wisdom Circle has received. Every two weeks for eighteen weeks, the participating Elders received a new "assignment" of ten letters that would form the core of our nine theme chapters, loosely arranged around life's major phases, from childhood through maturity, love, and, finally, loss. We invited all Elders to respond to any and all letters that spoke to them.

For some, that might have been only a few; others diligently applied their wisdom to letter after letter, continually delighting us with their strong and often conflicting opinions. Either via e-mail or through personal interviews, the Elders also took us behind the screen—that is, the computer screen—to provide us with telling insight into the life experiences that led to their answers.

In order to maintain the same anonymity of the Web site, in this book we refer to the Elders only by their pen names. Unfortunately, we could not include all of their responses, but for each question in the book we hope we have chosen a representative sample of the wisdom we received on the topic. Both letters and responses have been edited for space and occasionally for grammatical clarity, but both the letters and the advice are real.

The Circle Speaks

Elder Fran, eighty-three, is the oldest member of Gold and Wise, a three-member Elder Wisdom Circle group that meets in a nursing home in Sussex County, New Jersey. Fran was a young telephone operator during World War II, toiling at the switchboard while her husband was overseas serving as a tank driver in the U.S. Army.

"The system is so different now than it was then; I loved it, I really did," Fran reminisces. "I was working the switchboard the day my husband called to tell me he was back in the United States. That was very exciting—since I was working, I could call his mother and let her know he was back in the States, and the same with my family." Fran adds that as a local telephone operator, she couldn't help but know everybody else's business. "There were a lot of party lines," she says with a laugh.

Today Fran is part of a different sort of "party line"—the Elder Wisdom Circle. And she loves connecting with a younger generation via the Internet just as much as she loved connecting people with their friends and family at the switchboard in the 1940s. Like the other members of the Elder Wisdom Circle, she and the other two women of Gold and Wise say that through offering advice to a younger generation, they receive much more than they give.

"We have enjoyed it very much, and finding out the advice is read all over the country is amazing," Gold and Wise tell us through the facilitator of their group, Mary Ellen Quinlan, who coordinates volunteer activities for their residence. "Most of all, reading the questions people asked has helped take our minds off our problems as we try to help others. Even though some questions seemed to only need common sense, perhaps our advice has touched someone in a positive way and brightened someone's day."

The Elders range in age from sixty to over one hundred; they hail from small towns, big cities, various geographic regions, economic strata, and all walks of life. As such, they represent a tapestry of what it is like to grow old in America at the turn of a new century. But whatever their individual circumstances, they are drawn to the Elder Wisdom Circle for the same reason: to help others.

Members of another Elder group, the Heavensviewsages of Delta, Colorado, have this to say about being part of the Circle: "At first, we thought we had nothing of value for the younger generations. But when we got involved, we realized that we do have something to offer. If we can create something positive from the pain we have been through, and pass that knowledge on to another and help them deal with their problem, we feel that something good may have come from our suffering," the group says. "We really struggle to try to guide the children as best we can, and we worry about them long after we send replies to their letters."

Through gathering together to consider their responses, say the Heavensviewsages, "we gain a deeper sense of community and involvement in our lives. We learn things about one another and get to know our neighbors on a deeper, more personal level, which makes us closer. We also gain a better understanding of our society and how it is changing."

Elder Mort, seventy-three, a psychology professor from Madison, Wisconsin, finds himself changing along with society. He joined the Elder Wisdom Circle because, after a lifetime in clinical psychology, he has begun to doubt its effectiveness. "I've reached a place where I'm not sure that therapy is everything it's cracked up to be—I think we've gone overboard, oversold it without meaning to," Mort muses. "Much of what we're getting is no replacement for the wisdom of people who have been there, done that. A lot of it is just life."

Elder Seeley, sixty-five, of Tucson, Arizona, is another vocal advocate of "plain old concrete common sense." "I joined the Elder Wisdom Circle because I have experienced much of what concerns the majority of our 'clients,' " she says. "I also have a very low tolerance for fools, blowhards, grandstanders, and those who pad their resumes. My husband encouraged me because, as he told me, 'You can cut through the bullshit faster than anyone I know.'

"I just hope that I have helped those whose requests I am privileged to answer to find hope, the will and the ability to solve whatever problem brings them to us," Seeley adds. "That is enough for me."

Another Elder Wisdom Circle member, Elder Treefrog, sixty-five, of West Bloomfield, Michigan, has come to see the Elder Wisdom Circle as a calling of sorts. "Long ago I studied very hard for eight years to be a priest; it was not to be," Treefrog says. "However, the desire to reach out and help others with life's challenges on a personal level has always been on my mind, in my heart, and in my spirit."

Continues Treefrog: "I have gained the satisfaction that comes with knowing that all the life experiences I've had need not be relegated to some storage box in the dusty basement of my brain. I think it must be difficult for those who have experienced sixty, seventy, eighty, ninety years of life and, although they still have their wits about them, have no practical way to share this accumulated wisdom and knowledge. This is a modern tragedy."

Like Treefrog, Elder Jacobus, eighty-one, of Saskatoon, Saskatchewan, likes the opportunity to rummage around in the storage boxes of his mind with the goal of finding something useful. "When you're older, you like to think back," he says. "I've had problems with in-laws, I've had kids, and I've had grandchildren, siblings, and all this kind of misunderstanding that there is in families. There is a wealth of stuff in my cranium somewhere; all you have to do is dig it out. Why not share it?"

Adds Jacobus: "My wife died in November of 1999—my first wife, of course—after forty-six years of marriage. And when she died I said, 'Now what are you going to do?'

"I made a vow that what I'm going to do for the rest of my life, and try awfully hard is, whomever I meet, whether it's a cashier or whoever it is, that person shall have a better day because I met that person. That keeps a guy pretty busy."

Elder Dr. Sam, seventy-six, a retired physician of Harrisburg, Pennsylvania, observes that individual life experiences tend to make Elders better at answering some types of questions than others. His forte: advice to the lovelorn. "I used my own experiences with a young person who was infatuated with another," Dr. Sam says. "I remember going all the way up from Virginia to Philadelphia to see a young lady, and she announced to me out of the blue that she had gotten engaged! I can understand the advice seeker who is heartbroken, and has had the bottom drop out of his world."

Elder JeanMc, seventy-nine, of Sterling Heights, Michigan, observes a crying need for that reassurance from a generation that seems to have lost touch with the Elders within their own families. "What I have gained is the knowledge that a lot of people are confused and need help," says JeanMc. "I was shocked to discover that so many of them are so young. Where are their parents? Why can't they turn to them instead of online adoptive grandparents?"

Like JeanMc, a few other Elders express some discomfort in trying to provide a human touch via a computer screen. "I know it has to be done by e-mail, but I consider e-mail the coldest, most impersonal form of communication there is," says Elder Web, sixty-four, of Farmington Hills, Michigan. "These days, people are getting fired by e-mail. I've fired a lot of people in my time, but you always look the person in the eye and tell them—that's the way I am. I guess that's the only thing I don't like about this."

But, adds Web, the means of communication ceases to matter at the moment you make that special connection. "My attitude is, hey, if it's only one person, then I've done something," Web says. "I'm not trying to sound corny; if you've touched one, you've made the world a better place."

And the experience of offering advice has changed Web as well. "One of the reasons I'm doing this is, I hope to be a better person, more empathetic, more open to people than I have been in the past," Web says. "I was a sergeant in the Marine Corps; that takes a certain type of personality. But let's say I've evolved over the years; I'm a much different person than I was twenty years ago, ten years ago."

Elder Kriko, seventy-five, of Tempe, Arizona, celebrates the Internet as a tool with the power to connect, rather than to distance, the generations. "If they'd had it when I was growing up, I'd have been on it!" he exclaims. He adds wryly, "And I can't imagine talking to my real grandparents. My grandma was okay, but my grandfather was a real jerk."

Elder Anita, seventy-four, a clinical social worker of Brewster, New York, says the warm online feedback she gets from advice seekers serves as proof that it's possible to hold someone's hand in cyberspace. "I find that getting feedback from the writers of the letters and from the staff of the Elder Wisdom Circle is like getting hugs from the people I worked with at the clinic and in my private practice for so many years," Anita says. "Amazing how you can feel a hug in an e-mail. It works for me!

"If I have helped anyone to feel empowered, to make a choice to improve their life, then the process is working," Anita says. "One writer told me that she was going to carry my letter in her wallet and look at it whenever she wanted a boost.

"That is all I need."

Grandma Revay couldn't have said it better. Elders—this book is yours.

—Doug Meckelson

THE ELDER WISDOM CIRCLE™
GUIDE FOR A MEANINGFUL LIFE

CHAPTER

1

OBSTACLE COURSE
Wisdom for Overcoming the Unfair

I just wanted to say to all these seniors: Thank you. My generation often throws their grandparents away. You folks know something my generation will never get to taste: faithfulness, real family, discipline, knowing what it feels like to help your neighbor just because it was the humane thing to do. I was raised by my grandparents and I would give anything for five more minutes!

My name is "Lizzie" and I'm twenty-five and I personally salute every one of you fine relics.

—From "Feedback & Kudos"
www.ElderWisdomCircle.org

Do, or do not. There is no "try."

—Yoda,
Star Wars: The Empire Strikes Back

Brace Yourself

I'm fourteen years old and I have to wear a back brace. I have to keep it on for twenty-two to twenty-three hours a day for about a year and a half. I have to wear baggy clothes to cover it, so no boys will like me. Now I found out my best friend, and pretty much my only friend, will be moving to a state far away. I just want a boyfriend and more friends but I'm not sure if this brace is going to let me do that easily. What should I do?

For Elder Marble Rye, the words jump off the page. "That's exactly how I feel about this wheelchair," she exclaims.

Marble Rye is an actress. Not "retired" actress—actress. She made her mark late in life by playing everybody's favorite crazy old lady on stage, in sitcoms, and on film. She is well known to today's kids for her role as Adam Sandler's grandmother in the 1996 movie *Happy Gilmore*; their parents know her as the grandmother of Henry Winkler's "The Fonz" on the 1974 to 1984 sitcom *Happy Days*. And she has achieved cult status with both generations from her role on *Seinfeld* as "The Marble Rye Lady," Mabel Choate, a cranky dowager from whom Jerry snatches a loaf of marble rye bread because Mabel has bought the last one in the bakery in the classic episode "The Rye."

But that was before November 2003, just before Thanksgiving, when Marble Rye was mowed down by a seventeen-year-old driver as she was crossing a busy street. She suffered head injuries, multiple broken bones, and lost her right leg below the knee.

Acting parts remain scarce for an eighty-eight-year-old sparrow with one leg and a wicked sense of humor. And it's not just the casting directors who seem to have forgotten her number. "I love to be with people, I'm extremely social, but they are not calling me now," Marble Rye says wistfully. "I feel exactly like that little girl."

For Marble Rye, of Studio City, California, the obstacle is as obvious as the little girl's back brace: a physical disability resulting from a young driver's carelessness. But many who bring their problems to the Elder Wisdom Circle face far less visible obstacles. Paralyzing shyness. Sexual dysfunction. Fear of intimacy. Guilt. Shame. Compulsive behavior. Addictions.

Considering the problems presented in these letters represents Marble Rye's first experience with the Elder Wisdom Circle. Besides being a relatively new member of the organization, Marble Rye is also one of a handful of Elders—outside of those in senior-residence groups—who participate through a facilitator. She doesn't know how to use a computer. "I'm so eighteenth century; I don't use modern things," she sighs apologetically—although, with minor exceptions such as one unfortunate collision with a visitor's child, and once running over a German shepherd's tail, she's as handy with the controls on her electronic chair as any thirteen-year-old is with Nintendo.

Though she is new to the advice-giving game, Marble Rye finds that she loves it. Perhaps, she thinks, it's because of her training as an actress—she has learned not to rely solely on the words in the script, but to look for the unspoken meaning behind the words; to read between the lines. As actors are famously—and rather annoyingly— known to say when preparing for a role: "What's my *motivation?*" Maybe she's a bit more tuned in than most people to what these letter writers are *really* trying to say.

And, like the rest of the Elders who chose to offer their help to these particular advice seekers, Marble Rye has discovered that in most cases, when the letter is about overcoming a personal obstacle, the problem presented is usually not really the problem at all.

Marble Rye's accident occurred less than a year after she lost her husband, who was her childhood sweetheart growing up in Dauphin, Manitoba, Canada. She insists that she knew she would marry him from the time she was nine years old. As she lay in a coma, friends wondered whether she'd ever recover from suffering two crushing blows in such a short time.

But Marble Rye surprised everyone by coming out of her coma with her determination intact. It wasn't long before she was fussing at the nurses to bring her mascara and lipstick, watching films on videotape in the hospital to fulfill her obligation as a voting member of the Academy of Motion Picture Arts and Sciences, and getting on the phone to her agent looking for roles. "I'm still an actress—I'm just an old one," she tartly told a reporter for the *Toronto Globe and Mail* in 2004. It was her passion to get back to acting despite her new handicap that kept her from giving up.

In her reply, Marble Rye encourages the young girl to find a similar passion to take her mind off the ugly corrective device. Marble Rye was about the same age as this girl when a favorite teacher put her in her first play and, she observes with a wry laugh, "damned me for the rest of my life." She remembers how she felt when she first stepped on the stage and all her early-teenage self-consciousness melted like the Manitoba snow. That happy time floods her mind when she answers the girl's letter.

> *Dear little girl,*
>
> *In high school in my small town, I was popular. I was class secretary and I did a lot—but at the back of my mind I always felt inadequate. My image of myself was far less than what other people thought of me. But when my teacher encouraged me to go on the stage, I did—and from there on, acting was all I cared about. Being an old woman now, I know that there are some things that I've got to offer that are particular to me.*
>
> *I'm not pushing you to be an actress, but what are you interested in? Do you like to draw, are you a good writer? Can you look at yourself and see what qualities you might have that would appeal to people? You are worried that your friend is moving away and you won't be able to meet other people—well, getting involved in a group activity is the natural way to do it.*

As a character actress who's played everything from kindly grandmas to "bitches and witches," Marble Rye also knows that putting on high heels, a scarlet scarf, a pair of spectacles, or a pointy black hat can entirely change the way she feels about herself. The same is true, she believes, of the teenager's clothes.

You have to wear baggy clothes—why not turn that around and see that baggy clothes can be very fashionable? It's all about how you play the part.

Although it is the man of the house who offers the advice, Elder Gpa of Rochester Hills, Michigan, eighty-five, now prefers to sign his letters "Gpa-and-Gma," because, as he puts it, "I find my wife's input—especially, but not always limited to, the fairer sex—is enormously helpful in achieving balance in our advice-giving." Gpa-and-Gma, to date the only married couple among the Elders who both serve as advice givers, celebrated their sixtieth wedding anniversary on September 1, 2006.

In advising this young member of the fairer sex, however, Gpa borrows from his own experience, not Gma's, in handling his own occasionally frustrating obstacle.

Er, could you repeat that, please?

My hearing is impaired and I have found that people can become quite annoyed with it. So I tell them jokingly: "The hearing in my right ear is that of a young man. My left ear is like an old fence post." Almost everyone cooperates willingly by speaking up, or positioning themselves on the side of the good ear.

For Gpa, honesty is the best policy, even if you have to say it twice.

Tell them why you have a brace and why you must wear baggy clothing for eighteen months. Use a little humor: "I should be ready to run in the marathon in the 2008 Summer Olympics."

Although he had recently celebrated his eightieth birthday when he answered this letter, Elder Jacobus of Saskatoon, Saskatchewan, Canada, now eighty-one and a retired high-school counselor, has no problem remembering what it was like to be fourteen, anxiously trying to view oneself through the eyes of the opposite sex.

Although I am a grandfather, I can remember what it was like to be a teenaged boy like it was yesterday. Would the fact that a fourteen-year-old girl was wearing a back brace keep me from wanting to get to know her?

I don't think it would have bothered me very much at all if she had her hair and face done up nicely, and if she had a nice smile. If she was friendly, I would probably already kind of like her before I noticed that she was wearing a back brace.

Then there is the matter of learning to say one or two words that make people feel at home talking to you. You could say something like, "Hi, how are you?" or "What a lousy windy day!" or anything else in a nice, friendly way.

Who knows, pretty soon the other person may start chatting with you. If he doesn't, don't worry about it. Try it with the next guy and so on until you get the hang of it.

I'm glad you wrote the Elder Wisdom Circle. We Elders are always here to "listen." May I take this opportunity to wish you all the best.

Elder Rose, sixty-four, a retired teacher from Calgary, Canada, knows from personal experience that the way for an impatient fourteen-year-old to accept her back brace is to remember that she is bracing herself for the future.

Dear young lady,

This June I will be watching my daughter walk toward her fiancé. I know I will have tears as I watch her walk erectly, easily, to meet her beloved. She has had to battle scoliosis: In eighth grade, at fourteen, she was told that her spine was crooked. Of course she didn't want the treatment. She hated being different. She cried many nights.

Please try to consider the positives. This is more than cosmetic. Without the brace you may end up crippled. No friend would want that for you.

What should you do? Stand up straight. Every day thank God that your spine is getting strong and beautiful. As for socializing? Be yourself. Look people in the eye. Smile. Remember that all the others your age are self-conscious about something.

Remember, this brace is external. You'll have it off by the end of high school. And that is exactly the time when you want to do more than hold hands.

A Thirty-One-Year-Old Jar of Apple Butter

LETTER: PACKRAT HERITAGE

I, like many packrats, was raised by Depression-era parents and grandparents. I have "save it, you might need it someday" deeply engrained in my psyche. I am now thirty-six, married, and in medical school. My family keeps everything and for them, I suppose, it is not a problem because they are where they are going to live for the rest of their lives.

For me and my husband, however, keeping all this "stuff" just means moving it! We will move again in three more years when I finish medical school. Then we will move again after residency. But my issue is really bigger than all the moves. I WANT to get rid of stuff . . . but the guilt holds me back. "What would my mother say if she knew I was getting rid of this?"

We do not (cannot) have children and so all of the things that I saved as a younger woman, thinking that I would someday give them to my children, will not happen. I suspect that the pain of the finality of getting rid of those things that I had such hopes for, also keeps me from getting rid of many things.

How do I get rid of the guilt I feel about getting rid of things? What things do I keep and what things do I get rid of? How much of the things that you got rid of in your life did you regret later? Thanks so much for listening to my ramblings and for your time to advise me.

This letter *does* ramble on, suggesting that the writer can't bear to part with unnecessary words any more than old clothes and broken toys. And this is the abridged version.

Detroit Elder Jangela, sixty-six, believes that there's a way to save objects of sentimental value without becoming the leader of the pack-rats—even though her thirty-plus-year-old jar of apple butter lends new meaning to the word *preserves*.

Before I dispense any words of wisdom, I will freely admit the following: My mother died in 1975. She loved apple butter and had a jar of it in her refrigerator. I have that jar in my refrigerator today. I have a coat she bought for me that I have not worn in twenty-five years and I have a bowl she had in her house. Except for pictures, I don't have anything else of hers. Everything else I have either given away or thrown away.

The words of wisdom would be, I think, that it is okay to save a few things. It is more than okay to throw away or give away the rest.

In a 102-bed nursing home in northwestern New Jersey, three resident women, aged seventy-four, seventy-six, and eighty-two, gather with a facilitator to answer questions for the Elder Wisdom Circle. They call themselves Gold and Wise. And if anyone knows how to get rid of stuff, it's these Golden Girls.

Dear Packrat Heritage,

We moved from a house into half a room in a nursing home. We have a small closet and a few shelves. We had to get rid of most of our things before coming here.

Find a niece or nephew with kids that can use the items you have been saving. Since you are in med school, see if the pediatric unit can use anything.

You need to stop thinking about holding on to things. It's difficult to go forward with all that stuff weighing you down. Remember, your parents and grandparents lived in a different world.

This letter also struck a chord with many of the Elders who had Depression-era parents, or lived through it themselves. There are plenty of "rats" in the Elder pack. One of those is Elder JeanMc, seventy-nine, of Sterling Heights, Michigan.

Since most of the stuff you're keeping means nothing to you and you have no children (unless you adopt) to pass it on to, my suggestion is you give your family a heads-up that you intend to rid yourself of this accumulation and invite them over to sort through it and take what they want. (You can word it much more diplomatically, I'm sure.)

Take pictures if you want. Perhaps your mother would be pleased. But don't waste too much time on it. Now, can you tell me how to unburden myself? Happy unpacking.

Another senior residence group, the Rockymountain Owls of Montrose, Colorado, whose ages range from late sixties to early nineties, offers an idea that might help the writer both clean out her closets as well as provide a constructive channel for her admitted sorrow over being unable to bear children.

Children's things may be greatly appreciated at a children's hospital where they can be used to comfort a frightened and hurting child.

Memories are really in your heart and not in your boxes. The photograph and scrapbook idea would allow you to hold those memories close to your heart, and you would have what is important. Just take your time and follow your heart.

Worried that your crowded closets are a sign of deep-rooted neurosis? Listen to Professor Packrat: Elder Mort, seventy-three, a psychologist and professor emeritus of the University of Wisconsin at Madison.

I'm one of those "save it you might need it" folks; we were as poor as everyone around us and sometimes I act as if I never grew up. I'm not so sure it's about feeling that we might need the stuff as being anxious about giving up a part of ourselves. I still have all my class notes from 1960 to 1964.

Don't pathologize! You're not nuts. More people than you know hoard stuff simply because we are attached to our stuff and attachments are not easily broken. No matter what you do you're going to feel bad and good—guilty and sad for having gotten rid of "really important" stuff that, as both you and I know, you'll never need for the rest of your life.

It's time to leave home. I'll bet that hanging on to that stuff the way your folks do is a way of feeling like you're still part of the family. I'll also bet that when you visit them, you think you're "going home." Well, you're not. Home is where you and your husband live. Mom and Dad live in their home and you merely go to visit.

Feel bad about that? You should. Feel good about that? You should. "I wanted the author to know that her feelings and behavior are not necessarily 'sick' and that therapy is therefore not the best, or even the only, answer to her dilemma," Mort says. "Because I am a therapist, I am aware of what therapy can and cannot do."

Do any of the Elders regret giving up the things they've stopped packing away? Only one: Elder Imelda-Rose, seventy-four, a former "play advocate," therapist, and artist of Edmonds, Washington, said in her reply to "Dear Concerned Packrat" that the only thing she later regretted giving up was "a coat that I had made; everything else is unremembered."

When asked about the coat, Imelda-Rose recalled: "I was in my thirties and had used a coat of my grandmother's that was made of black plush; I redesigned it and lined it with a leopard plush lining. I gave it away when I moved to California from the Midwest. There was a time when I would have worn it again if I still had it."

But, Imelda-Rose admits, "It was just something I remembered when I was answering the letter the other day. I haven't thought about it for years."

Bad Timing

LETTER: PROBLEMS IN THE BEDROOM

I don't know if anyone will be able to help me out on this one, but I have a severe premature ejaculation problem. I have tried many things, medicine, thought concentration, masturbation, and such, but whenever I am with a girl, it's over before it has begun.

What makes matters even worse is that I am only twenty years old, so I should have some more vigor, right? I have confidence, charisma, and intelligence. I cannot see any psychological reasoning behind my problem; all I know is that I am becoming increasingly annoyed and actually starting to dislike sex because of it. Any suggestions?

This question drew a polite lack of response from the Elders—that is, except for spunky Elder Helen, sixty-eight, of Sierra Vista, Arizona. She writes:

Premature ejaculation (PE) is common in men younger than forty.

You may reach climax after eight minutes, but this is not premature ejaculation if your partner regularly climaxes in five minutes and you're both satisfied. Another guy might delay his ejaculation for twenty minutes, yet he may consider this premature if his partner, even with foreplay, requires thirty-five minutes of stimulation.

Premature ejaculation has historically been considered a psychological disorder. One theory is males are conditioned by societal pressures to climax in a short time because of fear of discovery when masturbating as teenagers, or during early sexual experiences in the back seat of a car or with a prostitute.

Some men don't discuss it with their doctors because they're embarrassed or feel that no treatment is available. You should consider seeing a doctor who will explore your sexual history, your general medical history, and screen for other medical conditions. This is what I suggest.

From her answer, it would appear that Helen has done her research. She has. "I responded this way because I had this kind of discussion with my grandson," she explains.

But isn't this the kind of discussion a boy usually has with his father? "My son-in-law was killed in a hit-and-run accident when my grandson was a year old," says Helen. "My grandson has only recently met any of his male relatives and they do not live near him. We have always been able to discuss any subject and I guess at the time we had this discussion, he did not feel comfortable speaking to his mother about it. I didn't question him about why he didn't talk to his mother. I just gave him the information I thought he needed to have."

Making Sense of Touch

LETTER: FEAR OF TOUCH?

Hello. I'm a sixteen-year-old female and I struggle with a sort of odd issue. I guess this might sound weird, but I feel entirely strange about people touching me. It doesn't really matter who it is, friends, adults, relatives, anyone.

Today in gym, my teacher walked over to where I was standing and went to put her arm around me to ask me a question, and I literally jumped like three feet back. She gave me the oddest look, and I just acted like I wanted to play basketball and ran the other way.

Maybe it's because no one in my family touches each other. Well, my father tries to touch me, but I haven't let him in a long time. I have a really bad relationship with my father, he's always been verbally abusive, and used to beat my brothers up for bad grades, though he hasn't hit *me* in a really long time.

The strange thing is, I want to be touched. I fall asleep every night clinging to one stuffed animal or another (it's a juvenile habit I've yet to break).

I want to enjoy being around people. I want to be able to sit close to someone without moving away. I want to be able to hug my friends when they're crying, but I don't know how to do it. Is this something I can control, or improve if I'm willing to work at it?

Sorry if this is confusing. It's something I've been carrying around in my mind forever and I need some input. I don't know who else to ask.

Collectively, the Elders who chose to reply to this letter seemed to agree that even the hint of mental and physical abuse on the part of the father suggested the teenager should seek out professional help.

Elder Sylvia, seventy-three, a retired teacher who lives in Hillsboro, Oregon, was among those to recognize that the sixteen-year-old has most likely suffered from child abuse and is headed for future problems without proper counseling. As a former teacher, she urges the girl to use the resources provided by her school.

I'm really glad you have written for advice. Your fear of touch is not the normal thing for anyone, but particularly for a young woman your age who is obviously intelligent and sensitive. Ignoring it will only worsen the problem as you get older and you might well be tempted to try to get past it in ways that would only be to your detriment.

In spite of being a former teacher, I am not a professional counselor and don't want to counsel you beyond urging you to, please, try to see a counselor at your school or see if they can recommend [someone to] you. You sound like such a lovely young woman who deserves not only an abundance of love and hugs and understanding, but also the ability to enjoy them. Don't be afraid to reach out for help. You've gone this far, now take one more step or as many as it takes, but one at a time.

While members of the Circle preferred to defer to the professionals on the issue of child abuse, they were, however, more willing to offer their hints on the less complicated business of learning how to hug.

Although she was not a victim of child abuse, Elder Michelle, sixty-four, a retired high-school counselor from Portland, Oregon, says that she, too, grew up in a family of non-touchers, always yearning for an embrace. Writes Michelle:

The only person in your family who tries to touch you is also the one who disrespects you and abuses you emotionally and has hit you. No wonder you have developed a protective cover. As a child, you needed to protect yourself to keep yourself from giving in to the comfort of touch that could turn instantly to pain.

Now, you need to teach yourself that there are touches that are good and even healing. You have to teach yourself that you can tell the difference.

You are so astute to realize that you have been conditioned to avoid affectionate contact. That means you can recondition yourself to feel comfortable with a quick touch on a friend's arm or eventually a hug. If you know any little kids, try hugging them or tapping them on the arm or holding their hands. Kids are usually great huggers.

Practice on them. And practice on yourself. Yup. Hug yourself. Just put your arms around yourself and give yourself a great big hug. When you wake up, do the same thing. You deserve that hug. You deserve all the good hugs waiting for you. You are on your way.

Elder Dixie, seventy-one, of Pittsburg, California, has been an insurance agent for thirty years. As she does for her clients, she wants to make the sixteen-year-old feel safe. "After reading this girl's letter, I realized that I had grown up in such a household—no touching," she recalls. "I wish I had had someone to encourage me."

You say you were raised in a household where there was no touching. I was, too. How sad for us. We missed out on a lot, and my father was abusive, too.

I eventually learned to reach out to people. I learned to touch them and hug them. It's the best feeling in the world.

Can you start by offering your hand to shake when you are introduced to someone? Some people like to be touched by family, but not by strangers, so watch out for that.

I guess this all comes down to reaching out; this confronts your fear, doesn't it? You know, most of us have fears of some kind, whether it's spiders or ghosts or fear of the dark. But at some time we must confront those fears and we find that it really wasn't all that scary.

So take that first step. Start by touching your friend. High fives or something like that. You'll like it.

Write us again anytime. We're here for you.

And the Elders agree, it's okay to hold on to that teddy bear. Just ask Elder Shekina of Springfield, Illinois:

By the way, you don't have to give up sleeping with a stuffed animal. I'm sixty-two and I still have one!☺

—◄○►—

The Perfect Mother

LETTER: GUILT ABOUT DISABILITY

I am thirty-eight and found out I have multiple sclerosis about eight years ago. I cannot get over feeling guilty about having it, like there was something I did to deserve to be sick. I dread becoming more of a burden than I already am on my family and, now, my new husband of just over a year and my baby that will be here in just three months. I even feel guilty about wanting a baby and getting pregnant when I am not 100 percent whole. I worry a lot about failing my baby by not being able to take care of her properly. I know there are those worse off than me, but somehow that just doesn't make it better. Is there a way for me to get over feeling guilty . . . as though I have failed by getting this disease?

The writer is a member of Generation X—a group, it often seems, that feels entitled to perfection: perfect teeth, perfect SAT scores, perfect job, perfect cell phone reception. But if there's one thing the Elders have learned through years of experience, it's that there's no such thing as a perfect parent. Just ask their children.

Elder Scribe, seventy-one, of Seal Beach, California, a former commercial salesman who now works as a community liaison for California State University, Long Beach, has two adult children, two grandsons under the age of ten, and another grandchild on the way. He tells a worried mother-to-be not to sell herself short.

In college, we learned that the politically correct term to use for "people with disabilities" was PWDs. Curiously enough, those of us without (visible) disabilities were referred to as TABS, which stood for "temporarily able-bodied." Any or all of us TABS could become PWDs in the blink of an eye through accident, illness, or unforeseen circumstance.

Right now, you are 100 percent "whole," just not 100 percent "perfect," whatever that may be. You're obviously perfect enough for your husband to love you and I can guarantee you that your new baby will love you absolutely and completely. Why not accept their love,

and love yourself as well? You sound "perfect" enough for me. So con-
gratulations and enjoy life without guilt, mommy.

Writes Elder Michelle:

Of course you don't want to be a burden, any more than your baby
would want to be a burden. But then he or she will also be a blessing,
won't she?
   That baby will wake you in the night and you may grumble, but
you will not want it any other way. Then you will know what a bless-
ing it is for those who love you to be able to love you.

Should a young woman with MS have a child if she wants one?
Marble Rye had a very short answer. In a word: *Yes.*
   Because Marble Rye misses her own son so very, very much.
   The auto accident that cost her her leg is not the only tragedy in
her life. "I had a child and I lost him—not a baby, he was twenty-three
years old," she says of her only son, a suicide. "I talk to other people and
they say, 'Oh, my son is coming around' and I get *so jealous*," she says,
her voice dropping to a whisper. "I feel so inadequate.
   "I'm going to be sloppy on this—if she is going to give that child,
with however little time she has, a lot of love, that can't be a threat to
that child," Marble Rye says firmly, her eyes full of tears but her voice
regaining its usual strength. "If she wants a baby, and apparently she
does, she should have one."
   Elder Barbara, sixty-two, of rural Greene, New York, was always
sure that she would die before her husband. "My first husband was such
a healthy person, he used to call himself the man of iron, and I was not
a healthy person," she recalls. Instead, he succumbed to a rare form of
cancer at age forty-one, leaving Barbara, then thirty-eight, to raise
their two sons on her own.

After my first husband died, I blamed myself; I was sure that if I had
just done something different, I would have been able to save him.
That was factually incorrect, but I wasted years believing it. The
world is less scary if we can blame someone, even ourselves.
   It is really too bad that you have MS. Rotten luck. You have my
sympathy; why don't you have your own? Are you afraid that if you

orry for yourself you will just dissolve into a lump and cry? Or *that* feeling sorry for yourself is self-indulgent? You may be feeling guilty because that is more comfortable for you than feeling sorry for yourself. You want to have a child, are full of love; there is no reason for you to feel guilty about those emotions.

Raising children is a hard job and your family's life may be more difficult because of your health issues. But now I know that the single most important thing a parent can do for a child is to encourage the child to be his or her own person. My children had to help cook and clean because their father died when they were in elementary school and I needed to work full time to support our family. I felt really bad about that, but it turned out it gave them self-confidence.

One final piece of advice, this time from the perspective of a care-giver: I suggest you and your husband talk openly about your illness. You are feeling guilty about being a burden on him, but he may be having some powerful feelings of grief or guilt or worry, too.

I have a cousin who has MS, and she and her partner share in her care. When it is a good day, they enjoy themselves immensely. When it is a bad day, they work together to make their life as easy as possible.

Food Fight

LETTER: WILL I EVER SUCCEED?

I weigh two hundred pounds and I have tried every diet and even eating balanced meals and exercise and have lost and gained back again and again. I can't keep up with any diet for very long.

I feel like giving up. I feel like I need someone to monitor my every move. I would like to lose weight and quit smoking and be an overall healthy person again but I just don't know how to do it on my own.

Do you have any advice for me?

This was another question that spoke directly to Barbara.

Barbara's life is happy now. She remarried in 2000 and she and her new husband fled Manhattan for the country, where, after working as a computer software writer most of her life, she has developed a second career as a glass artist. She got through the depression that accompanied losing her first husband. But she still struggles with the fat.

The only thing that makes people slim (aside from lucky genes) is eating well and getting plenty of exercise. But when I'd try to diet, there seemed to be some part of me that was always messing up.

So I set about trying to find that part of me, and it turned out to be a little child that didn't want to grow up. That child demanded the comfort of food, food like ice cream and lollipops.

The bottom line is how you feel about yourself. I have a sister who is good at punishing herself; when she gets fat, she goes on a starvation diet and it works. For me, the only time I can lose weight is when I feel good about myself. So my advice is to forgive yourself for gaining weight and stay conscious. If you see yourself starting to eat something, check to see if you are hungry, and if the food that you've chosen will help with that hunger.

More Vice Advice

LETTER: ADDICTION

I am a forty-three-year-old male with a healthy family of a wife and three children ages four to nine. I am what some call a functional addict.

I have been abusing substances since I was very young (marijuana and alcohol since my early teens, food before that). I have participated in therapy, A.A., journaling, and many attempts at self-governance. Whenever I successfully address one addictive pattern (e.g., I quit drinking alcohol) I soon abuse another substance or behavior. I alternately use marijuana, alcohol, food, and pornography.

I have occasionally abused pain medication, though only when it was legitimately prescribed. I know I have unresolved anger over some things in my childhood (untreated chronic bedwetting into my late teens, divorced parents—alcoholic mother and emotionally absent father).

My understanding of these things has not led or enabled me to move past them with several years of therapy. I appreciate any advice you can offer. Thank you.

When she read this letter, Elder Walk-On, seventy-two, a retired teacher and retired medical office administrator who lives in Bethesda, Maryland, just couldn't walk on without offering a helping hand. She is a food addict. Her adopted daughter has abused alcohol and drugs. This young father might well have been a member of her family.

Thank you for presenting this very challenging issue to the Elder Wisdom Circle. We are not professionals, but try to answer requests for advice by sharing our experience, strength, and hope.

Your request caught my attention because I am a compulsive overeater and have been working in a 12-Step program for three and a half years. I also have an adopted daughter who is an alcoholic and drug addict, in and out of recovery. I have been working in another 12-Step program to deal with my issues surrounding her addiction. I have been able to achieve emotional sobriety and go on with my life whether my daughter is in recovery or not.

It is quite common for addicts who become clean and/or sober from one substance to begin abusing another. Many people I have met in my program have come after years of sobriety because they are not ready to deal with food addiction.

I learn from your letter that you have explored many avenues for recovery from your addiction, but something struck me in your account. I did not get the impression you had worked the A.A. program. To me, participation in A.A. and working the program are two distinct practices. I wonder if you had a sponsor, how many meetings you attended each week. It takes most addicts at least three years to achieve sobriety with any hope of maintaining it. Then, they have to continue working the program every day for the rest of their lives.

Addiction is a family disease. The 12-Step programs understand this. There is help for the addict, and there is help for the family of the addict. I wish you success in dealing with this crippling disease.

A Message in a Balloon

LETTER: HOW TO OVERCOME INFERIORITY

Hello. I hope you are doing well. My name is "Mary Lou" and I am twenty-six years old. My problem is I am a very shy person. I do not seem to have the ability to make friends.

After losing my job, I have taken to holing myself up at home. I never go out, and the few times I venture outside, I am afraid to look at people in the eye, I do not like to ask for anything in stores and/or over the telephone. I am not assertive at all, my eleven-year-old sister, who is actually taller than me, walks all over me.

I feel dead inside. I feel for people, I am just afraid to touch people and to be vulnerable in front of others. Please please help me. I am not happy this way. I really really want to change. Thank you.

I have even gone so far as to release a balloon with my address on it, just so someone will write to me.

—Sad and Lonely in Arizona

The balloon probably never made it to the Arizona border—but this letter went straight to the hearts of the three wise women in a nursing home in New Jersey.

Dear Sad and Lonely in Arizona,

You must realize two things: First, it doesn't show that you feel inferior. Others cannot tell how you feel by looking at you. The other thing to keep in mind is that everyone has feelings of inferiority at times. Letting those feelings consume you is the problem.

If you want to build confidence, you cannot wait for others to hand it to you. Do special things for yourself such as buying something special or looking up an old friend to talk to. Tell yourself you are doing this because you deserve it and are special.

Force yourself to do things you are not comfortable doing. Find a job. Join a club or church. Volunteer at a library. Get out of the house and away from your family. Measure yourself by your own terms and not your family's.

Remember, you are special. You need to be around people who recognize this. We suggest professional counseling.

—Gold and Wise

Except for that question about erectile dysfunction ("that's really not for me to say; he should go to whatever kind of doctors men go to"), Marble Rye found herself answering every question in this chapter, filling hours of late-night insomnia poring over the letters, jotting down pages of notes in defiance of the arthritis in her fingers before sitting down to compose a reply.

Since her accident, Marble Rye has had a little trouble with her hearing, but her memory is pretty sharp. Still, more often than a few years ago, the word she's grasping for seems to wander off just out of reach—kind of like the telephone on the end table by her living room sofa, which always seems to end up just an inch or two farther away than her fingertips can stretch. It just sits there, ringing.

Though her short-term memory has acquired a slightly duller edge, thinking about these questions brought her own youthful insecurities back into clear focus. Through those memories, it became easy for Marble Rye to figure out that in every case, the important element was how the writers felt about themselves.

In many life situations, Marble Rye recalls, it didn't take a wheelchair for her to feel self-conscious and awkward. "It seems that the whole feeling about these letters is a lack of . . . what's the word, *self-esteem*," Marble Rye says. "The letter about the back brace sets the tone for many of them, basically. Where they're hurting is in self-image.

"I probably shouldn't be admitting this, but it's true; I identify with that completely," she adds. "I've always wondered about this—is it the reverse, is it extreme egotism that makes me feel like I'm inadequate?

"One of the letters was about being terribly shy; I've discovered through the years that I'm tongue-tied around people that I would like to be attractive to, sometimes people who are more prominent in the theater than I am," she adds. "I met Hume Cronyn and Jessica Tandy doing a film, and I didn't know what to say to them. And with another prominent actress, I said, 'I don't know what to say to you.' And she said, 'How about hello?' "

In writing back to the little girl with the back brace, Marble Rye considered ending the letter with "break a leg," the phrase stage actors use to mean "good luck" because saying "good luck" means *bad* luck—but figures this fourteen-year-old must be too young to be familiar with that dusty old theater expression. But as she thinks about the irony in a one-legged actress saying "break a leg," she realizes she has answered the girl's letter without once mentioning her wheelchair.

PARENTAL GUIDANCE SUGGESTED

Wisdom for Parents and Children

Oh my God! You elders are angels. Many times I would need advice and didn't have anyone to turn to, although I have my parents but I can't talk to them because they don't understand. . . . The fact that you are here to listen makes me feel like I'm not alone. Keep up the good advice because you are truly making a difference! Thank you from the bottom of my heart. . . .

—From "Feedback & Kudos"
www.ElderWisdomCircle.org

Having children makes you no more a parent than having a piano makes you a pianist.

—Michael Levine, composer

One of "Those Kids"

Hi, I am a mom of seven. I know that is a bit unusual these days, so I often do not have moms my age to turn to that have as many children as I do.

Six of my children are very well behaved, well bonded to my husband and myself and to each other. They always seem to be going together in the same direction as we are. They are a joy to us most of the time with few problems.

The seventh child age six (he is a twin) has been the opposite since he was a baby. I think he is becoming our "black sheep." He is forever in trouble and very difficult to love. I feel awful that I do not feel very bonded to this child and I am afraid of what he will grow up to be. He has never been cuddly and resists our attempts to hug him or cuddle him. He does well at school most of the time. He eats well and sleeps most of the night.

I am looking for help in bonding with him more, helping him to go along with the others during family activities (he throws a tantrum every time things don't go his way) and I hope to keep him from a life of being a misfit.

Thank you for your help.

Nowhere are generational differences more obvious than when it comes to raising children.

These days, a child like this one probably would be whisked immediately to a psychologist or psychiatrist and diagnosed with a clinical problem: Attention Deficit Disorder (ADD), Attention Deficit Hyperactivity Disorder (ADHD), Oppositional Defiant Disorder (ODD), Obsessive-Compulsive Disorder (OCD), or some combination of the above.

In fact, quite a few of the Elders in their sixties who answered this letter—including Elder Rose, sixty-four, a retired teacher of Calgary, Canada—tried to steer the mother toward a professional evaluation of her son's behavior. So did seventy-year-old Elder Grammypam, of Hancock, New Hampshire—although this former psychotherapist also offers this common sense observation: "If you are the youngest of seven, how do you get any special attention *without* 'pitching a fit'?!"

But Rose and Grammypam are years younger than Elder Heart of Texas, eighty-one, who raised her five children in several different Iowa communities during an era when the closest most frustrated parents got to a professional diagnosis was the neighbor who clucked, "Boys will be boys."

"We never heard of Attention Deficit Disorder, or autism either," Heart of Texas recalls. "We just knew that he was hyperactive and we tried to channel his interests. He never tried to hurt himself, but it happened sometimes because of his curiosity," she says. "Like when he wanted to see what was in a can he found and dropped a match into it and it exploded. It singed off the front of his hair, eyebrows, and lashes—but no burns. These were the kinds of incidents he got into."

In her letter, she tells the story of her energetic boy, growing up in the 1950s:

Our second child, a boy, demanded attention even as a baby. Our first born was a girl and was even tempered, so this was something new. He came out kicking and screaming and never let up. He did everything fast, ate fast, crawled fast, walked fast, and climbed on everything. We knew he would need lots of attention, so we tried to focus his energy on things to keep him occupied. This included games, sports like swimming, golf, Little League baseball.

Our other four children were more easy-going and easy to discipline, but each personality was different. I learned early to find something each of them were good at and help develop those traits.

I did learn as he progressed through school that he was a hard worker, bright, got along with others, excelled in sports, and made the honor roll. We were very pleased that he adjusted to his personal nature, finished college, and now has a successful career. He is a workaholic and still goes full speed but has a lovely wife who understands him and they have a great family. Don't be afraid of an active child, they may be hard to cuddle and live with but they have much to give this world.

You don't need to bond the same with each child; you can show your love in so many other ways. You sound like a very concerned mother and I wish you the best. This child will not be a "misfit" or a "black sheep" but a mover and shaker, so guide him well.

Heart of Texas declares that she would use the same approach if she were raising her son today. "I must tell you about my daughter's son while he was in elementary school in the 1980s," she says. "They thought he had ADD and he was on Ritalin for many years. I really was not in favor of this, but that's what the school suggested. The Ritalin just slowed him down so much that he gave up. I am not in favor of drugs to calm down students just to make them easier for the teachers to handle. Hyperactive children have much to give to this world— they are creative, hard working, and many times are bored with school as it moves too slowly for them."

Rose, however, does not believe that common sense alone would have helped her troubled son.

Hi Valiant Mother,

I too had an "odd child out." I thought of him as my little bird with a broken wing. He was so bright, so funny, so quick, and so exasperating. What was wrong with me that my son refused to cuddle, couldn't be soothed? Why couldn't I teach him how to get along? He scared me. I had so many trips to the emergency room that I was investigated by child family services. Imagine my relief when they told me that he was "one of those kids." Imagine my confusion when that's ALL they told me!

"Those kids." What "kids"? What was wrong with my baby? And so I started my trek from doctor to pediatrician to child behavioral specialist.

People told me to relax. He'd grow out of it. He was "just a boy." I was offered Valium by one doctor. Another told me that I didn't like boys. I heard "You're a bad mother" in so many subtle ways.

I'm describing how I saw the symptoms of ADHD as my son grew up in the 1970s. I do hope that thirty years later, teachers and pediatricians now are so educated about this that you have already considered this diagnosis. If not, I suggest you look at this. Attention Deficit Disorder (with or without Hyperactivity) is a kind of hidden disability.

I do know that if you, the mother of seven children, have not been able to feel warm toward this one child, it is worth investigating. He needs you as his advocate. He needs you to keep asking for help for him.

He isn't easy; he is valuable. You, accepting that he is different, will find out what those differences are. You and your family will someday say that he is the odd man out—and extraordinary.

Only the Lonely?

LETTER: LIFE AS AN ONLY CHILD

> I am going to be forty in January. My son is now six years old. I felt strongly all along that I only wanted one child, so we could provide much more for him and he would have our undivided attention. Now friends and relatives say I am selfish and not thinking about how lonely he will be in life when we are no longer around. I feel very pressured to have another child before my biological clock runs out! I don't really want to have another child, but I feel guilty that he has no siblings! I feel at forty, I can't do anymore night feedings. Should I be content with what I have now or have a sibling for my son? I really don't want to be in my sixties when my child graduates college. Please advise.

Is it harder to be the "black sheep," or the only sheep? Elder Ken, seventy-four, a military-officer-turned-school-administrator who lives in Royersford, Pennsylvania, is something of an expert on whether sheep—that is, children—can be happy without being part of a herd.

Ken points out that in the days when more parents opted for larger families, there was often such a wide age spread between siblings that they were not really playmates, anyway. "I have three brothers, and each of us were only children, I think," Ken says.

"I was thirteen when my brother was born, and he was ten when our third brother was born. In 1952, when I went to tell my mother I was going to be married at Christmastime, she started to cry. I said, 'Why are you crying?' " recalls Ken, laughing. "And she said, 'Because I'm going to have a baby then!' My mother and my grandmother carried babies at the same time, and then my grandmother had two after that. I have two aunts that are younger than I am."

Ken and his bride were married in February 1952—after his mom had her baby.

I have been on both sides of your concern. I was the only child in my family until I was thirteen and, at age seventy-three, I am the adoptive father of my fifteen-year-old granddaughter (how does eighty at college graduation time sound?).

Let me tell you that being the parent of a teenager in your later years can be hell or heaven, depending on the child's attitude. (For me it is heaven—thank God.) And I know from experience that even the best of families sometimes have a difficult child for reasons which seem to be beyond comprehension. In other words, this part of the equation can be pretty much of a crap shoot.

As to the next issue: May I list in order the people who will be most discomforted by your son not having a sibling: your friends and relatives who would like to provide you with the knowledge they presume that you do not have; you, if you are not mature enough to determine such things for yourself; and, lastly, your son, if you make it an issue. If you do not make it an issue and treat him as a child who is deserving of unrestricted love, you will find that the question of siblings never comes up.

If he feels lonely when you are not around, it will be because you have not allowed him to become an independent man and not because of a lack of siblings.

In short, the only problem I find in your question is your lack of confidence in yourself and your ability to make your own decisions. This is not a dress rehearsal, you only get one chance at life, don't let others lead it for you.

Ken, a remarried widower, has two biological children aged fifty and forty. He became the father of his fifteen-year-old granddaughter—the biological daughter of his second wife—when his second wife's daughter, the girl's mother, passed away (pay attention, there will be a quiz on Ken's family tree). Like Ken, his teenage daughter has siblings, but is still, in effect, an only child.

"And she has turned out to be just a beautiful young lady," Ken says proudly. "I feel that the prime problem here is not the future of the six-year-old son, but the future of the forty-year-old mother."

Ken is not the only one who believes that the mother should follow her own instincts, not the opinions of others. Writes Grammypam:

My immediate response to your letter is: Are the friends and relatives who are urging you to have another child going to be there to take care of it? My guess is no. I think THEY are the selfish ones, imposing their values on you. Every child should be a wanted child and every parent wise enough to know how many is right for them. One is fine!

Elder Dawn, seventy-four, of Rockville, Maryland is an only child—and proud of it.

That's ridiculous and quite rude of those relatives and friends to say you are selfish for wanting just one child. In fact, there are several positives in being an "only." He gets a lot of adult attention, which gives him excellent social skills and an above average vocabulary. He also doesn't have to worry who Mom and Dad love best. He has space to think, to dream.

Stick to your gut feeling. We're not all "Mother Earth" types. Good luck and keep me posted.

◄o►

Step-dancing

Help! I am a stepmother to a nine-year-old daughter. We cannot get along.

I have a thirteen-year-old boy from a previous marriage, and a seven-year-old stepson. The boys and I get along great. My daughter and I fight about everything. My husband says it's because two women can't live in the same house and get along.

I don't remember fighting with my mother like we do. I am in tears about it at least twice a week. My husband is not home right now, he is truck-driving. So I am here alone to deal with her. The kids see their birth mother every other Saturday for twenty-four hours, that's all she can handle, and they idolize her. I tell my daughter every day that I love her; I give her hugs and kisses just like the boys.

My son from my previous marriage gets along great with my husband, calls him Dad, and they never argue. I want the same relationship with my daughter. I know a lot of her anger with me is because she's angry with her birth mother, but I'm tired of taking the lashing. Please help, I'm at my wits' end.

Says Elder Michelle, sixty-four, of Portland, Oregon, "I raised a daughter and watched both my brothers try to parent stepdaughters—not listening to me—and I still have that good advice waiting for someone to take." Here it is:

You want to mother your stepdaughter, but she doesn't want you mothering her, exactly. Of course the children adore [their biological mother]. She is not there to discipline them, wipe their noses, and be patient when they are upset. She gets to be the "good guy." This is actually not a bad thing. They need to see their mother as the "good guy."

Unfortunately, I am guessing they also know that she "should" be there for them and is not. You are. You are giving them individual time and attention. You might add to that, especially with your daughter, an

*effort to let her know you understand how hard it is to leave her mom
behind when she has to come home. You don't have to make a big thing
of it, just so she knows you understand. You might ask her what her
mom does, or what she cooks that she particularly likes. You might ask
her to help you with something you know she is interested in.*

*It is very hard for someone to parent stepchildren. It is generally
better to leave that to their natural parent. Unfortunately, you do not
have that luxury since he is on the road a lot. But he should do most
of the disciplining when he is home. This leaves you time to be the
"good guy."*

*It is not an easy journey under the best of circumstances, but you
seem to have the mettle for it. Reach out to her with understanding
and compassion and respond to her reaching out to you. Good luck.*

The Heavensviewsages—a twelve-member Elder group, aged seventy to ninety-three, in small-town Delta, Colorado—think the stepdaughter may have an ulterior motive.

Dear Mom,

*Your daughter may be taking out her frustration and anger over the
divorce on you, thinking that if you and Dad break up, her mom will
get back together with her dad. You and your husband need to sit
down and explore this issue with her.*

*It is said: "Two women can't live in the same house." But a nine-
year-old is not a woman.*

Taking the Wheel

LETTER: OVERPROTECTIVE DAD

Basically, my father will not allow me to hold a driver's license,
join the military, or go to the college I wished to go to, even though
I already hit the age of eighteen almost nine months ago and graduated from high school four months ago. He keeps on freaking out
whenever I drive for a few laughs, so much to the point where we

have not driven for at least five months now. The last time we did, it was with a '91 Honda Civic. I kept on stalling because I couldn't get used to the car. He picked me up from church, and without warning, he turned onto a side street, asked to switch seats, and said, "Drive." I tried and tried. Now my father repeatedly promises me that he'll sell one of our "sticks" and buy an automatic.

If you didn't know already, I live with my father. He also wants me to stay in town and go to a community college (which he went to) so I can be an engineer (like him). What I really want to do is go to a culinary school and learn to be a chef.

I've heard of honoring my parents, but isn't this going too far?

Basically, the Elders tell this "kid" that it's time to switch gears. Writes Rose:

You are a man now. You are over eighteen. You now have adult privileges, such as driving, and responsibilities, too. Yet you are still at home, living with your father and fighting with him. Why is that? Are you trying to please your father or convince him to support you financially or gain his approval?

You must know that you cannot change your father. He is what he is.

You must give up trying to get money or cars from your father. It's his money, and he's using it to control you, like a carrot. Stop wanting that carrot. Claim your freedom. Get a job, find a place to live, and start working for what you want. You want culinary school; get a job in a kitchen. Maybe someday you will have the resources to attend a prestigious school; for now learn as you go. It will be hard, but it will be on your terms.

Yes, you are to honor your father; that does not mean being his slave. It will take courage, but in the end you will perhaps earn his respect. First you have to respect yourself.

"This is a kid who doesn't want to grow up," says Elder Web, sixty-four, of Farmington Hills, Michigan. "He's looking for excuses to do nothing, so I keep the options short and sweet."

At eighteen, you are considered a legal adult and can obtain a driver's license, join the military, etc. In order to do this you will need to break away, get a job and follow your dreams.

If you want to become a chef you can always get a job in a restaurant. You will probably begin as a dishwasher, but if you show an interest and aptitude, you can move up the ladder. You need to see if any local college offers a culinary program. Also, you could become a cook in the military.

If you do not want to be an engineer, you will probably fail, and even if you don't would be unhappy. Regardless of what you do with your education, you need to make some important life decisions. Your father may mean well, but should not be making decisions for you. Don't do anything rash. Rather, check out everything first, make the life decision that is best for you, and then proceed.

I wish you the best and trust you will have a bright and productive future.

Elders Gpa-and-Gma, eighty-one and eighty-five, of Rochester Hills, Michigan, think this dad may be misreading his son's Career Aptitude Test results:

I wonder if it has occurred to Dad that if, at eighteen, you cannot master driving a stick shift car, perhaps you are not cut out for engineering? Perhaps a chef would be more appropriate for you. Can you devise a plan whereby you can work your way through culinary school?

When our granddaughter was eighteen, she went to work in a restaurant where she was taught how to make salads and desserts. In a week, she was in charge of preparing salads and desserts.

You have our best wishes for success in your chosen career.

Elder Helen, sixty-eight, of Sierra Vista, Arizona, agrees that the eighteen-year-old needs to pursue his own desires in order to become a man. But she sides with Dad on one point:

It is my opinion you should know how to drive a stick. I learned to drive a stick, both of my daughters learned to drive a stick, and you can, too. If your dad buys an automatic for you, this will just be *another way that he is in control. If you want to be in control, you will be patient, and learn.*

Too Much Information

LETTER: OUR DAUGHTER SAW US HAVING SEX

Our daughter is nine years old and the incident happened two-plus years ago. At the time she surprised us; we had just finished and were getting dressed. We knew there was a possibility that she saw something but then concluded that we had finished before she arrived. We now know our assumption was wrong. Over the past couple of years our daughter started to take an interest in sex . . . meaning she inquired about it on the playground, and then wrote what she learned in her diary. We had the "talk" and have followed up by asking if she wants to know more; she always declines. Today I found erotic pictures (both male and female, private parts labeled) she drew. When asked why she drew it, she said it was right after she saw Lisa (her stepmother) and me in our room at Aunt Shelly's house. We are concerned about the impact that this has had. How do we address this old issue with her?

The Rockymountain Owls group of Montrose, Colorado, aged early sixties through mid–nineties, wants to help the little girl reconcile what she saw "in a healthy way."

Dear Dad,

You and your wife need to sit down with your daughter, maybe more than once, and explain that this is a normal, natural part of life. It is not wrong or dirty.

Explain that this is also a very private, personal thing between two people and she should not have seen it, but it is not her fault. It just needs to be stressed that this is one of the ways that mommies and daddies love each other and is normal for married people.

Make sure there is an open line of communication. This may take more than one conversation for her to understand.

Sincerely,
Rockymountain Owls
P.S. Buy a lock for the bedroom door!

Two Moms

LETTER: NONCONVENTIONAL

> I am looking to have a family without the presence of a male father figure; instead, I will be raising children with another woman. Do you believe that I can raise my children with two moms?

The following letter was written by Elder "Gogently," who hails from the Midwest. She uses another pen name on the EWC Web site, but asked to use this one for the book to further protect the identity of her and her partner.

I am a lesbian. I have some experience in this area, and some thoughts that I will share with you.

First of all, I commend you for thinking ahead as to what this might mean for your child. Second, where you live might also be a consideration. There are places that are more accepting than others.

I was married to a man for twenty-six years and my sons were twenty-five, twenty-three, and fifteen when the marriage ended. After that, I was in a relationship with a woman for many years. We live in the Midwest and it was a very difficult time for all my sons. I had shared custody of my youngest son, and he now says (at thirty) that his life was enriched by being reared part time in a two-woman household, although he had to put up with remarks and lots of ridiculous questions in his high school. Small town, star basketball player, and he expected us at all his games. The only time he ever had a detention was when he hit someone who called me names. My pacifist son . . . he had some tough times!

My thoughts are that children need stability . . . and love. If you can provide that, they can make it through a lot of tough times. Although attitudes are changing somewhat, there is a lot of negativity out there. Pick your school system wisely, and find out up front if you will be supported as a two-mom family there.

I also really believe that children need both male and female influences in their lives. It can be provided in a lot of ways . . . family members, friends, whatever. It is good for them to see interactions between all kinds of people.

Blessings on your life journey. May it be filled with joy, love, peace, and acceptance.

Elder Barbara, sixty-two, of Greene, New York, answered this question "because of my aversion to rules about having children that emphasize anything other than loving your child."

I definitely think it is okay to raise children with two moms. To me the definition of a family is a loving unit of parents and children. The only problems a two-mother family might have would be caused by other, ignorant people.

My husband died when my sons were very young and I raised them by myself. I remember asking my older son when he was an adult if he was having problems with his girlfriend because he did not grow up in a family with two parents. He told me no, that his friends who had a mother and father were having more problems with their relationships because their parents were screwed up.

So good luck with having a child and I hope you enjoy motherhood.

◄○►

Sixteen

LETTER: HOW DO I TELL MY MOM I'VE HAD SEX?

I'm sixteen years old, but I lost my virginity at age fifteen to my boyfriend of almost six months. I know that seems like a short time, but I loved him and he felt the same. Should I tell my mom that I have had sex? And if I should, how? I don't want my parents to hate me because I had sex and didn't wait like they've said I should a million times, but it felt right then and it still does. I mean, I'm not a bad kid; I'm popular in high school, I'm always on the honor roll. I love my parents, and I know they have a right to know. I don't want to lie to them anymore, but I'm scared of the aftermath. Please help me.

The Heavensviewsages answered this question "because this girl needs some hard advice or she's going to be in trouble quick."

Dear Sixteen,

If your parents really love you, they will be shocked, but they won't stop loving you.

Now, just imagine telling your parents that you are pregnant. That is where you are headed if you don't start thinking clearly about this whole sex issue. The Love you are talking about is spelled L U S T. If you have sex with everyone you "love" for six months, you are in for a lot more heartache in your young life.

We have all known people who missed out on their high school/ teenage years because of ONE bad choice. Don't lose these years, they are some of the most fun and enjoyable you will have in your lifetime.

If you are determined to continue this route, go with your mother to see a doctor and at least take precautions with some kind of birth control, although we think that would not be the best course for a smart, popular girl like you.

Elder Rinchu, seventy-eight, of Albuquerque, New Mexico, however, would not be so quick to run to Mother. The Brooklyn-born jewelry artist—who can boast the distinction of being only the second woman in New York City to become a professional Checker cab driver—is a nonconformist, and her advice often reflects it. "It always comes as such a jolt to realize that my responses are different from almost everyone's," she says. "They seem so apparent to *me*."

> *Hello. Thank you for writing to us. In my opinion, having sex is an ADULT thing to do. So, I would treat it in an ADULT manner. That means I would not suggest that you tell your parents . . . or anyone because sex is a very personal and intimate experience, and should not be discussed with anyone. It also means that you have sex in a responsible adult manner . . . pregnancy and sexual disease protection. I'm sure most people would NOT agree with my advice to you, but if you tell your parents, I'm afraid that the results will be devastating to ALL concerned. Good luck!*

"The Talk"

LETTER: WHEN TO HAVE *THE TALK* WITH MY KIDS

My two oldest daughters are ages five and a half and six and a half (I also have a seventeen-month-old), and I'd like to discuss where babies come from with them before they hear about it elsewhere.

I'm concerned because I am pregnant (with baby number 4), and they have not asked one question, so I wonder if they "heard" about it at school, and think they know all the facts.

My mom told me the facts in first grade, but my mother-in-law waited until her kids were in fourth grade (which I feel is WAY too late). Kids today seem to grow up so much faster, and I just don't know what to do. Should I wait until they ask questions, or talk about it now?

As the previous letter from the sixteen-year-old suggests, many parents do a better job communicating to their children that sex is "bad" than they do at explaining what sex is all about. This parent is looking for some ground rules.

A few of the Elders—including Elder Seeley, sixty-five, of Tucson, Arizona, Elder Myra, seventy, of Providence, Rhode Island, and the Wizeones group of Albuquerque, New Mexico, aged seventy-eight to ninety-three—must own the same joke book. In their responses, they recall the story of a child asking where he or she came from, only to receive a nervous "birds and bees" lecture from their parents. "Oh," replies the confused child. "I asked because today at school Jimmy said he comes from Chicago, and Billy said he comes from New York."

Even though they invoke the same old gag, the Elders who answered this question came down on opposite sides of the fence as to whether it is better to offer the facts of life to children at an appropriate age, or to wait until they ask.

Seeley advises waiting.

Your daughters are quite young yet and probably cannot process an in-depth clinical discussion of sexuality and the birth of babies.

You say you are concerned that you want to tell them before they hear it elsewhere. Each child is different and will want to know in his or her own good time; for some that may not be until they are ten or so. I would suggest that you wait until they ask you, and then have a simple explanation prepared.

You are concerned that they have not mentioned your pregnancy. I can tell you from my own personal experience that they may not recognize it. I was nine years old and did not know that my mother was pregnant until one of Mother's friends asked me what I thought about having a new baby brother or sister. I ran to Mother and she then told me. We tend to see only what we expect to see and until that moment I had not noticed my mother's change of clothing and protruding belly.

If I were you, I would simply tell them that they are going to have a sibling in X number of months or so. That will produce "the question"! The answer is: "It is growing inside of me." Wait for the questions, answer them honestly, matter-of-factly, and as simply as possible and tell your wonderful little daughters that they can and should always come to you with their questions, that you will always give them the honest answer. Period.

Myra, however, believes that the parent should take responsibility for bringing it up. "My own mother never talked about sex; the few times I asked questions, she said little and managed to change the subject," Myra says. "I think it's important to find ways of comfortably discussing this topic with children and not always to wait until the child asks a question." Her letter:

I'm wondering how far along you are in your pregnancy. When you've reached the stage of "showing," that would be a good time to raise the subject. One way this could happen is for you to encourage your five- and six-year-olds to feel the baby kick, which could lead to a natural conversation about the baby growing inside your body. There are also excellent books for young children on this topic.

At ages five and six, the children may not know how to ask or they may feel they shouldn't ask even if you have done nothing to make them feel that way. The most important point to remember is to take the lead from the children and not overwhelm them with information they are not ready for. For this reason you may want to do this individually because each child is different, even those who are close in age. Also, your tone of voice and body language provide even more information than your words, especially to a young child.

Elder Arianne, sixty-seven, of Wyncote, Pennsylvania, agrees with Myra. In fact, her beliefs led to an unfortunate clash with her nanny.

Children should be taught that childbirth is a glorious process that brings delight to families, not something that should be hidden and not talked about. When my two younger children were younger than your two, they began to ask questions. Feeling that I needed some help in answering their questions, I went to a few bookstores to find a book that would be appropriate for children of their ages.

I did find a good book, one with words, and many lovely pictures of the pregnancy, the birth, and the new family all together. I put the book on a lower shelf of our bookcases, so that if the children wanted to look at it, they could get to it. Then, if they had questions, I was happy to respond to them at the level they were asked, and in terms they could understand.

One evening I came home from work to see that the book had been placed on the top of our bookshelves. When I asked why it was there, the nanny told me that it had been very careless of me to have put the book where the children could get it and look at it, that children "shouldn't read about that stuff." I explained to her that it was indeed meant for children, and had been bought for my children. Regrettably, she promptly quit in disappointment because our children were being allowed to look at a "dirty" book. I was quite happy to have discovered this aspect of her before it caused problems in our family.

Sex is one of the most basic acts of life, yet for so many years women were compelled to hide their pregnancy, not appear in public, and certainly it was not discussed with children. This is the basis of tales of the stork, or the cabbage patch, or other nonsensical stories of where the baby came from, told to children by adults who did not understand or respect a child's curiosity and desire to learn.

Since your children have shown no curiosity about your pregnancy, you should perhaps sit down with them and mention the new baby that will soon join your family, and see where it goes from there, letting them feel or pat the baby now. It is very good for children to learn the facts of life from loving parents instead of an ill-informed child at school, or people who will give them the wrong idea.

Elder JeanMc, seventy-nine, of Sterling Heights, Michigan, says it is important to be honest to protect today's children from being introduced to sex the way *she* was—as a teenager.

The old advice was to answer questions when they're asked. From personal experience, I can tell you that is really bad advice. When I was sixteen, my mother finally decided to tell me how babies got into mommies' tummies. Mind you—and I swear this is true—I still believed God planted a seed under your heart. Well! When she told me, not sparing any details, I was shocked. I asked her why she would tell me such an awful thing. When I realized she meant it, I said that no way would I ever get married! Well, I did. And I had four children and there were no seeds under my heart involved.

Years later, I told my mother I must have been a really dumb kid not to ask. She said, "Oh, you did. I just thought you were too little for me to tell you the truth." Moral of the story: Don't wait.

And as soon as they understand—and before dating—work in the subject of birth control and STDs. Better too early than too late.

Oh, yes: Don't assume they really understand what you have explained. Go over it with them again, have them tell you what they think they understand, and iron out the wrinkles. Believe me, there will be some.

Elder Barbara, sixty-two, of Greene, New York, believes this parent has already provided the right answer to the question.

You wrote that you feel that fourth grade is WAY too late to tell your children about sex. So clearly you know you don't want to wait until your children are that old.

You also wrote that you were told the facts of life when you were in first grade. How did that work out for you? If you found that hearing about where children came from was helpful, then it is certainly safe to tell your children about the birds and bees now. If it was too upsetting for you, then you should wait. Trust your own feelings. What worried me as I read your letter was that it felt to me that you were polling other people rather than making up your mind yourself.

I told my older son about babies growing in their mother's stomach when he was a two-year-old because I was pregnant. He didn't understand much, but was not at all upset and assured me that he had a baby growing in his stomach, too. I bought a doll, which his father "delivered" while I was in the hospital so we would both get our babies out of our stomachs together. The fact that his baby was born by saying a magic spell from Sesame Street didn't cause any long-term problems. He learned the real facts of life when he was ready. It all goes to show that when anyone tries to give a young child more information than he can process, he works it out some way, and it doesn't bother him.

◄○►

Video Violence

LETTER: VIOLENCE FOR KIDS

> What actions should we take to prevent kids from watching too much violence in video games?

Not surprisingly, advice-seeking parents are as concerned about exposing kids to violence as they are about introducing them to sex. Elder Emme, sixty-three, of Bel Air, Maryland, is a former speech and communications teacher who has devoted much class time to media violence and its effects on children. "It is a problem that continues to grow, and something all parents should be aware of," she says.

Let's face it, there's no way we can keep kids completely away from violent content, whether it's in movies, on TV, or in video games. We know that the American Academy of Pediatricians is very concerned about the violence kids are exposed to. We even know that some children are likely to act violently—hitting, kicking, scratching, and so on—after viewing violence. The good news is that there are several things you can do to lessen the amount of violent game-playing and the effects that seeing such violence can have.

It's a good idea to have computers out in "public" space in your home rather than in kids' bedrooms. This will allow you to monitor what games the kids are playing. You also need to be aware of the content on any hand-held games your kids might have. Of course you can use parental blocking devices to prevent the downloading of violent games, just as you might to protect your kids from porn.

The most important thing adults can do is to have an ongoing dialogue with their children about media violence in general as well as video game violence. Tell the kids exactly what you don't like and explain why. When our daughters were children, we didn't allow them to watch music videos at home, explaining that too many of the videos degraded women and glorified violence against them. Interestingly, one of our girls now does volunteer shifts on a domestic violence hotline.

Your kids might say that they know what they're watching isn't real and that they know the violence portrayed is wrong. That's when you talk with them about how the more violence kids view, the more immune they become to violence in real life.

Another thing that you can do about this problem is to talk with the parents of your children's friends. You may be able to come to an agreement about not allowing the playing of violent video games in your homes.

Remember: Be aware of content, and keep the channels of communication open. Good luck!

Elder Barbara answered this question because "I hate violent video games."

The simple answer is not to buy any violent video games, but of course that doesn't stop kids from playing them at their friends' houses. So, I think the family needs to inoculate its children against violence by talking about what is really happening in those games. That means asking your kids what is so exciting about them and talking about what violence does to both the victim and to the violent person. But the first step is to raise your child in a loving, nonviolent family. If there is any abuse, verbal or physical, that child will be longing for an outlet for his impotent anger. If the household is loving, the child will have less of a need to kill imaginary people.

If you make things taboo, sometimes they become very attractive. My husband and I did not allow our sons to have toy guns; they used their Legos and Tinkertoys to build weapons for themselves. We decided not to forbid that; they have grown up to be caring, nonviolent adults.

The Elders didn't have video games to play when they were growing up, and most are old enough that their children didn't have them either. In giving advice on that subject, they must draw on their general attitudes about violence in entertainment, or rely on what they've read in the media about the games.

But the next question deals with a subject common to all generations—the family pet.

◄○►

"Louie"

LETTER: OUR DOG WAS KILLED AND THE KIDS WANT A NEW ONE

My ex is a very distant man and can be verbally abusive, especially toward my thirteen-year-old son (Child Protection Services kept him away for a year because of this). "Brad," my son, has suffered greatly in the past, but with tons of individual and group therapy with his father, he can accept his dad's problems, but it still hurts. I figured you have to know this part to help.

Anyway, Brad has had a black Lab, Louie, for the last five years. They were very close. Louie slept with him every night, went camping, was his buddy. Brad has very few friends, and has relied on Louie for companionship. Last week, Lou was hit by a car and died instantly. Brad cried for about a minute, then refused to even speak of the dog. He is very upset, snapping at his sister, very quiet (not like the boy at all) and withdrawn. Two days ago, when we were alone, he cried briefly and told me he missed Louie so much it hurt. He asked if he could have another dog. We live in the country, have a beagle and three cats, but Louie's absence seems to be everywhere. Is it too soon to replace the dog? Will getting a new one now just further push the loss inside? I want him to grieve and I want to make everything all right again. I have asked friends and everyone is split on the decision. What do I do?

Thank you for your help in advance.

All of the Elders seem to have a dog story; Jangela's yellow Labrador, who lived to be fifteen ("If I'm going to have a dog, it has to be a big dog; I think the little ones are pathetic"); the Great Danes and boxers to whom Elder Michelle of Portland, Oregon, told her childhood woes; Elder Grandma Dan's little dachshund, who was hit by a car: "I can remember crying just as hard as I did when people I was close to passed," she writes. Elder Shekinah, sixty-two, of Springfield, Illinois, calls them "angels in fur."

For Elder Dr. Sam, seventy-six, a retired family physician in Harrisburg, Pennsylvania, it wasn't a dog—it was a young Angus steer. "I happened to have been given a 4H-Club calf, I guess when I was about ten years old," Dr. Sam recalls. "I grew very fond of this calf. I used to put him on a halter and lead him out across the farm, and I used to clean his stall. He used to lick my trousers and was affectionate, in his own way. The calf won the state championship, and I had to sell him— that was really hard.

"So I stood up in front of a couple of hundred people and said, 'No!' And the next thing I knew, there was a senior person saying, 'Yes, you will!' "

Despite his protests, Dr. Sam had to sell the calf—and has not forgotten how it felt. And he joins the Elders in their unanimous vote: It's time to get the boy another dog.

Says Elder Jacobus, eighty-one, of Saskatoon, Saskatchewan: "The mother seems to be aware of the steps involved in the grieving process, but I am concerned that she feels Brad needs to grieve according to the book, instead of allowing him to grieve in his own way. By wanting to 'fix' things for Brad, she is adding to his stress."

It is very thoughtful of you to want to do everything you can to help your son deal with his trauma. It is important to realize that although there are certain steps that every person may go through, every person goes through these phases of grief at a different rate. Sometimes a person may go through one phase so quickly that it seems he is missing that phase entirely. That happens to be the way that person deals with his grief. It is important to allow each person to grieve at his own pace.

Therefore, instead of assuming it is too soon to replace the dog he lost, I suggest you allow Brad to make that decision. It is important to allow Brad to pick the dog he wants when he feels he is ready for it.

That is the way I see it. I hope it helps. Brad is lucky to have an understanding mother.

Elder Ruthie, sixty-four, of Swanton, Ohio, grew up on a farm and had several dogs. During the past sixteen years, her family has lost two dogs and she has had to deal with the effect on her children. "Between the lines, I sense that it is the mother who is not ready for a new dog," Ruthie says. "It always took me longer than it did my children to adjust to the loss of a pet. My children have often been the ones to force me to move on after a difficult period."

*First of all, my sympathy at the loss of Louie. Dogs leave big holes in
our hearts when they leave us.*

*You have answered your own question, in a way. Louie was a
companion to Brad. Brad feels the need for that companionship and
expresses that he is ready for another dog. At his age he certainly
knows his own feelings.*

*I do not believe the new dog will drive the grief inward but will give
him a living being he can let out that grief with. I believe Brad understands he will not be replacing Louie, just filling his need for a warm
fuzzy creature to run with, laugh with, and cry with. As it is with humans, no two dogs have the same personality. Nonetheless, the new
dog will most likely sleep with him and camp with him and do the
things that Brad wants the dog to do with him. Dogs are that way.
They adapt to the activities of their humans. What Brad has not experienced from his father can be experienced in loving and caring for his
dog.*

Elder Helen just doesn't get why this mother feels the need to con-
sult anyone but her son on this decision. Her strong opinion is reflected in exclamation points:

*Brad asked for another dog. All I can think is: "WHAT ARE YOU
WAITING FOR!!??"*

Whether they are raised with the knowledge of contemporary psychology or just traditional common sense, the Elders seem to agree that
when there is love in the household, the kids turn out all right.

Whatever happened to Heart of Texas's "odd child out," who is now
in his late fifties? "He was an exciting child and he is still an exciting
adult," Heart of Texas says. "He lives his life to the fullest. I would say
he is a workaholic, but he loves his family and raised them in his own
style. He is a banker in Chicago and travels a lot and that is something
that suits him. Never a dull moment!"

And how about Rose's son, whose hyperactivity was treated with a
different approach? For the record, Rose acknowledges that it's still a
struggle many years later—but that the combination of professional
help and compassion seems to have led him into productive adulthood.

"He's now thirty-four. He has children. He struggles every day to function as a wage earner and father," Rose says. "His high energy and mechanical talents allow him to do very challenging and dangerous work. He still has the disturbed sleep patterns, attention problems, problems with impulse control and OCD. His wife is struggling to live with and love him despite these challenges."

Adds Rose: "He is funny, witty, intelligent, generous, kind, sweet, and cuddly. He and I have managed to hold on to the truth that I love him. Without him, I'd never have grown as I have."

SIBLING STORIES

Wisdom for Brothers and Sisters

Where do you find these Elders? They are so much better than Dear Abby and Ann Landers it hurts! Keep up the good work.

"Hannah," NYC

—From "Feedback & Kudos"
www.ElderWisdomCircle.org

Mom always liked you best.

—Tommy Smothers

Bully Pulpit

LETTER: I THINK I RUINED MY BROTHER'S LIFE

Hello,

I am in my forties and come from a large family. I only recently admitted to myself that I bullied my little brother, "Ed," terribly when we were kids. Nothing physical, just belittlement, playing tricks on him, making him look like an idiot. I grew into a kind-hearted adult, so I don't know why I was such a rotten kid. Anyway, Ed and I are not close today.

About ten years ago he married "Sue" after a whirlwind courtship. They have no kids. She turned out to be one of the most mean-spirited, nasty, manipulative, childish, and self-centered people I've ever met. He adores her and seems to be completely under her thumb.

The thing is, I feel like maybe I caused this. Maybe his idea about what a relationship is got damaged by how I treated him. Even when I was tormenting him, I did love him, so maybe his ideas about love got mixed up with the feeling of being bullied.

Anyway, my question is this. Ed and Sue are pretty much estranged from the rest of the family, because she has picked fights with everyone in the family, including my extremely mild-mannered and bewildered parents. I imagine that after my parents die Ed and Sue will cut all connection with me and my siblings.

Before that happens, I would like to apologize to Ed for bullying him. But I would also feel tempted to explain to him that maybe that is why he married a bully. I would like him to realize that he doesn't have to stay tied to this person. But maybe it would be awful for him to realize that, because he's already put so much time in with her and he does seem content with her (they both have medical problems and they do seem to take care of each other in a caring way).

Should I tell him I'm sorry about the bullying but not say anything about Sue? Or should I not say anything at all?

When it comes to issues involving siblings, it seems that we never quite grow up. Octogenarians can still recall hair-pulling, name-calling, spitball-throwing battles with their brothers and sisters as though it were yesterday.

Many of the Elders report that it took them until they were grandparents—and, sometimes, that many years of therapy—to discover who they were as individuals, rather than being forever defined by their childhood place in the family.

At eighty-one, Elder Jacobus of Saskatoon, Saskatchewan, is perhaps twice as old as this advice seeker. Still, the story of "Ed" transports him back through time to the 1930s, to the family farm in the village of Blumenheim, Saskatchewan, where children learned their lessons in a one-room schoolhouse, hunted gophers and rabbits with single-shot .22 caliber rifles, and observed the strict teachings of the Old Colony Mennonite Church.

In the winter, village families took turns transporting the children to school in an open grain box atop a bobsled drawn by horses. To prevent the children's toes from freezing in the bitter cold, the floor of the grain box would be lined with fresh straw. When the children arrived at school, they gathered around the round, black furnace to warm their hands and were told sub-zero horror stories of digging out through the deep morning snow.

Metal syrup and honey pails served as their lunch kits. Since this was the Depression, lunch for most consisted of jam or syrup sandwiches; the lucky ones got a smear of peanut butter. Because the cloak room was on the opposite end of the room from the furnace, the sandwiches were usually frostbitten by the time noon rolled around.

Most young men in Blumenheim couldn't wait to drop out of school at fifteen to go to work on the farm. But Jacobus loved school—even though a case of scarlet fever at the age of four left him with a permanent hearing impairment, and triggered chronic ear and throat infections that delayed his entry into elementary school by one year. Jacobus eventually worked his way through college and became a teacher and counselor. In fact, his first teaching job was in the very schoolhouse where he began his own education.

These details come from Jacobus's forty-seven-page, self-published autobiography, *Growing up in Blumenheim, Saskatchewan: Life in an Old Colony Mennonite Village During the Thirties and Forties*. It is not surprising that Jacobus would choose to record his story in detail; always a history buff, Jacobus now works as a guide at a Saskatoon museum devoted to one hundred years of the history of Saskatchewan—aptly dressed in period costume.

Jacobus was the youngest of four brothers. And he was not the bully—he was the bullied. The bad boy was his always-rebellious eldest brother, Willie. You couldn't call it sibling rivalry, exactly, because quiet Jacobus took whatever Willie dished out. And, more than sixty years later, Jacobus believes that the bullying shaped many of his own most important relationships. Writes Jacobus:

> *Allow me to speak from my experience.*
>
> *I grew up with a brother four years my senior. He made me feel inferior most of my life. I have realized for years that I have always had low self esteem because of the way my brother always put me down.*
>
> *After I was married, my wife couldn't stand my brother. She told me he was always putting me down. As I looked back, I realized it was true.*
>
> *Fortunately, my brother did not ruin my life, although he affected it no doubt. Even today, people who know me tell me that I hold back.*
>
> *My brother and I are now good friends. As we were reminiscing one day, I told him that I remember the day when we were around eight and twelve years old. We were sitting in the back seat of the car while our parents sat in front. I guess I was talking too much and my brother told me he wished I would shut up because my voice irritated him. When I told my brother about this incident he burst out laughing: "No wonder you never said anything!"*

It is possible that your brother learned that your attitude toward him is the normal way for people to react to him. He probably held you in high esteem, as I did my brother. Hence, when he met this lady who was similar to you, he may have fallen in love with her immediately.

In my opinion, it would be a good idea for you to tell your brother Ed how you feel about the way you treated him. Tell him that you have always actually loved him.

I don't think I would suggest to him that this may have led him to marry his wife or that it is why he adores her even though she mistreats him. It could be a little too much for Ed to absorb at one time.

For the time being, I would leave it as an apology for the way you treated him. He may recognize later that the relationship with his wife may be a repeat of his relationship with you.

If, at a later date, you feel you should raise that issue with Ed, I would do so in the form of a question for him to think about. Should his relationship with his wife become intolerable in the future, it may help Ed to understand what is happening is not his fault.

Elder Helen, sixty-eight, of Sierra Vista, Arizona, answers this letter from the point of view of the bully. Born and raised in Harlem, New York City, this former tomboy recalls playing stickball in the streets, hitching rides holding onto the back of buses while wearing her roller skates—and torturing her only sibling, a brother thirteen months her junior, without mercy.

"I used to take his allowance, and I'd say, 'If you tell Daddy, I'm going to beat you up,'" recalls Helen. "And once he did tell, and I beat him up—he hid under the bed. I just did what kids do. And I did it until I was about twelve or thirteen and he hit me back. And then I stopped, because boys can hit harder than girls."

The very independent Helen—mother of two daughters, grandmother of three boys, and great grandmother to one more—lives alone and describes herself as "divorced for a hundred years." She believes that her tomboy past and admitted family status as a "Daddy's girl" probably rescues her from the constant self-doubt and self-blame she observes in her female friends. "They seem to me to be wishy-washy and have no backbone whatever," she observes, laughing. "I had boyfriends, but I was never like some of my friends were when the relationship ended, crying and carrying on. I felt like it was *his* loss, not mine."

Helen brings a similarly straightforward attitude to her response to the letter: Forget the guilt, and move forward. And, like Jacobus, she suggests that the writer forget about trying to fix his brother's marriage and concentrate on his own relationship with his brother.

I bullied my brother in the same way you describe. He has been married four times, none of which worked out for him. He is also alcoholic, has heart problems, and suffers from anxiety attacks. Do I blame myself for any of this—NO WAY!

I can't answer as to why some people's lives turn out to be what they are. The bottom line is that we all make our own choices.

You were no more of a rotten kid than a lot of other kids. Your brother may not even think of you as bullying him when he was little. Some men like dominant women. This may be why he chose Sue.

You said he adores her. She may be the one with the problem. Perhaps she has issues that do not allow her to be close to you and the rest of your family. Perhaps she would be the same way if she were married to someone other than your brother. I agree that it would be nice if she could be closer to your family, but you have to remember that she married your brother, not you and your family.

If you're concerned that Ed and Sue will cut all connections with you and your children, talk to him about that. Let him know that you feel that when your parents are gone, you will always want him and his wife to be a part of your family. That is all you can do. It will be his choice to be a part of your family or not.

Give your brother some credit. Assume that he knows he doesn't have to remain in his present situation.

Admitting your feelings to him may ease your conscience. I would not suggest to him that he married a bully for that reason. You can just let him know that whatever the circumstances, you will always be there for him. That is all he needs to know.

Elder L. David, seventy-one, of Monterey Park, California—retired from thirty-five years in financial management and another ten years as an art dealer and art framer—was bullied by an older sister.

I was exactly three and a half years younger than my sister—just about the right difference to really be resented by a sibling who hated losing her status as an only child. My parents would tell me, "Don't hit your sister, boys don't hit girls"—although I was half her size.

You are not responsible for his actions today, and it is probably time that you worked on your guilt feelings. I really believe that it is more important that you feel good about yourself than that you try to "fix" your brother. He is old enough to take care of himself.

About apologizing to him: Yes, I think that would probably be a good idea, it certainly couldn't do any harm, and it might help you feel better about things as well as possibly relieving the strain in your relationship.

Just remember, though, you can't control his feelings, and I don't think that you should interfere in any way with his relationship with his wife. My sister married a man totally lacking in any social graces, and who has alienated almost all of her friends, and the rest of our family. Her attitude is that we either receive her husband of almost fifty years uncritically and on his terms, or forget about seeing her. Although no one in the family wants to be around him, it still wasn't worth it to criticize her husband to my sister.

I hope that you will do whatever personal work needs to be done to get rid of your guilt. Good luck.

Mean Girl

LETTER: MY SISTER IS A BRAT

I have a little sister named "Heidi." Now, don't get me wrong, I would take a bullet for her any day but she is the loudest, most bad tempered little brat I ever met. She is sooo territorial. She can come up and touch my crap but when I go to get something from her stuff, she throws a fit. Whenever my parents leave me home with this devil child, she thinks she's in charge and all big and bad. When she gets mad —and I mean mad—she'll bite, kick, SCREAM, and punch me, sometimes till I'm black and blue. How should I deal with this demon child from hell?

Says Elder Grammypam, seventy, of Hancock, New Hampshire, "I was both amused and challenged by this letter. Everyone thinks their younger siblings are brats at some point, but I'm also concerned about the physical violence and abuse that is going on. Why hasn't the writer talked to her parents?"

You sound like a pretty good big sister, handling a very difficult situation. I wonder how your parents respond to Heidi abusing you and leaving marks on you. What would happen if you suggested to your parents that you really didn't want to stay alone with Heidi unless they made some real consequences for her behavior, both in not respecting you and physically abusing you? It is very bad for Heidi to be such a bully. This kind of behavior carries over outside the home and can get her into real trouble. So my advice is to talk with your parents and also to make sure that there is nothing in your behavior that is a model for this kind of behavior in her. Good luck!

Grammypam suspects that the problem between the older and younger sister might not be all one-sided. "I get a big clue from the language she uses," Grammypam says. "I want her to engage her parents in working with Heidi, but I also point out that the girl needs to be accountable for her own behavior."

A Tangled Web-Search

LETTER: SHOULD I TELL MY BROTHER?

Browsing through the Internet the other day, I inadvertently and unintentionally came across some information regarding my future sister-in-law's past. This information is posted in the form of court documents, and various Web sites. Without being too specific, this girl (several years ago) was involved with some scary people, one of whom is now sitting on death row. There have been books written about her and her "friends," as well as movies. While I do not believe that my brother is in any danger, I can't shake the feeling that this is something he should know about the girl he plans to marry. I have no idea whether he knows or not, it's not the type of thing that ever comes up in conversation. I like his fiancée and am not trying to get them to call off their wedding. Do I tell my brother about what I found or just let it go?

The Rockymountain Owls of Montrose, Colorado, aged sixty to ninty-five, think this marriage could be headed for disaster if the advice seeker doesn't speak up—preferably *before* the bachelor party.

In this situation, he really does need to know. They are engaged, not married, and this is the time for each of them to disclose information to the other partner. She may not be truthful with him, which is cause for pause right there.

Print out the documents and information and give it to him so he can make an informed decision. It is evidently public information, so give it to him.

Elder Walk-On, seventy-two, of Bethesda, Maryland, finds a credibility gap on the part of the writer.

If you feel obliged to tell your brother, do so. However, I would be prepared to have him find it difficult to believe that you found this information "unintentionally and inadvertently." If you expect him to believe you, then you will have to be honest about how you just happened to find these facts.

Also, be prepared for him to say that he does not care about her past. Whatever she has done, he forgives her. Are you ready to forgive her?

"I am eight years older than my twin sisters; although we did not have much in common growing up, we have chosen to forge close and supportive sibling relationships throughout our adulthood," says Elder Grandma-Dan, sixty-one, of Troy, Michigan. "A huge payoff from this was how we were able to handle things after our mother died; there was no fighting, no alienation, no division, and there could have been."

MY *advice is to let it go. This is your brother's ADULT life, not yours. It is very likely that he already knows about his fiancée's past and is choosing to marry her anyway. It is also highly probable that he is choosing to keep this matter private lest she be judged by her soon-to-be in-laws. It is clear that you care deeply for your brother, so I know how difficult it is to refrain from jumping in to "help" him out, but to do so would put you into the "buttinsky" category.*

This is one of those times in your life when you are being called to grow and become more mature in your adult relationship with your brother. I have learned again and again in my life that forging an adult relationship with my sisters has been staying out of their business, rather than getting into it.

In other words, my sisters did not need to hear things about their spouses from me that, I came to learn, they already knew. But my "being there" meant everything.

Well, no one else came up with this practical solution. Writes Grammypam:

If you feel you have to do something, why not ask your future sister-in-law about what you have discovered? If you like her, as you say, let her decide how and when her history should be shared with her future husband.

Crisis-in-Law

LETTER: HOW SHOULD I TALK TO MY SISTER-IN-LAW ABOUT A PROBLEM?

My younger brother, "Jordan," is forty with a wife and two young kids. He lives in Montana and the rest of the family lives on the East Coast. Jordan was diagnosed with ALS. He is now unable to walk and eating and talking is very difficult. He has also lost a lot of weight. His wife works as a pharmacist from 10 a.m. to 10 p.m. four days a week and is home the other three.

Jordan does NOT want to move east, he is very adamant about it. So our folks retired and bought a home four miles from him, to help out and spend his last months, hopefully years, with him.

My problem: Mom has learned through a friend of Jordan's that his wife was very upset that they were moving there and has made Mom feel very unwelcome. She has also learned that when Jordan dies, his wife plans to sever all ties with our family.

I am so confused and hurt by this news that I can't sleep. When I call she is always too busy to talk. I've always made her feel welcome. She knows we love her, she is our sister (she only has a brother and there are seven of us), I thought she was our friend.

My son and I plan to visit them for Easter this year and don't know if I should bring up this news or let it lie and enjoy our visit.

Please help us.

It is unusual for an Elder to get involved in an extended conversation with an advice seeker, but with this letter it happened for Elder Web, sixty-four, of Farmington Hills, Michigan.

When it comes to the fallout of a family member's illness, Web has had more than his share of experience. "My father had three brain-tumor operations while I was growing up—he was supposed to be dead at forty, but he lived to be eighty," Web says. "The first one was in the 1940s, when it was almost a miracle to survive that kind of operation—luckily none of them was malignant. It had a major impact on family dynamics."

Web wrote:

I am sorry to hear about your brother's illness and can appreciate the anxiety it has caused your family.

Although an illness of this type has an effect on all family members, ultimately it comes down to your brother and his wife. It sounds as if she is coping the best way she can, providing an income, raising the children, and dealing with Jordan's illness. She sounds like a strong woman dealing with a most difficult situation.

You did not mention the circumstances under which your parents moved to Montana. Since Jordan does not want to move back east, it sounds as if he wants to spend the time he has left with the life he knows, including his wife and children. If they just decided to move, without asking, his wife may resent this. The most important thing at this time is to try and keep a sense of unity. This is no time for family battles, ego or otherwise. Continue to be supportive and empathetic to the situation.

I would not bring up what you have heard during your vacation. Be upbeat and positive. Let her know you are there for her but don't force yourself on her. While you are there, don't dwell on the illness. Get their minds off the day-to-day problems, even if it's only for a few hours. I would think that this would be greatly appreciated.

The intentions of your family are good, but you need to view the situation from her perspective, giving her the support she needs, and not what you, or some other family member, THINK she needs. The feelings and desires of the one with the illness and the spouse and children need to take precedence over anyone else's, including the parents.

I'll be thinking of all of your family, wishing you all the best and hoping that Jordan has many more years.

Best regards,
Web

The advice seeker eagerly wrote back:

Hello,

I want to thank you for your great and quick response. You asked if Mom and Dad moved uninvited. In November, they were invited to stay for five to six weeks and spend Christmas and the New Year. During the visit they realized that "Jordan" and "Loraine" needed help and basically decided to be the ones to provide it. Loraine told me that she was feeling as though they were imposing on friends, so having Mom and Dad there was a relief. That is when they decided to move out there and buy a house. Mom has been making food that Jordan can eat easily and will "stick to his ribs." He is gaining weight again.

I understand you are not a psychologist, but you seem to know what you are talking about. If you want to elaborate on your answer with this new information, please do!

The advice seeker seemed to be hoping to sway Web into her parents' camp. Web didn't budge.

Thank you for the follow-up. I've read through it several times and my original advice is unchanged.

Since you said she had indicated that she intended to cut all ties when Jordan passes, she is obviously upset about something. As an example, has some type of "guilt trip," either stated or implied, been laid on her over Jordan's weight issue?

Remember the old expression about the road to hell being paved with good intentions? It might be best for your parents to sit down with Loraine and discuss parameters. They are there to assist, not to become part of the problem.

I would like to hear from you when things get worked out. It sounds as if you have a great family and with everyone's love, support, and understanding, I'm sure the problem will be resolved.

The advice seeker responded again:

Thank you so much for your understanding and compassion. I will use your advice, as I think it is great and I agree with everything you say. I just needed an unbiased opinion. I will let you know how we make out.

Web did not get another letter—but that's okay with him. "This was a letter that really drew me in, and I had to try, to the best of my ability, to provide what I thought might be helpful to a family in pain," Web says. "I may never hear from her, but I feel good about this one."

Most other Elders who answered this letter agreed with Web that the advice seeker should try her best to see the situation from Loraine's point of view. But they also jumped all over the unnamed gossip who gave a push to this family's house of cards in the first place. Writes Elder Barbara, sixty-two, of Greene, New York, whose brother-in-law died of ALS:

I hope you can be a loving presence, there for your sister-in-law, and allow her to cope the way she needs to. And I think you should tell whoever is talking to your mother to keep quiet.

Where Did She Go Right?

LETTER: LIVING MY SISTER'S LIFE

This may sound bizarre, but I feel as though I've been living the life my younger sister should be living.

My sister has always been the good girl. She spent her childhood getting in little trouble and was without a doubt the easiest to raise of three children. My brother has a problem with drugs. And I, the middle child, spent my teen years arguing with my mom, treating her terribly. At nineteen I dated a guy my parents pleaded with me not to see. Of course I had to run off, move in with him, and come home knocked up.

My parents were wonderful letting me stay with them and helping me take care of my baby. It was then I realized how much I loved them and gained an appreciation for them that I regretfully didn't have before.

When my daughter was three I met a military man and fell in love. We were married a year later and ten months after that I had my second child, a son. My husband, being the wonderful person he is, adopted my daughter.

This is where my sister comes in. You see, she has done everything the way you're supposed to. She went to college, got married, started a career, and couldn't wait to start a family. But she's had trouble getting pregnant and she's had miscarriages. Her husband is emotionally abusive. She has even told me that she is afraid to leave him because she thinks if she did he would hurt either himself or her. My sister is a smart girl with a degree in psychology. But she still doesn't see the signs of abuse when they are staring her in the face.

I feel like I am so lucky and that I am living a life that my sister deserves to be living. I really love my sister so much that I would do anything for her. I would even carry a child for her if she needed me to. I just want her to have the life I always wanted her to. What can I do to help her see that her husband is getting in the way of her dreams coming true?

"This writer has not only gotten off the track, but she's gotten stuck in quicksand," says Barbara. "I found myself wanting to yell at this woman, because I felt that she was ruining her life. I wanted to know why she felt the need to punish herself the way she has."

When I read your letter, I was struck by how well your life was going and how determined you are not to enjoy it. When you were young, you made some mistakes, but you learned from them and turned into a good person.

It would be easy to see how silly this was if your sister were a billionaire and you were miserable because she had more money than you did. It's not so easy to spot the absurdity if you feel that your motivation is concern for your sister who is having a difficult life. Being sympathetic is terrific; beating yourself up is not.

We always see what is right for other people. The best thing you can do for your sister is to be there for her as her friend and, well, sister. But that doesn't mean forgetting that you are two different people. You are seeing her as an extension of yourself.

She is an adult and will either figure out how to change her life or continue living as she has decided to live. In the meantime, you have a responsibility to yourself and to your own family to drop your useless guilt. If you find that hard to do, I suggest you see a counselor or a therapist. Good luck.

◄○►

Sworn to Secrecy

LETTER: HARD-TO-KEEP SECRET

My brother found out he has cancer, and the prognosis is not good. He didn't want anyone to find out, but his wife told me and swore me to secrecy. The thing is, there are four other siblings besides my brother and me, and our elderly mother is still living. It bothers me to keep this secret, because I feel like they would want to know. I don't want to make him mad, especially when I'm going to lose him. But I don't want my family to end up feeling betrayed by me because of this secret either. So far I have kept the secret because I feel his wishes, under these sad circumstances, should take priority over anything, even if I don't necessarily agree with them. He is only trying to protect his family from pain. At some point they will have to be told, of course, and I guess his wife and I will just have to use our best judgment about that. So what do you think of my keeping this secret in the meantime? It's hard to try to act like everything is normal when I talk to my family.

Elder Tina, seventy-three, of Greensboro, North Carolina, had a mother who died of cancer and has several family members currently struggling with the disease.

I'm sorry to hear that your brother has cancer and that his prognosis is not very good. By telling you about his illness and then swearing you to secrecy, your sister-in-law has put an almost unfair burden on you. She probably needs someone to talk to about it, and that's understandable.

You're right when you say that sometimes there are no easy answers, but I personally feel that you should abide by your brother's wishes. His family and closest friends deserve to know the truth, but your brother may be having a hard time coping with his new reality. He may feel that he can't cope with his family members' sadness if they were to find out about his condition. Respect his decision to be silent, at least for the time being. If and when his condition deteriorates, the family may sense that something is wrong, even if they don't see him often. He may change his mind over the course of his illness and decide after all that he would like to say his "good-byes" to his loved ones. The choice should be his. We all handle illness in our own personal way.

In the meantime, be there for your sister-in-law if she needs a shoulder to cry on, and try to be strong in the face of these sad circumstances. Hospices are a wonderful resource for helping both the patient and the survivors cope before and after death. There's also a possibility that by some miracle, things will turn around for your brother. We never know. Perhaps he can gain strength from the people around him who show courage and faith.

I wish you all well. Let us know how you're doing.

Best regards,
Tina

Writes Elder Michelle, sixty-four, of Portland, Oregon:

Secrets are, of course, meant to be kept, but they hardly ever are, for good or ill. We do not usually share secrets because someone needs to know them. We usually share secrets because we need to share them.

Your brother and his wife will know when it is time to share with the rest of the family, or maybe they already have and everyone is keeping his or her own counsel. That would be amazing, but it is possible. It is hard to act like everything is normal when you talk to your family. It must be hard for him, too. But by doing this, he can live a life devoted to living rather than to dying. He does not have to see his disease in others' eyes. He can just be your brother. Please let him have this. Respect his wishes and keep your own counsel. It is a great, albeit painful, gift you give him.

Elder Barbara also believes that a promise is a promise, but urges the advice seeker to appeal to his brother and sister-in-law to change their minds.

I got the impression from your letter that it is your sister-in-law who makes most of the decisions. Can you talk to her or to your brother honestly? You could then describe how uncomfortable you feel about

*having to keep quiet. You could also maybe help them understand
that keeping secrets from family members does not spare anyone anything. Any pain that your family may be spared right now will be
canceled out by the pain that they will feel about being kept out of the
loop.*

*I hope that your sister-in-law and brother see that the best thing
would be to tell all of your family. You can offer to do the telling if they
feel it would be too painful for them. If they do not want the rest of the
family to know, however, you will have to keep the secret, as tough as
that is. Good luck.*

Hip-Deep Gumbo

LETTER: SISTER SUICIDE

Hi. I am a nineteen-year-old college student with one sibling, a
twenty-one-year-old sister. Both of us have spent the past ten years
struggling with depression and eating disorders.

I have searched for relief through medication and therapy, but
nothing seems to make a dent. My sister, for her part, has refused to
take such measures. Lately she's revealed to me that she is considering suicide. Honestly, I think it might be the thing to do—I don't
think she'll ever really be happy. I don't see this world as a place
where optimism and hope is well-founded. We don't believe in
God, we don't take great joy out of anything in particular; we struggle through cruel people and mundane days—so why shouldn't
she get the final rest? I personally would have probably done it
years ago if it wasn't for a sense of responsibility for my parents. I
don't know what I'm asking really. Moral guidance? How to elec-
troshock both our lives so that it isn't the same exhausting sludge of
emptiness and painful emotion?

At any suggestion of suicide, alarms go off for the Elders. Those
who responded to this letter almost unanimously recommended an

immediate call to a suicide hotline for the sister, and professional help for the advice seeker to help her recover from what appears to be clinical depression—a condition that Elder Rose, sixty-four, of Calgary, Alberta, aptly describes in her response as "slogging through hip-deep gumbo." Once that was said, some Elders empathized by describing their own bouts with depression and how they sought treatment.

Elders Gpa, eighty-five, and Gma, eighty-one, of Rochester Hills, Michigan, also called upon personal experience—not their own, but that of their child. "This letter spoke to our heart. We tried to light a path for these girls modeled on our daughter's history of success in fighting depression," Gpa says.

We speak from our experience with our daughter who at fourteen was diagnosed manic-depressive after several suicide attempts. After many frustrating attempts we were able to find a comfortable (for her) therapist. She went on to finish high school and college, graduating with a master's in psychology. She married and had two lovely girls, our granddaughters. She practiced for fifteen years as a clinical psychologist. Today she continues on medication and some therapy and has a vital, healthy life, looking forward to weddings and grandchildren.

We found that disciplining yourself to a rigid timetable for medication is absolutely essential. Strong physical activity can be highly beneficial in containing mood swings. Talking it out with therapists and loved ones is helpful in keeping the demons at bay.

Suicide is only one way out of the darkness. A better way is to fight as hard and as smart as you can. Gather a support group consisting of your parents, family, sister, therapist, psychiatrist, mental health support group, and empathetic friends to help you.

It will take many small steps to climb up into the sunshine; reaching out to us like this was a big, strong stride. Our very best wishes go with you.

Elder Ruthie, sixty-four, of Swanton, Ohio, however, says she believes this letter requires a "politically incorrect" answer. "The line that struck me in the midst of their pain was they did not believe in God," she says. "Without my faith in God, I could easily be where they are. If this young lady came to me, this is exactly what I would tell her. I really don't expect this response to make it to publication."

The Elder Wisdom Circle does, in fact, have a policy on addressing religious matters. Elders are instructed to remain open-minded at all times and to avoid promoting personal religious standards, beliefs, and practices unless specifically requested by an advice seeker. The service does not promote any one faith.

In this letter, Ruthie adheres to that policy by discussing the issue of God in a general way, as well as making it clear that she is describing her own experience with faith, rather than proselytizing. She offers that trusting in God might be an option worth pursuing, rather than threatening some form of afterlife suffering if the advice seeker does not choose a religious path. There seems nothing "politically incorrect" in presenting that view.

So here it is, Elder Ruthie:

You question if you are seeking moral guidance; it would be logical to me that you came seeking wisdom from the "Elder WISDOM Circle."

For my part there can be no wisdom outside of God. All the things you describe are what life is like without God. At the same time a moral life grows out of a relationship to a higher power. All 12-Step programs have that premise. If there is such a thing as Suicide Anonymous (and I think there is), that is where you might start to find help. There are many paths to a relationship with God and at this point I would suggest you have nothing to lose. Try starting a search. At ages nineteen and twenty-one both of you are very young and have plenty of time to seek out a spiritual life. Start looking into the philosophies of various religions that seek ways to give meaning to life.

Bottom line, even if there were no afterlife and no God, those who live as if there were, from my observation, are happier and more fulfilled. Give it a try, after all—as I said, what have you got to lose?

◄○►

When We Grow Up

Hello. Thanks for your wonderful Web site. I need to know how to deal with an older sister who is constantly "bad-mouthing" me to our mother. She is fifty-five, I am thirty-seven. The things she says are quite venomous. This has been going on for about ten years, and I have not confronted her mainly because it would make things very uncomfortable for other members of the family. She is also very passive-aggressive and many of her harsh words are cloaked in humor or teasing.

I know she harbors a great deal of resentment toward me as well, but for things that are beyond my control. She believes my parents spoiled me, were more lenient with me, and have given me more than they gave her. All this may be true, but these are issues she should have resolved with my parents long ago, rather than hating me.

My basic question is: Should I confront her? If so, how? And second: How do I deal with this intense frustration and anger I feel? I look forward to your words of wisdom!

Writes Elder Barbara:

My older sister resented me for similar reasons; she told me often when we were both adults that I had ruined her life. Finally, when we were in our sixties, we had it out on the telephone. We both alternated yelling at each other. I got out all of my resentments about a half hour before she got out all of hers. So I listened quietly; I must confess that I was smiling toward the end of our talk. As wrong as she was about some of her resentments, she needed to air them. A couple of months later she called to talk to me about how she'd just realized that she'd been unfair to me. We now are building a good relationship for the first time.

It will be easier if you can see how emotionally crippled your sister is. If she is fifty-five years old and still is filled with anger at her parents, whom she does not even have the courage to confront, then she cannot be a happy person. As hard as it is for you, if you can look at her with sympathy, it will be easier for you to deal with your own anger.

Says Elder Michelle, "My mother loved my brother best. But he thinks she loved *me* best. Go figure."

Who is happier, the child who was loved best or the one who was not? The answer is the one for whom it is a past issue. Your sister is still trying to equalize the two of you by bad-mouthing you to your mother. Tacky. She is still living her childhood resentment.

Your sister needs to forgive you for coming along and stealing your mother's heart. Your sister needs to know that there is room in there for both of you.

I am wondering how you know that your sister bad-mouths you to your mom. My guess is that your mom tells you. Tell your mother kindly that it hurts you too much to hear about your sister's bad-mouthing and to please not share that information. Your mother could tell your sister that she needs to get over the past and stop bad-mouthing her sister, but that is your mother's choice.

Your question is "Should I confront her?" No. However, it may be helpful to make peace with her. You might say that you know there are many years between you and it must have been hard having a sister come into her life when she could have been having her own child. Then let her talk and just listen. You are so right that she needs to let this go and to grow up and respect you, but she needs your help to do it.

Now, in his eighties, Jacobus is learning something about respect for a sibling.

His brother Willie was the first of the two to join the Elder Wisdom Circle—under the dashing pen name Horatio Victor; he brought Jacobus into the fold. Even though Willie had run away from home at age seventeen, and homebody Jacobus never strayed any farther from Blumenheim than nearby Saskatoon, the two forged a late-life bond. Jacobus's wife died in 1999 after a happy marriage of forty-six years; Willie, less successful at traditional domesticity, had been divorced for what seemed like forever and has had difficult relationships with his offspring. Now, both were living alone and took comfort in communicating by phone or e-mail almost every day.

That's why Jacobus recommended that the writer of the letter "I Think I Ruined My Brother's Life" might better worry more about his relationship with his own brother than that brother's relationship with his wife. "My relationship with my brother has turned 180 degrees plus, I guess you might say," Jacobus observes. "His memory is failing, and I can reminisce about the old days. We grew up in this very conservative environment, which he totally rejected. He can talk to me, and tell me things—like our parents had it right in the first place."

The two brothers are now a long way from the back seat of the family car in Blumenheim. "Now he *likes* to hear my voice," Jacobus says, with a laugh.

MEETING YOURSELF HALFWAY
Wisdom for Self-Discovery

I must say that I am delighted to have found your Web site. The response I received was logical and straightforward. I was looking for a miraculous panacea to solve my dilemma. What I got was a charming, compassionate tousle on the top of my head and an answer like the squeeze of a hand to let me know I might have the skill to work this out.

Grateful,
"Louise"

—From "Feedback & Kudos"
www.ElderWisdomCircle.org

How does it feel
To be on your own
—Bob Dylan,
"Like a Rolling Stone"

Inside Story

I'm an eighteen-year-old male on the brink of high school graduation. I'm gay and have yet to come out.

I would love the life of a heterosexual. I would love to be married
and have children without being discriminated against. I know coming out would pretty much ruin my chances of that. My family frequently speaks poorly of homosexuals. My friends are all expecting
me to grow up as the cliché role model—having a successful career
and "normal" family life.

I've read stories about people who have overcome homosexuality through years and years of abstinence and religious devotion.
I just don't have that devotion nor do I have the willpower to ab-
stain from every thought that crosses my mind for the necessary
amount of time to "train" my brain.

I can come out, or continue living a lie and perhaps marry as an
attempt to overcome my lifestyle (marriage may not be the best
choice for my potential spouse's sake, I know). I'm not asking for
you to make the decision for me. I just wish I had someone or
something to point me in the right direction.

The first answer comes from an Elder who calls herself Silver Sun
Woman. A friend argues that "silver" is the wrong element, the sun is

gold—but Silver Sun Woman loves the way the sun dances on silver when it catches the light.

She also has adopted the name Silver Sun Woman for a less attractive reason: Now in her late seventies, Silver Sun Woman resides in a conservative senior community where, she believes, the other residents would reject her if they discovered that she is a lesbian. Too many people already know her by the pen name she uses when offering advice through the Elder Wisdom Circle. So for the purposes of this book, she will borrow her name from sunlight on silver.

What makes Silver Sun Woman different from the young man concerned about "coming out" is that, while she has made a practical decision to stay in the closet as far as her neighbors are concerned, she has learned over the course of many years to be comfortable in her own skin.

Like the other Elders responding to this collection of letters, all from advice seekers confused in one way or another about their identity, Silver Sun Woman advises self-acceptance—but combined with some street smarts to help navigate a world that may not always be so accepting.

Silver (for short) and her partner (whom we'll call "Gold") reside in separate apartments in the community, on different floors—but both inhabit the same closet; in this environment, it is not okay to be old and gay. But affordable senior housing is hard to come by, so Silver and Gold live with their secret.

It is somewhat ironic for Silver to find herself back in the closet after coming out more than forty years ago. She discovered her own lesbian yearnings in the late 1950s, after more than ten years of marriage and two children.

During that period, Silver saw a male therapist to discuss her newly discovered sexual identity. "He asked me two questions: 'Did you ever have sex with a woman?' and 'When you see a woman walking down the street, do you want to go to bed with her?' My answer was no to both. He proclaimed me 'not a lesbian.' "

Knowing better, Silver came out to her husband in 1964. "He said I was sick, and needed to go to a straight therapist and not see any women for a year," she says. "I complied. I was also in a weekly group therapy with straight people who knew my husband and children and were very hostile toward me. It was hell, but I accepted it because I felt terrible about what I was doing to my family."

After her year of therapy, Silver's husband asked her how she felt. Her feelings had not changed. Then her sexually conservative spouse shocked her with an idea that he thought would take care of the problem. "He said, 'Well, why don't you just get involved in a relationship and bring her home, and we can have a threesome?' " Silver recalls. "I said, 'I'm sorry, that's not the way I do things.' So I left without any money, and I lost custody of my kids."

Silver threw herself into the Gay Liberation Movement, counseling gay youth and participating in the first Stonewall March in 1969. "This was way before the AIDS epidemic. The chant was 'Out of the closet and into the streets,' " she reminisces. "I can still cry when I remember that, because we would hold out our hands to the people we knew, and they would hesitate—and then they would reach out and take our hands."

Because of her own struggles with the consequences of coming out, Silver Sun Woman has devoted herself to answering the questions of young gays and lesbians who ask for guidance from the Elder Wisdom Circle—or from their hysterical parents: "Oh my God, I just found out my son is *gay!*" She grows impatient with what seem to her the trivial matters that seem to occupy many heterosexual teens and preteens. "My least favorite questions are from the young people who say, 'Joe smiled at me but Paul also smiled at me and now I don't know who to smile at,' " she sniffs. She knows the more difficult question is what to do when Joe and Paul begin smiling at each other.

Along with her personal story, Silver often refers gay people, as well as their family and friends, to the national organization Parents, Families and Friends of Lesbians and Gays (PFLAG) and other support groups.

Hello. Thanks for writing to us. I totally shared most of your concerns as a middle-aged lesbian when I first came out. Where you and I disagree is where you state that people are able to overcome homosexuality through various means. In my opinion, that is not so. They are able to suppress their feelings and actions, but not their basic nature.

Yes, it would be unfair to your spouse, as well as to yourself, to marry into a heterosexual alliance. The good news is that you still are in a position to have a successful career as well as a normal family life . . . and come out. If you lived in a largely gay and lesbian society, you would be considered the norm. Some of those societies are: the Bay Area (San Francisco and environs); Greenwich Village (New York City); Madison, Wisconsin; and Hillcrest (San Diego).

As for your losing your mother and brother: They may be distressed, at first, but if you treat yourself with respect and dignity . . . and with pride, rather than shame, they most likely will eventually feel your influence.

I hope that I was able to point you in the right direction. Take care . . . you have a great and wonderful adventure ahead of you, and you deserve it.

Elder Emme, sixty-three, of Bel Air, Maryland, brings a different sort of personal experience to the young man's dilemma.

You have a big decision to make. As you've implied, no one can make the decision for you, but I'd like to give you some ideas to reflect on while you're determining your next move.

First, a little about me. I'm a recently retired high school teacher. The last few years of my career, I became involved with gay youth and their friends by volunteering to be the faculty sponsor for the first high school Gay-Straight Alliance (GSA) in our city. It's the best thing I ever did in my career, and I'm proud to still be an activist for gay issues.

You mention having read stories about people who have "overcome" being gay. How one behaves sexually is a choice. But who you're attracted to really isn't a choice—most people who have studied homosexuality agree that you were born that way. There's also the possibility that some of the people you have read about who "overcame" are bisexuals who choose to ignore the same sex attractions they feel.

Probably the most difficult part of your decision is going to be how your family might react if you come out. This is where you have to choose between living a lie or possibly losing some family members' respect and love. Coming out could be the most painful experience you'll ever have. You have to decide whether you're ready to handle the consequences.

You mention that you would like to have a normal life with children. You also know that it would be wrong to marry under false pretenses. But don't give up on having children. Many gay couples adopt, and are excellent parents. I once had a straight student who was in foster care with two fathers, and they did a fine job. It's even possible for a single gay person to adopt.

Have you looked in your area for support groups for young adults who are gay? Check your local library, too, for information on coming out. (You may not want to do this if you live in a town where everybody knows everybody.)

My personal bias is probably toward your coming out, but you have to weigh all the possible ramifications of doing so for yourself. Coming out can be more difficult and heart-wrenching than most of us could possibly understand, but it could also lead to fulfillment you can only dream about right now.

My heart goes out to you. Please know that there are many of us out here who care about you and your struggles. I'll be thinking about you—may you find well-being in your life.

From the Parent's Point of View

LETTER: HELPING ME GUIDE MY SON

I am a woman of strong faith who believes everyone falls short and who is loving of all people. With that out the way, I came across my thirteen-year-old boy watching gay porn the other day. I am understandably disturbed. Watching porn is bad enough, but I have some idea of how to approach it and possibly even expected it of a young boy with changing hormones. I do not know where he would be exposed to gay porn enough to even know to look it up and this disturbs me as well. He lives with his dad and stepmom who are very traditional, so I know it doesn't come from home.

I have a brother who is gay and I love him, too; I do not seem to my son that I will love him any less if he is gay. But just as I would feel if my daughter fell for an adult, or a married man, or her brother, or if my child fell into drugs, I feel a need to try and intervene somehow.

I just don't want to overreact if this is just curiosity on his part. My heart is very broken over this, I love my son so much, I want to do all I can to guide his choices to be healthy ones spiritually, as well as physically and mentally. Please give me some options on dealing with this in a way that is spiritually sound. I understand tolerance as my brother is gay, and this is not the type of advice I need.

In her response, Silver Sun Woman takes the advice seeker at her word. Silver does not hazard a guess as to whether the son is gay, nor does she lecture the mother on the issue of acceptance.

Hello. Thanks for writing to us.

I think it is quite possible that your son heard about the Web site from his friends. I suspect that most young boys try all sorts of Web sites as experiments. You might bring it up by asking how he found the Web site and what he thought about it. His response might give you peace of mind. You might also mention that you do not approve of pornography. If you still are concerned, perhaps you could discuss it with a member of the clergy.

I also was under the impression that there were safety controls that could be installed on your computer to prevent him from watching that type of program. Speak to a computer dealer and your Internet service provider.

It is something most boys do, and many men, from what I understand. If he can talk to you without fear of ridicule, or punishment, he'll be okay. Good luck!

Other Elders, however, thought certain clues within the letter suggest that the mother may be more judgmental about sexual orientation than she realizes. Elder Kriko, seventy-five, of Tempe, Arizona, is among them. He writes:

This is not about spirituality or tolerance, it is about nature. If it is in your son's nature to be gay it would be a terrible disservice to him to add to his confusion and the ostracism he is bound to face. By intervening, whether you mean to or not, you will seem to disapprove of him as a human being.

Being gay in this culture, as your brother can tell you, is fraught with danger and exclusion. The last thing a gay man in this society needs is for his mother to reject him. When you say you believe that all people fall short, in this context that says to me that you feel that a gay person falls short of being acceptable. Your son will sense that.

At thirteen a boy is not fully formed. It may be that he is not at all interested in being gay but is simply curious and titillated by the forbidden. If so, your intervention would make him all the more curious.

It is comforting to hear you say that you are loving of all people. I know that you love your son. Give him the respect he deserves and let him be whatever he is to be.

Elder Holiday, eighty-six, of Tarzana, California, responds from the emotional perspective of a mother who raised a homosexual son.

You love your son very much and want to be close to him. That's reason enough to be open and honest with him. Despite the fact that you say you accept and love your gay brother, you still harbor fear and concern that your son might be gay.

I know only too well that parents don't want their children to be gay for numerous reasons. I went through all the stages of denial myself, since the youngest of my three sons was gay. However, I realized that there was nothing I could do to change that and so I joined a wonderful group called Parents, Families and Friends of Lesbians and Gays (PFLAG).

This was back in the early eighties when prejudice and discrimination were rampant. Also, at that time, AIDS had reared its ugly head. My son was one of the first doctors in New York City to treat AIDS, had already built up a great reputation, and had begun an enviable career when he died of AIDS in 1989 at age thirty-seven.

Thank God your son is alive and well and more education is available to him. If your son is, indeed, gay then you must talk to him openly about it, go to support group meetings with him, and learn to appreciate him for the human being he is. He needs your love and not your fears and condemnation. On the other hand, maybe he's watching gay porn as a matter of curiosity. He may be aware of his gay uncle and wants to know more about him.

However, gay men are human and have the same emotions as straight men; sex is only a part of their lives and not who they are. Don't lose your son because he's not the image you might have of him but love him and accept him as he is.

Light My Fire

LETTER: PERSONAL MOTIVATION.

My question is about personal motivation, procrastination, and achievement, and I hope it isn't too vague. I will turn forty this year, and it's been almost two years now that I'm at the first job I've truly loved. I'm attending an accredited online school and will finally have my bachelor's degree next year (hopefully). I've been married for thirteen years, and most of that time has been a financial struggle. We've lived in a mobile home for about eight years and went through a bankruptcy when we moved in here. I was unemployed for about eighteen months after 9/11, then struggled at $8 an hour jobs for another year. I have steadily gained weight since we got married, and I'm now up to about 270 pounds.

I feel that the reason my career has taken so long to get off the ground, the reason we live in a cruddy old mobile home, and the reason I've gotten so out of shape is because of my lack of personal motivation. The thing is, I know how to work. I'm not lazy. I have goals. I want to get in shape, get a home, and finish my degree. But there are a lot of things in my life that I want that I don't take action on. I want to get in shape, but I don't go to the gym. I want to invest in real estate, but I don't put in the time doing the activities that will allow me to be successful at it. What do I need to do to light a fire under my butt to get moving?

Elder Frank, seventy-two, of Greensboro, North Carolina, drove a big white Harley Electra Glide tour bike until recent heart problems caused him to undergo a quintuple bypass and the insertion of a pacemaker. He sold the motorcycle, but has not lost his sense of adventure. "I like an active life," he says.

This is an understatement. Retired from the electronics business, Frank's varied career has also included an eight-year stint in naval aviation as an air crew member, as well as a number of years as an auxiliary police officer in Nassau County, New York. Though this was a volunteer position, Frank was often called into service when the police department was short-handed, or when special events brought extra crowds to the city. "I was armed, and trained," he asserts. Frank, who later lived in the Los Angeles area, has also served as a bodyguard to "a lot of Hollywood people." Now, Frank uses the knowledge he gained in the Navy as a tour guide for an aviation museum.

Coming from the strict disciplines of police work and the military, Frank is the last person you'd expect to lack motivation. But he says that the stress of the electronics business often sapped his energy. That's why he's always had so many outside interests: "In retrospect, that's why I tried to leave work at the office," he says.

As a man of many interests, Frank knows how easy it is to lose focus. His answer to this advice seeker, he says, "directly relates to my need to continually monitor my activity, even in retirement. One can spend hours at a computer playing if not organized."

It is to your credit that you have recognized the need for change in your life at the young age of forty. I think we can both agree that the root cause is a form of depression. Your cup runneth over!

Let's take one step at a time. Food is a comfort. When we get sad or depressed, we tend to graze in the kitchen. I win with 277 at my max. Excess weight will slow you down for sure and may cause health problems. If diets work for you, do it. If not, try a change of lifestyle. Go to a swap meet and get a used bike. Bike to the store for milk as a fun thing (it also saves money on gas). You might try having a contest with a friend or coworker with weekly weigh-ins, which can be the one losing the least having to wash the other one's car or put their trash out. Money need not be involved, which leads us to the next facet.

Financial struggles have a snowballing tendency. Solving the financial dilemma also requires support. One must first analyze money outlay for a budget, and then team up to achieving a goal. You do not mention if your spouse works or if there are children. If he or she is able to contribute by working and you work a second part-time job, the results might amaze you. Even if it is only putting your pocket change in a mayonnaise jar each night or twenty-five cents for each time you sneeze, start saving.

Kudos to you my friend for continuing your education in the face of despair; that takes guts! So you see, you DO have motivation! Just transfer a piece of it to everyday living and chores.

Lastly, your "cruddy old mobile home." If you are paying a space rental fee for your mobile home, you may want to look for a lease option where the money goes to a better end. Just because one has declared a bankruptcy, it does not mean doomsday. Find someone with good knowledge first. YOU CAN DO IT!

Consider the butt fire ignited. Our thoughts and best wishes are with you.

Worth It

My husband and I both work forty-plus hours a week. We have a medium-size house and large yard. Sometimes I feel overwhelmed by the daily routine of going to work and caring for the house and yard, pets, bills, laundry, food prep etc., etc. I recently went to a weekend intensive learning and spiritual retreat that felt like a life-changing experience, but now that I am back, my life hasn't changed. I think about selling everything I own and scaling down drastically, but then I look at my home, yard, and pets and I love the comforts and spaciousness I have.

I am the primary breadwinner, so I can't quit or go part time. How can I resolve the inner conflict between material things that give me pleasure and wanting more time for the intangibles like spirituality and my personal journey?

Elder Tina, seventy-three, has been on a personal spirituality quest for about fifty years now. Most recently, she has been on that journey with Frank, her companion and housemate of several years.

Tina and Frank attended the same high school on Long Island, New York, class of 1951—but they weren't an item back then. They did not meet again until their fiftieth high school reunion in 2001. Tina attended with her then-husband, and Frank, a widower, came with a date.

But one year later, Tina's forty-eight-year marriage had ended, and Frank was no longer involved with his companion for the reunion. So Frank, then living near Los Angeles, moved to North Carolina to be with Tina, who had lived in the state since 1972. Frank roared into town on his Harley—not the usual style for Tina, a former medical transcriptionist with formidable spelling skills who prefers a quiet life and a workspace alone in a corner.

The two have not married because, at this stage of their lives, it doesn't make good financial sense. "But that don't mean we don't love each other," Frank jokes.

While Tina has on occasion been persuaded to ride the Harley with Frank, she much prefers the sanctuary of her "sacred space"—a stone patio nestled among the trees in her backyard, near the lake. "That works for me," she says.

"I think it's even worse than when we were younger, with our young families," Tina adds. "Now it's like everybody has to have a TV for every person in the house, a computer for every person in the house, a cell phone for everybody, all that *stuff*—so many material things to keep up with. I think we spent more time together; now, everything is on your own."

Life is stressful and complicated nowadays. From my own experience, I would say that a spiritual retreat or a book is not going to change your life.

Look around you, review your life, and write down what you spend the 1,440 minutes in each day doing. Where can you gain more time? Most of us can gain time by turning off the television or limiting time spent on the computer or telephone.

Now that you feel that something is missing from your life, you have to take steps to initiate changes. It can be something simple like lighting a candle, saying grace before a meal, saying bedtime prayers, taking time to reflect quietly, or starting a journal where you write down all the things that you are grateful for every day. Set aside time to go for a walk or to meditate. Learn tai chi. Find some time for solitude. Set aside a space in your backyard for a sanctuary where you can sit quietly and enjoy nature. That always seems to nourish my soul.

Then track your expenses for a month and see where you can cut back. Ask your husband for his ideas on simplifying your lives. It's not necessary to live an austere life, but see if you can separate your wants from your needs. There's a big difference between the two. If you can hire someone to help with the yard work or housecleaning, you could probably free up quite a bit of time.

I believe each of us has to do our own soul searching and we have to find our own path. Listen to your own inner voice. If you want to make your life more meaningful, figure out what's important to you and go for it. Enjoy the journey!

If you're too busy for spiritual things, then you're too busy.
—Asbury Friends group,
Gaithersburg, Maryland

From the exhausted JeanMc, seventy-nine, of Sterling Heights, Michigan:

My husband is quite ill, can't drive anymore, and everything falls on my shoulders. I keep a calendar where everything "medical" is written in red. My calendar looks like a bloody crime scene . . . mostly red. Unless you are a hermit living in the woods somewhere, you are going to be inundated with paperwork, cooking, cleaning, shopping, laundry, or whatever.

If you are truly overwhelmed and it is making you miserable, you must choose what to eliminate from your life.

As for me, I continue on, doing the paperwork, taking my husband to doctors' appointments, cleaning the house, shopping and cooking, caring for the pets, gardening. I finally relax in the evening, watch a TV show or two, and do what reading I want to do after I go to bed.

So, you see, life goes on, we do what we need to do and what we want to do. We must choose which is which. No easy answer.

Elder Lester, sixty-nine, of Roswell, Georgia, is retired from a highly stressful career in automobile sales; at one time, he was one of the top Cadillac salesmen in the country, and he says you can't sell a big-ticket item like a luxury car without the ability to inspire trust in the nervous buyer. Lester has penned two books on personal motivation and taught evening courses on stress management. He writes:

When we let society condition us to believe that success is measured in terms of power, money, and status, we will never find true happiness. It's the fear of failure that slows us down and prevents us from moving forward.

By comparing ourselves to others we are inadvertently trying to be THE BEST and that just brings us down. This is the reason we must stop trying to be THE BEST and only try to be OUR BEST.

Don't let the fear of failure prevent you from following your dreams. Turn your "I should" in to "I must." And, as I said before, stop comparing your situation to that of others. It's my opinion that once you put these things into action, your mind and your body (the weight) will all become healthier.

"That was me, twenty years ago," says Grandma-Dan, sixty-one, of Troy, Michigan. Her advice for learning to rest in peace, so to speak:

I have written my obituary at a couple of retreats as part of an exercise they gave me to do, and found it very revealing. It was a perfect way for me to begin realigning my values, goals, and expectations. Perhaps that would be helpful to you as well.

—◄○►—

An Underlying Problem

LETTER: LINGERIE

Why is it so wrong for men to wear women's lingerie?

The Elders who chose to reply to this letter think there's nothing wrong with men wearing women's lingerie—but suggest that there is a good argument for keeping it in the boudoir.

Your Grandparents—an Elder group that can boast some members in their mid-nineties—weigh in from their assisted living residence in Pleasant Hill, California. They wonder if this writer might have more on his mind than whether or not he looks fetching in black lace.

We think the bigger question not being asked is "Does this mean I am gay?" Well, we are not experts, but we have heard that some straight men like to wear women's underwear.

We feel it is really important not to hide this kind of thing from your partner. As long as it works within the couple, we see nothing wrong with it. Frankly, it is nobody's business but yours!

Elder Barbara, sixty-two, of Greene, New York, answered this letter because "I know men who wear women's lingerie."

Men whom I know who routinely do wear women's clothing have told me that they enjoy how the silky fabrics feel and that they feel softer, more in touch with their feminine side and just plain happier when they dress up. If you do something that you enjoy, that doesn't hurt anyone else, what could be wrong with it?

I am answering you so easily now, but the first time in my life that I was faced with a partner who wanted to dress up, my answer was a categorical no. But he kept at me, nicely, and I slowly allowed him to wear women's clothes; I remember approving of one article of clothing at a time. Once I was no longer threatened by it, I realized that when he was dressed that way I saw a different, softer, and appealing side of him. That's when I began to believe what I wrote in the first paragraph; there is nothing wrong with a man wearing women's clothing.

Muses Barbara after writing her response: "Funny, I feel 'outed' and a little bit uncomfortable that anyone might know that I allowed men to dress up in front of me. So I can imagine how difficult the issue is for the writer."

Elder Jangela, sixty-six, of Detroit, writes:

I don't think men wearing women's lingerie IS wrong. But I can't imagine why any man would want to wear women's lingerie. It is my personal belief that men created women's lingerie to punish women. I never met a bra I thought was comfortable nor have I ever worn a girdle or bodysuit that I thought was comfortable. Just like women's shoes. All men should be required to wear them and see if they can walk without falling.

Nine Lives

LETTER: STEPPING UP TO THE NINTH LIFE

A good friend told me I should open the ninth life cafe. I am sixty-two years young, vastly accomplished in my business career, have a loving family and grandchildren I love. I have survived sexual abuse at twelve to fourteen years of age, lung surgery, throat surgery, prostate surgery, and cancer. Two years ago I fell three stories from a building I was constructing. I pushed to get back to normal physically, still struggle with cognitive/vision/balance issues, but am pretty much okay on that, although I'm not who I once was.

Question is: How do I gear up for the ninth life when I am questioning my spiritual commitment, my interest in learning/growing, my value to my family, my financial future, and doubt the ability/willingness to kick it in gear once again?

I have active hobbies/interests and am a principal in my own business. I feel a bit let down by the man upstairs and a bit weary of these tests of character. Deep inside I am sad and don't feel there are many people who could grasp these experiences or would have the will to survive them.

Elder Web, sixty-four, of Farmington Hills, Michigan, says, "I chose this letter because I felt that the writer was feeling sorry for himself, while not really saying so. I felt a firm, friendly nudge might be in order.

"Life is difficult for all of us, in one way or another," Web adds. "Self-pity is unacceptable to me."

You certainly have experienced many things in your life and I congratulate you for having the strength to persevere through these difficult situations. I am just a little older than you and your letter caused me to look back over my life and think about things that have happened to me. Although I have been fortunate to enjoy good health, I have experienced many of these health issues with very close family members. I have also had many traumatic personal experiences in my life and always have been able to cope and move ahead.

My point is that everyone experiences pain in their life, and how they deal with it is a personal thing.

I feel you need to count your blessings, which by your own admission are plentiful, and make a decision to move ahead, one day at a time. Sometimes it's best not to overanalyze everything. There are more people like yourself than you might think, but truly strong people usually move ahead without advertising it (unlike the people we see on many TV programs).

Remember to always look for the good, learn from the bad, and try to live each day to its fullest. I wish you a long, happy, and productive life.

Elder Rechama, sixty-four, a retired attorney who lives in Berkeley, California, also thought the writer needed a nudge—and maybe not so gentle. "I responded in this way because I felt real compassion for the writer, combined with impatience at the self-congratulatory self-centered tone of his letter," Rechama says. "Also, I have a firm conviction that meaning is something we create, not something we discover."

I am going to be honest, even brutally honest with you. The source of your problem is evident in the words of your letter. It is filled with "I" and "my." The tone and content combine pride with having overcome so much adversity with resentment at having been forced to do so. A lethal combination. Why? Because both force you to focus almost entirely on yourself.

My first advice is that you have yourself checked for clinical depression. It's possible that the stress you have experienced may have caused a chemical or situational depression than can be helped with medical treatment or therapy.

If, as I suspect, your problem is not clinical depression but spiritual malaise, then I advise you to stop asking questions about yourself, including "why me?" and "what will my future be like?" and start asking questions about what you can give in return for the life you have repeatedly been blessed with. Recovery from your self-absorption doesn't mean just a superficial counting of your blessings. It will require a deep recognition that we're all here on borrowed time and this ninth life, like the eight before it, is not something you've earned. If you begin to concentrate on what you can give back, rather than on what you are entitled to, at the very least you'll escape the boredom of worrying about yourself.

I hope this helps. It worked for me.

At Cross-Purposes

LETTER: CROSS-CULTURAL COMMUNICATION

Dear Elder Wisdom Circle member,

I come from Asia and am currently living in United States. The Eastern culture is quite different from Western culture. During the past six years, I have met some Americans who communicate with me perfectly well; some are my friends for years now. But with some people, I feel it's so hard to communicate. How do you make people understand you, and not judge you in their own culture? My current work involves working with different people, so this is very important for my career; I can't simply keep away from the people who are culturally ignorant. Thank you very much for your advice.

JeanMc knows this story first hand.

My daughter-in-law is Chinese. She has been in this country for al-
most seven years. But, still, there are cultural conflicts. Birthdays are
not important to her. In my family, they are very important. I recog-
nize the Chinese New Year . . . in her honor. I buy Chinese New
Year's stamps and offer them as an "extra" as a Christmas gift. I am
hearing impaired, which makes it even more difficult to communicate.
Now that she and my son have a daughter, it is even more important
for me to connect.

I understand where you are coming from. The cultures are ex-
tremely different. Unfortunately, you must learn to put up with those
Americans who don't want to, or can't, understand who you are and
what your culture is. I can't imagine how I would fare if I were to live
in Beijing. I would have to depend on the kindness of those I met. As
you must.

The people you work with are well aware of the cultural divide.
Some will willingly accommodate you, others won't. But if you are
good at what you do, you will be successful. Just don't let the ones
who are truly ignorant get to you. They don't matter. They really
don't.

I wish you well.

In her eighty-eight years, Elder Marble Rye of Studio City, California,
has learned that there are some people you get along with, and some you
don't—regardless of what country they hail from.

Who can make it with everybody? In a social situation or at work,
there are some you are naturally attracted to. You are blaming it on
being Asian, but if a person feels at ease with some people but not oth-
ers, that's chemistry.

Of course, Marble Rye believes that with age comes a certain degree
of privilege. She says, "Now, if I came across someone who was intoler-
ant, I would just shout them down."

◄○►

From the Heart

LETTER: ATTITUDE

I find that I am not the person that I wanted to be. I am pretty, successful, and smart. I am considered a nice, caring person. And I do try to do unto others as I would have done to me. However, the truth is my heart is full of anger, hate, jealousy, insecurity, and criticism. If people knew some of the things I feel and think, I do not think they would like me so much. I do not like having a hateful heart. I want to be beautiful on the inside. I want to know from your life experience, how did you find true peace and love? How did you stay optimistic when there is so much anger and hate in the world?

Says Elder Ruthie, sixty-four, of Swanton, Ohio, "I believe most people are much better than they will give themselves credit for. Self-forgiveness is not a popular phrase in today's world, and self-acceptance is not far ahead of it."

Before I go to the sharing that you asked for, I want to say I am greatly impressed by your openness and honesty. Many of us are not as nice on the inside as we show on the outside, but it takes a very honest person to admit to that.

You are already doing the most important thing in becoming beautiful on the inside. You have heard the saying that beauty is as beauty does. You are doing, and that doing will grow inward.

Yes, there is much anger and hate in the world; in our small town just this weekend a domestic disturbance led to the death of two children at the hand of their father, who in turn took his own life. This, after the father attempted to kill his wife (their mother). We are all shocked and tearfully asking how this could happen. Yet in this same weekend I saw people reaching out to make Mother's Day better for women in isolated situations. Even at our church I found hope in a teen asking for support as he is preparing to go on a mission to Guatemala.

Your last question is the hardest to answer in that I am not really there yet. There are many parts of my heart that are not yet loving enough and so many of my intentions are not yet pure. It is a lifelong work. I will not say struggle, as that is a bit too dramatic a word for the process. It is more like taking the time to weed the garden as well as to fertilize and water it.

Your letter gives me a lot of hope in our younger generation. Thank you so much for contacting the Elder Wisdom Circle.

Elders Gpa-and-Gma of Rochester Hills, Michigan, eighty-five and eighty-one, say that through their work for the Elder Wisdom Circle, they have discovered that even two people in their eighties can find joy in helping others. "We tried to guide the writer to think in terms of giving as a path to personal peace and happiness," the Elders say.

As you get older, you learn the good in people and the environment far outweighs the evil, despite what the news media tells you. So inside your heart you reserve a small space for anger and resentment against injustice and immorality that motivates you to speak out and act.

You may find in helping others that the hateful heart will soften. There are many hungry, hurting men, women, and children around you who need a helping hand and will hold you in their hearts. Giving a few hours a week to community services, the Salvation Army, a soup kitchen, crisis hotline, or other charitable organization can help you find a peaceful, loving heart.

24/7

LETTER: HOW DO I SLOW DOWN AND SMELL THE ROSES?

Dear Elders,

I love my family, my friends, and my job. Yet I am one of those fast-moving, nervous energy people who never can rest for more than five minutes. Sometimes I say or do things on impulse that hurt others.

How can I teach myself to slow down, to smile more, allow myself to get fat? I want to be the guy who can take an insult with a smile, keep cool in a bad situation, etc. My fuse is too short. Any help is appreciated.

The Heavensviewsages of Delta, Colorado, advise the buyer to beware:

If you allow it, the pace of our Western culture will run you into the ground. Buy this, do that, feel this. Advertisers in all media want to create a feeling of panic so you won't miss this chance to buy, do, or see what they are selling.

Fortunately, you can take control, and you can smell the roses. Beware of how our culture can drive you 24/7 if you allow it to. Practice slowing things down deliberately and look at your life and your surroundings soberly and calmly.

Practice thinking, really thinking—and, as the old saying goes: "If you can't say anything nice, don't say anything at all." In our dining area we have a needlepoint that says "Lord, keep your arm around my shoulder and your hand over my mouth!"

Understand yourself and you naturally will come into your own rhythm, not one dictated to you by society. You can survive and thrive without half the things our culture says you have to have to be happy.

From the Asbury Friends:

As far as the impulse to make remarks that hurt others: Just count to ten before speaking. If that doesn't do it, make it twenty.

◄O►

God-forsaken

LETTER: IN THE ABSENCE OF GOD

Hello. Recently I finally gave up my long-held passion to seek God, to seek something beyond the earthly level of the human experience.

I realize that living without the divine presence is not entirely bad, but it is life brutally honest and in your face. I am not quite sure how to handle it.

I am now resigned to see religious and spiritual experience as means to soothe ourselves from the fragility and injustice in the world. The fact is, the world is not fair, not everyone enjoys equal rights, and more powerful people influence the less powerful.

Being a minority woman, I can no longer seek solace in justice after death, or striving for spiritual transcendence to explain my daily experience and the history of oppression toward minorities and women. The difference is finally the loss of hope for a fair God.

I grew up getting very little support and love from my parents. They were very unhappy people and excluded me from normal social life. I am very bad with maintaining friendships and am prone to depression. I am often left feeling empty and terrified. The thought of needing to make affiliations with like-minded people to stay afloat terrifies me—perhaps no one will care enough or for long enough, as I am not special enough. It is a very painful feeling.

Thank you for reading.

The Wizeones group of Albuquerque, New Mexico, whose ages range from seventy-eight to ninety-three, is led by Elder Rinchu, the baby at seventy-eight. Rinchu was frustrated and dispirited by the discussion that ensued when she brought this letter to her group. "We were unable to come up with one response that everyone agreed with," she says. "The majority of the Elders—six of us—are caring, good people who come from backgrounds of privilege and had problems truly understanding. Their response to her was, 'Everyone has problems in their lives. Don't be so self-centered. Try various churches until you find one that feels good to you.'

"However, the other Elders—three—said the following":

As a minority woman, we have no question that you have had a much more difficult time of life than most blue-eyed blondes from affluent families. However, that doesn't mean that they have happy, self-fulfilled lives. Just because a person has a lot of money and power is not an automatic key to a good future, a wonderful marriage, and a good life.

Life has been unfair to you for far too many years, but it is getting much better, finally. Colleges and universities are accepting minority students first. The same is true in businesses; they are hiring minorities at a greater rate to better jobs.

Your attitude makes a big difference. Become more optimistic and determined because you are strong and you deserve all the better things in life.

Now, to your feelings about God: All of us who are free-thinkers and seekers come up with our own explanations to the "Big Questions" . . . who am I, why am I here, and where am I going? We recommend that you check out two different groups. The Unitarian Church (they dislike being called a church because some of them are atheists and agnostics) is a group of people who are very welcoming to minority people, study all spiritual paths, are social activists and humanists, and have many good activities and classes. You don't have to be social, just join some of their classes or listen to their sermons. The other suggestion is to check out the Society of Friends (the Quakers). They are social activists, antiwar, antipower, and were the ones who ran the Underground Railroad during the days of slavery. Quakers believe in the "light" in each person, are very peace loving and big on political demonstrating. We know you will do well, because you will find a way. You deserve it.

Two Elder women—one white, and one who identifies herself as a member of a minority group—believe that the young woman's questions transcend the boundaries of race.

Writes Grammypam, seventy, of Hancock, New Hampshire:

I was very moved and touched by your letter, as it talks about many ideas and feelings that I have had. I am a privileged, educated elder white woman and have never had any problem in seeing the unfairness of life.

I always thought that religious beliefs were put into place to make sense of that which makes no sense, just is. However, if I live a totally "for me" life, it is certainly unrewarding. Something happens when you do something for someone else, sappy as that does sound.

I didn't design the universe, and if I had, many things would be different. But it is as it is and I must make as much sense of it as I can while I'm here.

Sounds like you are working on finding a "way," a path, that will help you make more sense of your life. Keep asking these questions, respect other folks' belief systems even if they aren't yours, and bits and pieces of YOUR truth will begin to form. Good luck!

From Elder Helen, sixty-eight, of Sierra Vista, Arizona:

I too chose to become a member of organized religion by participating in different religions and teachings. My father told me that the choice should be mine and I went about making that choice in much the same way you sought out the information you felt you needed. I chose the Catholic faith.

I too am a minority woman. Yes, we have to fight an uphill battle, but we must not lose hope. We must live in faith, hope, and love. I like to think of every day as a search-and-recovery mission, led by a divine rescue squad. No matter how many changes I have gone through, I have survived. I am still here. I have something to do and someone to be.

I try not to compare myself to anyone else. I have always been willing to work for what I wanted and I got it. I have never wanted something because someone else had it.

You also asked, "What about my idea of equality in life?" You do have equality in life. You have it more so than the people in Sudan. You may not have it as much as those people whose skin color is different from yours and who don't work as hard as you work. But you know what, that should not be of concern to you. For those who have less than I do, I try to help in the way that I'm able. For those who have more than I do—that's fine. I have what I want and I know I got it honestly. That is what's important to me.

As for your feelings regarding the fact that you grew up getting very little support and love from your parents, I can only say that you must forgive them. If you hold on to these feelings, you're only holding yourself hostage. You are no longer a child. You are responsible for your life now.

You must live in the present. You must forgive yourself for the judgments you've held against yourself. Try to realize that others need you as much as you need them. No matter what our station in life, what color or sex we are, we have much more in common than we have that's different.

The difference in our skin color is such a minor thing. The greatest service you can offer yourself is to eliminate your own self-doubt. Love yourself first. Then others will be able to love you and you will be open to maintaining friendships.

You are a child of God. How can you not be special?

After half a lifetime of counseling gay and lesbian youth, one might think that answering the letter from the young man torn about revealing his sexual identity would have been easy for Elder Silver Sun Woman. It was not. Despite having come out forty years ago, despite eventually reconciling with her children and watching them accept her partner, Gold, as one of the family, Silver knows how carefully the young man must weigh his decision.

A few days after filing her response, this e-mail from Silver—Sleepless in the Southwest—arrived to the Elder Wisdom Circle:

"Hello again. It is now 5:13 a.m. and I would like to make an addition to my response to the young man who is struggling with his sexual identity," Silver wrote.

Fortunately, in today's world, gay and lesbian people have many more options available to them than in the past. Many couples are made up of one lesbian and one gay man who get together to raise a family. They work out their joint lives and their independent lives to great advantage.

Another option is that someone, like your best friend, would marry you KNOWING your situation and be very comfortable with it.

The most important point I would like to leave you with is that MOST of the reactions that you will get from people will depend upon how YOU see yourself. If you see your sexuality with distaste and lack of respect, that is how you will be viewed. However, if you respect who you are as a total person . . . you will not lose ANY respect.

Your young age is very much to your advantage. You don't have to do anything but "find" yourself right now. Good luck!

5

US

Wisdom for Lasting Love

Thank you so very much. Not only have you answered my questions, but you have taken my breath away with your poetic response. To hear someone actually put my thoughts into words really confirms that LOVE exists. Thanks again.

—From "Feedback & Kudos"
www.ElderWisdomCircle.org

It is easy to halve the potato when there is love.

—Irish proverb

Where No Man Has Gone Before

As the title suggests, I am one of those who saved myself for my husband. He has only had one sexual partner in his lifetime. We are both twenty-five and are a God-loving couple. I expected difficulty in our first time(s) together and of course pain, but no one told us about the disappointment and frustration, anger, shame, and lack of interest that would suddenly pop up on us after several failed attempts. We somehow managed to have intercourse once, albeit a little uncomfortable for both of us. He can't maintain an erection for very long and it really hurts if he's unable to do so. It doesn't help that he is literally twice my size overall. (I am teeny at 105 pounds.) After that, more failed attempts and frustration, etc. So much so I don't even want him touching me now, and it breaks my heart. He assures me he didn't marry me for sex, but this is driving us crazy. I feel so depressed and I can't seem to focus on anything else. We have looked at books, I talked to some girlfriends who were married virgins, we have lubrication, etc. Any thoughts? I could really use some caring advice. I am sure it's all normal, but it was a surprise to me.

The Elder Wisdom Circle invites advice seekers on a broad range of topics, from self-improvement to parenting to auto repair. Still, most of the letters to the EWC, about 75 per cent, involve close relationships—

family, coworkers, and neighbors included. And within that group, the vast majority involve romantic love—spouse, boyfriend/girlfriend, or life partner.

Questions about love are tailor-made for Elder Arianne.

Arianne, sixty-seven, of Wyncote, Pennsylvania, borrows her pen-name Arianne from the old Johnny Mathis song. It's a beautiful song, a passionate song; a love song. Arianne could listen to those lyrics a thousand times: a rainbow in a puddle, the happiest of birthdays, cof-fee brewing, a kitten purring, going off on Friday morning and coming back on Monday with a tan, that's Arianne. She is a born romantic.

While there is much to be said for old-fashioned romance, however, there is also something to be said for sex education. Why, Arianne wonders when she reads a letter like this, didn't her mother, or an aunt or a friend or *someone*, tell this poor girl to see a gynecologist before her wedding night?

Arianne often answers letters from young women—to Arianne, no matter what their socioeconomic status, young women are a group at risk. "Many times, a girl is asking me a question that she really should be asking someone who loves her," Arianne says. "I say talk to your mother, talk to another adult whom you trust, talk to someone at school—and every single one of them will write back to me and say, 'I don't have anyone I can trust.'"

Arianne is appalled by some of the girls who write to the Elder Wis-dom Circle, concerned with nothing but playing mattress kitten in or-der to keep their man. They seemed perfectly happy to be some guy's "baby momma" instead of his partner and equal. To feminist and social activist Arianne, it sometimes seems that the Women's Liberation Movement is running in reverse, that women's self-respect is dying out faster than good grammar—and don't get Arianne started on, like, young people's *grammar*.

"It's as if the teenage girl's dream now is to show as much skin as possible," Arianne says. "We live very near a Catholic girls' high school, and you see the girls walking to school with their skirts up around their rear ends. And then, when they get to school, they pull them down where they belong."

It's not that she's a prude, insists Arianne. It's just that she hates to see today's young women squander their precious freedom. If only she'd had the choices *they* have, the kind of choices she and her husband have given *their* children—well, it can make her cry just to think about it.

A Southern girl, raised in Virginia, Arianne aspired to become an engineer. A high school graduate at age sixteen, she was accepted at the prestigious Massachusetts Institute of Technology, but her domineering father wouldn't hear of her going so far from home at such a tender age. In fact, he insisted she remain in high school for a postgraduate year. In 1957, Arianne, then seventeen, was finally allowed a taste of freedom, entering an engineering college that was only about an hour's drive from the family home.

It was a miserable freshman year. Arianne was one of only one hundred women among about five thousand men, and most of the other women majored in home economics. "I had professors who refused to have me in their classes because I cursed," recalls Arianne. Because she was vocal in her protests against stringent rules and curfews for female students, she was dismissed from the college.

When Arianne returned home, her father gave her the choice of studying to become a nurse or a secretary. She chose secretary—but instead ran away from home to marry an engineering student she'd met in a campus drama program during her short college career. Later in life, she returned to school, taking courses in English literature and creative writing, probably enough to add up to a degree or two by now. In a way, being thrown out of engineering school led her to pursue her love of words—but Arianne will always wonder what might have been.

Arianne married young—but unlike the confused letter writer, the rebellious Arianne was not a virgin. While she views neither choice as the "right" one, she is proud of this young woman for maintaining her own values in a "baby momma" world. But this girl needs some blunt advice, and fast, before her marriage blows up in her face.

First, let me assure you that there is help for you, and you must be aggressive to seek it out. There could be many reasons for this situation, and it isn't particularly uncommon. First and foremost, both of you must have a complete physical examination to determine if either of you has any physical reason for this difficulty. Yes, both you and he. There are many physical conditions that can cause a man to have this problem, and a good doctor will be able to answer the questions and determine the cause.

I am reminded of a friend of my younger days who had a complete checkup before her marriage, and was lucky enough to have a doctor who realized that her hymen was so strong that physical intercourse would have been almost impossible for her, certainly painful, and would have caused much grief and misunderstanding of her husband's inability to perform. She was in the hospital only overnight, and her problem was solved. In the meantime, they both were counseled by their doctor as to methods to use and how to minimize difficulties and pain.

Your marriage is much more than a sexual relationship, of course, but that doesn't mean that your sexual relationship is not important. A loving sexual relationship adds so much to a marriage and to the intimacy of the two partners. Never give it up until you are told by someone who knows that it is hopeless, and frankly, I do not believe this is ever true.

It is not the fault of anyone—it simply is—and it simply can be corrected. Please do as I suggest and find the greatest fulfillment of your lives, together.

A "virgin bride"? That's one question that sixty-five-year-old Elder Treefrog of West Bloomfield, Michigan, ought to be able to answer. When they married in 1965, Treefrog and his bride were both virgins, despite fogging up quite a few car windows on the way to their wedding day.

Of course, even for 1965, Treefrog might have been a little more innocent than most guys his age. He had spent his high school years in the seminary, intending to become a priest. The nuns and the parish priest all praised his decision; his family, they said, would be blessed. He entered the seminary at fourteen.

The law says you can't buy a beer or drive a car at fourteen; how, Treefrog wonders in retrospect, does anyone expect a fourteen-year-old kid to know he should become a priest? "The seminary in 1956 was much like a military academy," Treefrog recalls. "The only women around were three nuns who operated the infirmary; their cumulative age was greater than Methuselah's. Once in a while, the outside company that ran the kitchen, called a refectory, would hire an attractive girl to work in the cafeteria, dishing out the food. That usually slowed up the cafeteria line to a crawl."

It wasn't until his second year in college that Treefrog, as a student already wearing the priest's black cassock, realized that he didn't *know*. He would look around at families with children and the white collar would seem to tighten around his neck. It all seemed so unnatural. Obedience and poverty he could handle—it was chastity that posed the problem. "I am sure that, if it were not for celibacy, I would be a priest or a minister today, and a good one," says Treefrog, now retired from a career in the construction business that paid the family bills, but never offered much return in the department of happiness or personal fulfillment.

Treefrog admits that the "Newlywed Virgin" question is the kind of letter he might ordinarily leave for one of the ladies in the Elder Wisdom Circle. But then, had he become a priest—and a good one—a young woman might come to him with a question just like this, and he would never turn her away. This question, he decides, calls for a nonthreatening analogy, something soft and sweet.

Now that he has retired, Treefrog divides his time among three hobbies—fishing, gardening, and cooking. In offering advice, this time he turns to the kitchen.

Right now, I'm trying to make the perfect macadamia nut and white chocolate cookie. Hey, the recipe is pretty darn simple. I've made them too soft, burnt them, and gawd knows what else. But I will succeed! Failure only becomes frustrating when there is no learning.

It may sound a bit crazy, but I think intimate love may be a lot like that: only difference is, you have two people trying to make the ideal "cookie." It can be a wondrous adventure or an exasperating experience. It's all in how you approach it. My friend, these are some physical obstacles that can be overcome if you both decide to abide by the old cliché that "love conquers all."

Give it some time and decide that your intimacy is a "work of art" in the making. When you decide (together) that there might be a problem that needs help, do yourself a favor and seek out a physician or a counselor. There is no embarrassment or shame attached to the asking. You can do it!

I must be off now to make some macadamia nut cookies. (By the way, my wife and I are still working on the "perfect recipe" after forty years, YEAH!)

While Arianne and Treefrog both suggest medical attention and counseling, Elder Laura, sixty-four, of Detroit advises seeking another type of expert advice very specific to the problem.

You should find a certified sex therapist. Ask your doctor for a recommendation, or call your local medical society and get several names. Visit a few of them until you find one you can talk to comfortably. A sex therapist will work with you in a professional manner to assist you in developing a healthy sexual relationship. This will probably take time, but it will be worth the investment and is necessary if you are to have a strong marriage.

Money Talks

LETTER: SPOUSE'S SECRET BANK ACCOUNT

I recently discovered that my spouse of thirty years has a secret bank account with over $15,000 in it. It was opened three years ago and I do not know where the money came from. All our funds are kept in joint accounts and all our income is commingled. Should I confront her about this? I am very disappointed and hurt.

This is one of those questions where the younger Elders—that is, under seventy—hold a different opinion from the *elder* Elders, those on the other side of that birthday milestone.

While encouraging the writer to think positive, the younger writers pick up on the lack of trust on both sides.

Elder Jangela, sixty-six, of Detroit, writes:

There could be many reasons why your spouse has a separate bank account. Let me enumerate some of them: 1) your spouse has been "squirreling away" money over a period of years and just put the money in the bank three years ago. She has been saving to surprise

you with a retirement party or a wonderful trip; 2) perhaps you are
critical of money spending and she has just been putting money aside
for when she needs it: clothes, travel, etc.; 3) the money belongs to
someone else but she is keeping it for them; 4) she has a favorite char-
ity that you don't approve of and she is going to donate it; and 5) the
least likely, although you may think this is the number-one, reason:
she is going to leave you.

All of the above are the most common reasons women put money
aside independently and without telling their spouses. You should just
ask her about it. If you have a good marriage and have very open com-
munication with each other, then there is most likely a reasonable,
sensible explanation and you shouldn't be hurt.

Did you find out by accident or were you going through her things?
If the latter, then she will raise the trust issue with you, too.

Assuming you have a good marriage, then there is a very reason-
able explanation.

Elder Web, sixty-four, of Farmington Hills, Michigan, also wants to
know how the husband just happened to stumble upon his wife's little
secret.

I would think how you found out about the account is important.
Were you invading her privacy or did you find out about it by acci-
dent? The answer to this question would determine the approach you
might take with her.

It would seem that although she is keeping secrets from you, she
may have her reasons. Over three years the amount saved would
equate to $5,000 a year or $100 a week (excluding interest), and
even $15,000 dollars would not be enough for her to take off and
start a new life. I don't know the state of your finances, but that
would not be a difficult amount to save from grocery or household
funds if she manages the spending. Many people, especially wives,
like to have a "rainy day" fund. Maybe she is saving this for a spe-
cial gift for you or a vacation for the two of you. If this is the case,
you may ruin her surprise. You know the state of your relationship
and marriage, and if you think it is strong, my suggestion is to keep
quiet. However, if there is a lack of trust, you might want to ap-
proach her.

*My hope is that you both have a happy marriage and strong rela-
tionship and that you make the assumption that she has a good, as well
as positive, reason for this account. Sometimes it's best just to trust!*

The slightly-older Wizeones group of Albuquerque, New Mexico,
however, sees a secret stash as a woman's prerogative. To them, the
account is just a modern-day cookie jar, accessible by ATM.

*While it is a good bit of money, it is not unusual for women to save
money from their household expenses. All of us remember our mothers and grandmothers having jars full of coins in the cupboard. This
was typically a woman's cache that she used to give the children and
grandchildren special treats . . . or to get her hair done or to buy her
husband a birthday or anniversary present. Instead of confronting her
about it, speak to her gently and lovingly. Confrontation sounds very
hostile. There probably is a very logical and acceptable explanation for
it. Did she receive an inheritance three years ago?*

*We wondered whether in thirty years, you could honestly say that
you always put EVERY penny that you earned into your joint
account without withholding any of it for yourself?*

Elder Gpa, eighty-five, of Rochester Hills, Michigan, confides that
Elder Gma, eighty-one, has been leaving a paper trail for sixty years.

*Some women, you know, have an element of squirrellyness about
them. They like to squirrel away nuts for a rainy day. For years I have
been running across papers from banks I never heard of, and little insurance policies that my wife has taken out.*

*Yes, I would ask her off handedly, lightly, in a nonconfrontational
manner, about the strange bank account. But be prepared to explain
how you discovered the account and the amount. You can also indicate to her there may be income tax ramifications.*

*If she is a careful, prudent woman, I guess putting her loose
change in a little tin box over thirty years could do it. Or she could be
a lucky plunger and has hit it big betting on the nags at the race track.
In either case, we think you should congratulate her and be happy for
the addition to your nest egg.*

We sincerely hope the explanation for the funds is harmless and you enjoy the good fortune.

Plain Truth

LETTER: UGLY GUY

I'm twenty-five years old and walking on a cloud because I have met the most amazing guy, "A.J." The problem is that it has always been very important to me what other people think, and A.J. is just plain and simple not that attractive. He needs braces and his hair is thinning. I am attracted to him, but when other people look at him they will definitely not see what I see in him.

My family is the biggest problem. I have a very attractive family and I know that they are hard on people because of their appearances. I am feeling like I am a weak person and will never be able to face the world and their criticism.

What can I do to make myself stronger so I can be happy with A.J. and also stand up to the world? Probably the answer is that I don't deserve this guy because I am even having to ask this question. And I don't want to have to call my best friend and be like, "Listen I met this guy and he totally blows my mind and I want to spend the rest of my life with him, but just to warn you, he's not cute;" but with my selfish and insecure mind that's the only thing I can think of. Please help me. And please don't be too hard on me; I know that I am awful.

Elder Walk-On, seventy-two, of Bethesda, Maryland, was in college, maybe nineteen or twenty, when beauty met the beast. It was a blind date. "This young man had a dreamy voice and was the editor of a small-town newspaper. But I was truly shocked when I saw the face behind that dreamy voice," she says. "He was a gentleman—intelligent, interesting, and fun, but all I could think of was that face. I never thought about what others might think or say. It was solely my reaction of repulsion at his looks.

"When he took me home, I vanished without even a thank you for a nice evening. I was too ashamed to tell him politely and kindly that I was not interested in seeing him again. I never gave him a chance to grow on me. Today, I feel sorry that I was so unkind to a worthy human being."

Walk-On believes the advice seeker must be honest about her feelings, even if she isn't proud of them.

> *If your discomfort with this young man's looks is solely because of what your family and friends will say and think, I believe you could overcome your feelings. If you yourself are uncomfortable with his looks, that is a more difficult problem.*
>
> *You like what you like; you feel what you feel. You may not be able to get used to his looks. If you cannot accommodate to his physical appearance, you need to end the relationship or let him know that the relationship can be only a friendship and not a romance. After all, if you were to marry him and have children with him, your children would share his genes.*
>
> *So my advice is to do some serious thinking, and if necessary, take it to a therapist for help. You can take your time thinking and making the decision, but at some point you will have to decide which way to go. Don't drag it on for too long.*

"When I was in my twenties and thirties, looks meant everything—so much so that the inner person was overlooked all too often," says Grandma-Dan, sixty-one, of Troy, Michigan, the twice-divorced mother of two adult daughters. "I wish I had known then what I know now, because the decisions I made about whom I chose to spend my life with might have been different and divorce might have been avoided."

> *You are NOT awful; you just have some things that you must deal with inside of yourself if you are to go more deeply into a relationship with this man.*
>
> *Already being embarrassed by his looks tells you a lot. However, you are obviously very attracted to the person he is inside. What*

conflict! What emotion for you! Why can I say to this? Because, truly (and I am not proud to say this), I have been very much like you.

You may think I'm crazy, but honestly, professional help is probably the best approach toward dealing with the demons that cause you to feel embarrassed about his looks; to be uncomfortable about introducing him to your family and friends. If you don't deal with these things professionally, you will likely begin to nag him to have his teeth fixed eventually, to have his face operated on, whatever and whatever.

Finally, here is another possible approach you might wish to consider. I would venture to say that given time, your family and friends will see his beauty as they get to know him and will respect you for being "blind" to anything but his inner beauty. I know when it comes to my daughters, if they are happy and in love and loved by the men with whom they are in a relationship, I could care less how they look! My daughters' hearts are more important to me than anything! So why not square your shoulders and march forward proudly beside the man you love so much? Expect them to accept and respect him and to act accordingly. This is what growing up is all about.

Almost Paradise

LETTER: DATING AN ALMOST-DIVORCED MAN

I am a single yet extremely successful parent to a wonderful boy. I've been divorced for four years, and haven't found anyone to meet up to my standards, or someone that I am compatible with that would also be a great role model to my son until now.

I've met a wonderful and extremely successful man with a two-year-old daughter. We are only a couple of years apart (twenty-four and twenty-six) and we have so much in common. We've known each other for a short three weeks, but we've had some extremely deep talks, to the point where we could cry. I get lost in his eyes every time I look at him.

So, what's the problem? He is going through a divorce, and has been for six months. All the property and debt is split, but they are still debating on the custody issue. He is not living with her anymore, and emotionally, he says, they are divorced. The only thing that makes it not final is the stamp on the paper, which will happen just as soon as they reach a decision on custody.

The timing could have been better, but we met when we did. I consider myself to have high morals and I am feeling uneasy about this. I am experiencing feelings I have never, ever felt.

Elder Lester, sixty-nine, of Roswell, Georgia, has three grown boys from his first marriage of twenty-five years. "We got married when we were eighteen, and grew apart in our thirties," he says. Lester's fourth son is seventeen, the product of his second marriage, to a woman nineteen years his junior. He also has seven grandchildren. Despite this complicated family mix, Lester and his ex-wife remain friends, and everybody gets along just fine at weddings, bar mitzvahs, and birthday celebrations.

"Just be patient. Patience is what you need," Lester says.

You've found someone to love and he in turn feels the same way, and it all sounds good except for one huge, life-altering thing. He is going through a divorce and the most important thing of all has yet to be decided—the custody of his two-year-old daughter. I'm afraid if you aren't careful, things could turn ugly, but quick, during his divorce. If I were you, I'd lay low and let him get everything finalized before you go any further with this relationship.

I'd even go one step further if I were you and take a good hard look at how he's acting toward his soon-to-be ex and daughter. You can tell a lot about someone's character during a difficult time like this. Is your guy concerned about his daughter? Are his priorities in the right place? What is the relationship between his wife and him?

So, my best advice is to hang back a bit until he gets everything finalized. Three weeks is not that long, especially when you're talking about incorporating two young children's lives into yours and his. You'll need and want to have a working relationship with his ex-wife,

*so be respectful and give them this time to work things out. I hope he
is all you hoped for and more.*

Site Situation

LETTER: RELATIONSHIPS AND PORN

I have been with my boyfriend now for over a year, we are completely head over heels in love and have an amazing sex life. I am
very adventurous and will try anything, and have even told him to
try new things as well.

My boyfriend told me that he was never the porn type, that he
didn't need it because he always had girlfriends, and just didn't
find it necessary.

The other night I was viewing a short movie in Quick Time
Player, and noticed that on his recently played list there was a porn
movie. I proceeded to look elsewhere on the computer to see what
else he had. To my surprise I found over three hundred pictures and
sixty videos!

I went to him extremely upset and wanted to know why. He felt
very embarrassed, and said it means nothing and that it is just porn,
and he wasn't even aware that he had that much.

He was very supportive and told me that if he had known I was
going to be so upset and hurt by it he would have never had it. He
immediately deleted all the porn, and promised that he loves me
and only me, and that it really means nothing.

The problem? I still feel like it's cheating; going behind my back
and looking at other girls in such a sexual way makes me feel ill.
He knows that I wouldn't mind if we were to view it together, for
fun, but I really can't stand the thought of him viewing it. I want to
trust him, but only two days later I searched his history on his computer to make sure he hadn't been looking.

I don't want to be this neurotic girlfriend. I just want to know if my
feeling that he is cheating is out of line (I have a tendency to overreact).

Please help . . . thanks so much for your time!

Arianne knows that she can be a bit outspoken sometimes. Well, more than a bit. Arianne, a founding member of the Elder Wisdom Circle and former online editor for the Web site, knows all too well that at least in the early days, a few advice seekers protested her occasionally sharp-tongued advice.

The pettiest problems always seem to stir up the most trouble for Arianne. One such letter dealt with bridal shower etiquette: The bride-to-be wanted to know whether she'd been "tacky" in asking the guests to write their addresses on thank-you card envelopes at the shower. Obviously, the letter writer wanted an Elder to approve this decision, but she picked the wrong Elder—or, rather, the wrong Elder picked *her*. "If you don't have time to send thank-yous to people who give you gifts, then you don't deserve the gifts," Arianne wrote. "I'm tired of people who think they can be rude and crude and still be the recipients of gifts that have taken much time and consideration and expense. It's a big deal, girl. Deal with it."

Then there was the one from a vain young thing in her thirties who was terrified of losing her beauty. She wanted instruction on how to maintain her looks, possibly through plastic surgery. Arianne told her that she had the wrong idea about aging, that a woman in her sixties can be as beautiful as someone thirty years younger. She suggested that the woman focus more on her personality than her looks. The younger woman responded by filing a complaint letter, calling Arianne an old, dried-up hag who needed to get a life.

But then, some people are just asking to have some sense knocked into them—including the woman concerned about her boyfriend's taste for pornography. "I answered this letter because Internet pornography has become a very, very serious problem in our country, and is wreaking havoc not only on relationships, but also marriages and families," Arianne says. "I wanted to warn her that porn is very invasive and difficult to get rid of once it intrudes upon a relationship, though I doubt anything I say will make her more cautious."

Arianne writes:

Without doubt I agree that he is cheating on you each and every time he looks or thinks about his porn. I am very suspicious when he says the collection of porn "just accumulated." Nonsense! It was deliberate, not an accident he couldn't help.

Forget the idea that since your sex life is so good he wouldn't want to look at porn; it makes no difference whatsoever. In fact, I am disturbed by the fact that you talk so much about your sex life with him. Most likely, the man most interested in sex will be even more interested in porn. In time, porn often displaces sexual activity with a woman when the man decides he prefers fantasy porn, and satisfies himself while watching it.

Although you might not think so now, sexual attraction and activity does lessen as time goes by (hence his never being satisfied with any one woman). From your letter I can see only one aspect of your relationship: sex. When it lessens, will you two have other feelings for each other to maintain your relationship?

Invariably, men who are confronted by their partners about watching porn will lie. I say if he doesn't continue to watch porn, it will be a miracle. He didn't have a small amount of porn; he had a large amount—this indicates much more than a passing interest.

There is little I can say to you, my dear, with your deep trust in your boyfriend. All I will say is to be careful and take good care of yourself.

Unlike Arianne, Elder Dawn, seventy-four, of Rockville, Maryland, sees no red flags presented by the boyfriend's behavior. "I could see her ruining a perfectly good relationship," Dawn says.

Could this possibly be more of a control issue than one of cheating?

Men are created different from us—hallelujah! There're very visual and when they look at porn or other females, it's nothing we can take personally. You probably do satisfy him in more ways than he could ever have imagined; however, he's a male and unless you set him up with blindfolds, don't expect any miracles. He'll look.

Why do you feel dirty? He didn't touch anyone. No disease is implicated. He looked. Why do you feel that you're not enough? He swears that you are, and I'd leave it at that. If you pursue this any further you may find yourself in the uncomfortable position of being the porn police.

Your boyfriend probably was very attracted to you because you're a free spirit who enjoys sex with him and is uninhibited in love making. Don't allow yourself to turn into a shrew and send him into the closet for porn. Try real hard to lighten up.

Elder Horatio Victor concurs. And, unlike Dawn, he can speak from firsthand experience.

You have just found the difference between the genders. His interest in porn does not imply cheating. I'm a man in my eighties. We men (those who are honest) are charged up by porn; ladies are not. It is not cheating. Porn is not competition. All it does is rouse his appetite for you.

Elder Heart of Texas, eighty-one, of Salado, Texas, is not concerned about the boyfriend's taste for Internet porn. Rather, she worries that the letter indicates that the advice seeker herself suffers from an unhealthy obsession with physical sex. "Trust comes with accepting whatever your mate is personally and creating a loving relationship," Heart of Texas says. "I thought I could point that out, and give a short explanation of how fifty-eight years of marriage to the same man can create unbelievable sex when you completely love each another."

Being "head over heels in love" is a comment most young people make when only sex is involved. You bring up the subject of trust and you keep wondering if he could still be looking at other women. Don't you think it would have been better to find this out before a full year of wild and wonderful sex?

Since this is still a boyfriend-girlfriend relationship, you do not own this person or control his actions. Even when married, you must let your mate be their own person. You did not know what type of person this boyfriend was until you found a lot of porn and videos on his computer.

I must say I have not had an experience like this, as in our day, living together was frowned upon. My husband and I grew up in the same community and knew each other as children. We married young and raised five children; adventurous sex between two happily married people is far better than what you described here.

Your obsession with sex during the one year of knowing this man has left doubts that you really don't know him and trust him. I would suggest easing up on the sex and try to find out just what kind of person this man really is. A couple counseling session may help if you really believe you want a long-term commitment and marriage. If all you want is a relationship of wild sex and fun times, then forget the trust and just lay back and enjoy the ride.

Barking Up the Wrong Tree?

LETTER: THE DOG SEEMS TO COME BEFORE ME!

My boyfriend and I have been dating for a little over a year. We have lived together for about six months. He has a dog. While I love the dog, I am sick of my boyfriend putting the dog before me! He stays at home to spend time with the dog rather than go somewhere with me. My son has been asking my boyfriend to watch him play soccer for eight weeks now, but the dog comes first. I am divorced and don't want to become engaged or married to a man who is not going to love me at least as much as the dog. I am not saying that he has to love me more. I just want the same attention. Sorry. I'm obviously very frustrated.

None of the Elders who responded to this letter suggest trying to resolve this issue in a frank discussion with the boyfriend; instead, they urge the advice seeker to cut her losses and move on. Says Elder Michelle, sixty-four, of Portland, Oregon, "My dad definitely liked the dogs better than anyone in the family. I need to let the writer know that this will not change."

This man loves his dog. He chooses the dog before you or your son. Even after you speak to him, this man is not going to change. It certainly is easier to have a relationship with a dog than with a human—not nearly as satisfying, but easier. This man is also rude and insensitive. It is really himself he puts first and he always will.

You cannot change people. The older they get, the more like themselves they become. Eight weeks and he could not attend one soccer game. How much more evidence do you need that you do not need this guy in your life? Get a dog and take him to the soccer games.

Elder Sylvia, seventy-three, of Hillsboro, Oregon, is a dog lover— but recognizes that this boyfriend doesn't know how to keep a reasonable perspective on his affection for his pet. And she sees the woman's willingness to put up with it until this point as a sign of weak self-esteem.

I would like to see you care more about yourself and your son rather than accept what little this man is willing to offer. Believe me, you're both worth more than the dog. And what message are you sending to your son by remaining with a man who seems to think more of his dog than he does of you and your son? Talking to a counselor might help you with these issues. This man may not put you first, but it is far more important that YOU put yourself and your son first.

From Grandma-Dan:

In order to get your boyfriend's love and attention, it sounds as though you must start acting like a dog (and even then, who knows?). So here is another big question: Do you want to do this?

The Heavensviewsages, aged seventy to ninety-three, of Delta, Colorado, thought that the way in which the letter writer tells this dog story suggests that neither party is ready for a mature relationship.

Dear friend,
He obviously is not ready for this kind of commitment. Unless he is numb, he knows that you need and want more from him and he is unwilling or unable to provide that.
You say you love the dog, but you never say you love your boyfriend. Why is that, we wonder? We are worried that you are trying desperately to fill the role of "father" in your and your son's life.

You are absolutely correct in feeling that this is a losing battle and a sign of future problems. We feel you should extricate yourself and your son from this relationship as soon as possible.

In the future, don't rush a relationship that is supposed to last a lifetime. Love before marriage, and definitely marriage before cohabitation may sound old-fashioned, but it is the best way to be sure you are ready, and your chosen one is as well.

For now, devote yourself to your life with your son. The right man will come along, and you will know it . . . when the time is right!

May–December

LETTER: GERIATRIC LOVE

I am a twenty-eight-year-old female dating what was once a very healthy seventy-two-year-old man. He made love to me the way no other has before. And believe me I've had my share of men my age and even younger. But there was something about him that drove me wild. That's another story. But his health has gone downhill, and fast! He never took a pill before in his life and now he's on medication after medication and things are starting not to work right, if you know what I mean. I'm a young woman and have needs, too. Is it okay for a man his age to take Viagra? He now has high blood pressure and is taking medication for that. I can't believe he's so sick like this after just being so healthy. I love him a lot, really! But I want him around a long time because this man is va va voom! Is it fair to ask him to donate some of his sperm now instead of waiting until he can no longer do it?

An urgent reply from the Heavensviewsages: "We chose this letter to save a man's life!"

Hon, there are some facts of life and nature you really should think about. If you decide you can accept these unchangeable facts of life, then we wish you the best.

First, he is forty-four years older than you, which makes him old enough to be your grandfather. He is currently seventy-two. The average life expectancy in the United States is seventy-eight, we think. And you are wanting him to use Viagra for the va va voom? It's frankly amazing that he hasn't had more medical problems with that kind of carrying on than you report.

He will not be able to physically satisfy you sexually in the future if he can't now. We believe Viagra would put him at further risk if he has high blood pressure, but you should check with his physician.

You can have a relationship with this man if you understand these things, but don't kill him with sexual demands he cannot possibly fulfill! You may not have even reached your sexual prime yet, but his giddy-up has got-up and gone long ago! That is nature, and you can't change that with a pill of any color.

If you can accept that, and wish to continue with this relationship, we say good luck and may God bless!

And—not surprisingly—a stern talking-to from Arianne:

I find it rather amazing that this man, who "made love to me the way no other has before" . . . "there was something about him that drove me wild" is now simply someone who has disappointed you because he can no longer fulfill your "needs." Have you considered that he also can no longer fulfill HIS needs?? Obviously, you are very young.

Let me tell you a few facts: It is very common for a man who is on blood pressure medication to lose the ability to perform. Have you even considered this during your pity parties about your needs? Have you talked with his doctor? Have you discussed this with him? Maybe if you can consider this problem from HIS viewpoint instead of yours, you might find that you can be of help to him, as well as increasing his value to you as a great lover.

There are various methods you can use to help him, but you probably aren't too interested in that. So I suggest you talk with his doctor, with him, and with any other medical expert who might help this man so he can continue to satisfy you before you dump him. If only you had at least mentioned your concern about him and his unhappiness in this situation.

Elder Michelle says she answered this letter because "I have some-thing to say to this young whippersnapper." In her letter, she chal-lenges the young woman about whether she has any interest in the man beyond his ability to provide sexual pleasure, or perhaps sperm for future use.

If your gentleman friend has some sperm to spare, it certainly would be acceptable to ask him to donate it. Your letter is interesting because on one hand you discuss the "va va voom" aspect of this gentleman, and on the other hand, his sperm. You do not say what else you love about him or how long you have known him.

A person's health, even yours, can change in a matter of seconds. If it was your body that was starting not to work right, would his love be focused on sex? Would he want to harvest your eggs?

The One

LETTER: SOUL MATES?

I would like some advice from some of you who have been happily married. Do you think that one should wait for that person who from the onset you "just know" is "the one"? Or can your "soul mate" be a person that you are not in love with from the get-go, but that you grow fond of and grow to love over time and tribulations? I am a twenty-five-year-old woman who is currently in a relation-ship that is more of the latter. . . . Can, or does, a relationship that grows gradually like that ever match the love between two people who fall "madly in love"? Please respond and share your experi-ence, how long you have been married, etc. Thank you!

An anniversary toast to Gpa-and-Gma. Their letter:

Your inquiry is a good one. Stumbling on a soul mate from the git-go is a lucky accident and one can grow old and weary waiting for a lucky accident to happen. When you find a person whose character, habits, family history, physical presence, interests, and philosophy are in the general vicinity of your ballpark, it would be prudent and wise to develop a relationship and let it flower.

Much has been said about chemistry, soaring rockets, and heavenly violins, but personally we think it is wildly overrated. Yes, the initial contact between two people should have mutual attraction and liking. But that is only the first step along the path to love. As you stroll along the path and find you have common interests, like ice cream, roller coasters, children, golf, and mountain views, and together can overcome obstacles and "tribulations," love will come. If you let the relationship turn into a partnership where each carries out their duties and responsibilities to each other and to the home and family, love will be there and forever.

This year we celebrate our sixtieth anniversary, and it has never been better. We met during World War II, separated for long periods over four years, married penniless, had different faiths, raised four children, and had many ups and downs. Now in retirement we find our love still growing every day.

We want to wish you a happy, joyous life with your soul mate.

Elder Heart of Texas, eighty-one, of Salado, Texas, made it last for fifty-eight years.

A happy marriage seems to be the question in any young girl's mind. They are urged by every form of media, TV, newspaper, magazines, and Internet to look for ways to have a happy marriage. As for us elder women, in our youth it was just assumed that we would get married, raise a family, and hope it would be a happy union. I knew marriage would come at some later date, but lo and behold it came at age nineteen.

I had known this boy since early childhood; we belonged to the same church, so I was able to see him often. World War II was raging and he knew when he turned eighteen he would join the Navy. We became engaged and at nineteen were married, followed by his being sent to the Pacific War Zone.

One never thought of becoming a soul mate; in those days it was just expected of you to act like husband and wife. In those days a wife stayed home to be a homemaker. You accepted it and tried to make your home a happy place without complaints. We enjoyed our life together and became best friends. I suppose that is "soul mates."

Becoming best friends or soul mates doesn't just fall into place; it takes work. It means you become interested in the things your mate loves and he also gives you time for things you love to do.

I think the phrase "madly in love" is overrated. To me it says too much about me and not about us as a couple. It says you are being ruled by the head and not the heart. Becoming a best friend or soul mate comes from the heart and is longer lasting.

My husband and I remained best friends and soul mates until the end of fifty-eight years of married life. He passed away in 2003 after a long illness, but he was and always will remain my best friend. Of course I miss him, but the many long happy memories will be with me forever. I feel very blessed that we became best friends and always were comfortable with each other, even when no words were spoken. We did not need words. We always knew we cared deeply for each other, and that was all that was needed.

The Elders teach others through their advice, but they also learn. Arianne says she has learned a lot about the value of finding a softer way to express tough opinions.

These days, Arianne receives more kudos than complaints about her advice. Although it would be tough to find a subject about which she has no opinion, over time, she says, she has learned to express those opinions with greater tact. "I have tried to be a little less critical, and when I *am* critical, I try to still show that I empathize," she says. "I remind myself that many of our advice seekers are simply young and inexperienced, and perhaps have little guidance in their lives, and are therefore likely to make mistakes. I know I did."

Her response to this writer is blunt, and practical—but, like the song "Arianne," always, always romantic.

I'm going to first answer some of your questions. Then we'll discuss them.

Do you think that one should wait for that person who from the onset you "just know" is "the one"? NO.

Or can your "soul mate" be a person that you are not in love with from the get-go, but that you grow fond of and grow to love over time and tribulations? YES.

But basically, do you believe in "soul mates," or is a HAPPY marriage (I reiterate, a good, happy marriage) more about two people who grow to care and respect and love each other over time? NO and YES.

Can, or does, a relationship that grows gradually like that ever match the love between two people who from the get-go fall "madly in love"? GOOD GRIEF, YES! AND MORE SO!

Do you think that we FIND or can we DEVELOP a soul mate? NO and YES.

I think that people speak of "soul mates" when they are attempting to convince themselves that the person they have met and are now interested in is the "right" one for them, even if he is not. Let's get real— there are probably thousands of people who can make us happy, fulfilled, and delighted to be married to them. Why we insist on there being only "one" makes me wonder why people want to make life so difficult.

Second, I believe a "soul mate" is created, not found. When most people use the term "soul mate," they seem to think a raging crush on someone makes him a "soul mate." Please! Sexual attraction is sexual attraction; true love is love and is greater by far in both sexual attraction and love.

I have a soul mate, and I also am one. My husband and I married too young, and we paid for it. There were times in our lives together when the going got very rough; we were immature, we were overworked, we were scared, we were jealous, angry, selfish, inconsiderate. Yet, for all of that, neither of us would have changed partners. We learned, we taught each other, we helped each other, we shared all things, we survived, we laughed, we danced, we sang, and we triumphed. We raised three children who are terrific, involved with their communities, all kind and considerate, all full of hopes and dreams, and all succeeding in what they want to do. We are still very active in civic and charitable causes, we play tennis, we enjoy our many friends and our family, and we plan to live forever.

My husband and I are happier every day than the day before. We have been married forty-eight years, and we sincerely hope that we can say in another twenty-seven years that we have been married seventy-five years. We will be only ninety-five years old!

We had a great deal of adjustment to make to each other, and to family life as a whole. We were—and are—very different (and perhaps difficult) people. We have many areas of disagreement, but this doesn't endanger our marriage—they are simply obstacles to get over to get back on the right path. We continue to discuss, perhaps argue, certainly compromise, and most certainly have great respect and consideration for each other. Why? What makes it work for us? Because we love each other, and we value each other far beyond how we value our separateness.

I hope I have helped you.

Best wishes,

Arianne

6

MULTIPLE CHOICE TESTS
Wisdom for Making the Right Decision

Thank you so much for the helpful advice! I did follow it and I know it was the one right thing to do. Sometimes, even in trivial situations like mine, people need an objective point of view and you were there to provide it for me. Your help through this tough decision-making time was most valuable and appreciated!

Sincerely,
"Laura"

—From "Feedback & Kudos"
www.ElderWisdomCircle.org

When you come to a fork in the road, take it.

—Yogi Berra

With This Ring

Is it proper etiquette to give my prospective fiancée a ring that was originally bought for another eight years ago? The ring was returned to me seven years ago at the end of the engagement. It's beautiful, and that's why I'm considering it. The other woman lives in our town and it's possible that we'll see her at some time. My new lover has not seen the ring yet.

Before moving on to the advice seeker's dilemma, here's another question:

On a sunny summer afternoon, while his friends are probably working minimum-wage summer jobs or prowling the shopping mall, what is eighteen-year-old Bennett Meier doing in a retirement home?

Bennett is here to speak senior to senior—that is, high school senior to senior citizen. A recent St. Louis high school graduate headed for the University of Pennsylvania, Bennett became an Elder Wisdom Circle group facilitator during the final months of his senior year to fulfill an academic requirement.

At his high school, seniors finish their classes early and devote the month of May to extracurricular projects. While trying to decide what do to for his May Project, Bennett heard about the Elder Wisdom Circle on National Public Radio's *Morning Edition* program. "I thought, that's really cool—I wonder if I can get involved," Bennett recalls.

After finding out that no Elder Wisdom Circle groups existed in the St. Louis area, Bennett set about calling senior residences in the area to see where he might fit in. His May Project flowed into June, July, and August, leading two once-weekly groups at different senior residences.

While most Elder Wisdom Circle members operate independently from their home computers, the organization also includes more than forty groups that gather in retirement communities and nursing homes to discuss the advice seekers' problems.

Groups participating in this book include Bennett's Garden Villa Elders (his other group is called the Breeze Park Elders), both of St. Louis, Missouri; the Asbury Friends of Gaithersburg, Maryland; the Rockymountain Owls and the Heavensviewsages, both located in small towns in Colorado; the Gold and Wise group and the Chelsea Elders, both located in New Jersey; Webwisdom of Royersford, Pennsylvania, and the Wizeones of Albuquerque, New Mexico.

Collectively their ages range from early seventies to one hundredplus: Elder Dawn, of Rockville, Maryland, who heads the group along with offering her own individual advice, reports that the Asbury Friends includes one 105-year-old member. "She's amazing," Dawn says. "I'll throw out a letter to the group for discussion and she's right in there, giving her opinion."

Led by facilitators—or, as the EWC calls them, "scribes"—the groups hash out a problem until they come to a consensus, and the scribe composes a reply based on the input.

In some instances, a resident forms a group and serves the facilitator. Such is the case with the Wizeones, lead by Elder Rinchu, seventyeight, who also contributes individual advice. More often, groups are led by activity coordinators or other facility staffers who may be young enough to be the residents' sons and daughters. Bennett, by far the youngest facilitator, is more like their grandson—or maybe greatgrandson for some in his Garden Villa Elders group, which includes participants ranging from their seventies to mid–nineties.

Some advice seekers come to the Elder Wisdom Circle bringing questions of a more philosophical nature—queries about the meaning of life, the nature of faith, or the course of true love. Others, however, write in about concrete matters of choice, wanting to know whether to say yes or no, to stay or go, to turn left or right, to buy or sell, to confront or stay silent, to take it or leave it—and they want to know *now*.

Because there are two possible solutions—at least—suggested by such questions, they tend to provoke strong opinions. For this reason, they are just the type of letters that lend themselves to the sort of roundtable debate possible in the Elder Wisdom Circle groups. The effort does not always result in a consensus. Dawn says that when the Asbury Friends can't agree, "I record all their responses and that's what the letter writer gets: ALL the responses!"

While this chapter will include advice from both groups and individuals, much of the wisdom on making the right choice comes from these collaborative circles.

Bennett says that he is often surprised by the nonjudgmental views of people more than a half-century older than he. And he observes that the groups seem to have learned over their long lifetimes that the best "advice" is usually to nudge the advice seeker toward his or her own solution.

"A lot of the questions are not necessarily asking for direction as much as affirmation: 'Am I doing the right thing?'" Bennett says. "It's really easy to say we're here, we're supportive, and we think you're going in the right direction. Sometimes the people who are writing don't have anyone to do that, and I think that's what grandparents do best."

Bennett—Ben—is exactly the kind of young man to make a grandparent, or great-grandparent, proud: fresh-faced, well-spoken, and unfailingly polite, his clean-cut blond hair hidden under a Penn baseball cap. As the group members gather around the long, white folding tables in the activity room, set up to form a square—many arriving with the aid of canes or state-of-the-art motorized wheelchairs—you can almost hear them thinking, *Such a nice boy.*

This afternoon, Ben's group is large—eighteen attendees. Some are regulars, others are curious newcomers, responding to a loudspeaker announcing a group activity at 3 p.m.

One of the regulars is the ebullient Elder "Claudia," who parks her wheelchair next to Ben's right shoulder and proceeds to act as the unofficial assistant facilitator. "If you are going to fall asleep, you can't sit here," she scolds one of the ladies who is about to take another prime seat near Ben's chair.

Claudia, the proud owner of a new computer, has traded her bridge games for surfing the Internet. She is also an aspiring writer. "I'd like to write a short story or a play or a musical about a retirement center," she bubbles. In fact, she plans to base her characters on some of the residents right here in this room. For today, she is channeling her unstoppable energy not into musical theater, but to encouraging tentative seniors to speak their minds. She calls on them individually, like so many first graders: "What do *you* think, Grace?"

Which brings us to the question of the ring. Ben passes out copies of today's questions, but also reads it aloud to the group with the aid of a microphone. "I like this one," Ben says. "The real question is in the first line: 'Is it proper etiquette?' "

Not in the minds of several of the women at the table. Offers Elder "Hilda" in a musical accent that perhaps originates in Germany: "If he wants to keep the stones and have it redone in a different method, that's fine. But certainly not the same ring."

Bennett nods. "Maybe a different style, or metal, or setting," he says, scribbling notes.

That isn't enough for Elder "Louise." She shakes her head. "Even if he changes the style, she still may feel bad because he gave the diamond to somebody else," she says.

Elder "Bob," a newcomer in a bright orange shirt, doesn't let his relative inexperience keep him from donating his two cents. His advice? Tell the bride-to-be to get over it. "I personally think he has the right to give it to her," Bob says firmly. "After eight years? He says: 'The ring was returned to me seven years ago.' And diamonds are expensive."

"But if somebody else sees the ring, and knows it was used before, they might say, 'Oh, I know that ring—your fiancée had it,' " Hilda protests.

Bob defends his point. "I think he can solve both problems by saying, 'I bought this engagement ring eight years ago, so I'm giving it to you now.' You don't have to say you gave it to somebody else."

Nods and noises of approval come from several seated around the table. Claudia is not among them. "Why would you buy an engagement ring eight years ago?" she exclaims.

Bob doesn't have an answer to that—but he doesn't believe that the obvious question raised by an eight-year-old engagement ring to be an insurmountable problem. "Even if you *do* say you gave it to somebody else, if you've got two people who love each other," he argues, "why should it make such a big difference?"

"It could to somebody," Claudia says. "I think it's better to take the stones out and have it redone; then nobody's going to recognize it as something that was bought eight years ago."

Adds Elder "Louis", "Even though she hasn't seen it, *somebody* has seen it. The other woman had it for a year, and wore it for a year. And he's saying she still lives in the town."

Ben's next job is to turn this roundtable discussion into a letter. "Sometimes I'll have to remind myself that I'm going on *their* responses, because technically I'm not old enough to be in the group and answer the questions," Ben says. "It's a little difficult sometimes, being just the scribe."

Here is what Ben came up with:

This was a very interesting question, and it provoked some debate (mostly between the male and female members) in the group! Ultimately, we agreed that it would not be proper etiquette to give your fiancée the exact same ring.

You stated the first reason yourself: You still live in the same town with your former fiancée, and there's no telling how she would feel or react if she or one of her friends ever recognized the ring. You don't want a fiasco like that to disturb your current engagement.

In addition, your family would certainly recognize the ring (at least the women would). If news ever got back to your current fiancée about the origin of the ring, she may feel very hurt or react badly. You don't want to take that chance.

The ring is a very prominent symbol in a marriage. It ought to be individual and distinctive to the relationship. As such, it warrants a little effort on your part to present her with a ring that's unique. (Even if you don't necessarily feel this way, trust us, your fiancée will!)

However, this is not to say that you should completely abandon your current possession. It wouldn't be economically feasible (or necessary) to buy a completely new ring, especially if you like the diamond you currently have and feel that she would, too. So we are proposing a compromise. In our opinion, the best course of action would be to have the stone reset in a new band. This way, you can save the most beautiful (and valuable) part of the current ring while still making it sufficiently original for your new relationship. Your current fiancée may also be impressed with your ability to recognize a quality stone.

Trying to make the ring special for your new engagement does not have to break the bank. This compromise should help avoid any hurt feelings on either side.

The conclusion of the Garden Villa Elders seems to jibe nicely with that of most of the individual Elders who chose to answer this question. Most suggest that the writer keep the stones and lose the band, or get rid of the ring entirely, no matter what the cost.

Elder Elizabeth, eighty-six, a teacher and author who resides in Mission Viejo, California, has a personal reason for believing that the bride should not receive a ring with a "past": "My husband was a jeweler, and I have seen many brides break down in tears because they were forced to accept a ring that they disliked intensely," she says. "These rings were often 'lost' or hidden away."

Only one Elder Wisdom Circle member, Elder Jacobus, eighty-one, of Saskatoon, Saskatchewan, saw even a sliver of a chance of recycling the original ring as is, and then only with the blessing of the wife-to-be:

Maybe you should be honest with your prospective fiancée and tell her that you have this ring that was previously returned to you and you are wondering whether she would be comfortable with it. Emphasize to her that you want her to be completely happy about the ring you will be giving her. If she has any reservations at all, you will be more than happy to return the ring to the jeweler and buy her a new one.

Another group opinion comes from the Rockymountain Owls of Montrose, Colorado, aged sixty to ninety-five. Unlike the Garden Villa Elders, the Owls think even the stones should be sold, or saved for another less momentous occasion. "We chose to answer this letter because we would be hurt if this happened to us," say the Owls through their own scribe, Mark Deskin, a service coordinator for Volunteers of America, which manages both of the residences that house the two Colorado groups, the Owls and the Heavensviewsages. "We definitely wanted to get the message across that this ring must not be passed on, no matter what."

This ring is used goods, and in the worst way. Take the ring to the jeweler where you originally bought it and work out a trade or partial trade and pick out a ring that is new and special, just for your new fiancée. If that doesn't work, buy your fiancée a new ring, and sell the old one, or have the stones reset and save it for a gift for another occasion.

If it was a family heirloom, it might be different. But it is not, and absolutely do not give this ring again as a token of your love. You will be digging yourself a hole you will one day have to climb out of.

One Little Drink

LETTER: FRIEND CAN'T DRINK . . . CAN I?

My husband and I have joined a pool league. We recently had a baby (nine months old) and the pool league allows us a few hours one night a week to do a "grown-up" thing together.

Our friend who asked us to join has recently decided to stop drinking alcohol. He sought treatment for prescription medicine dependency and they informed him he shouldn't drink either. Now he has asked us not to drink when we are there around him.

We support his choice and never have alcohol when we go out to dinner or when he comes to our house, but I don't want to give up my one weekly vodka and tonic. I am a stay-at-home mom and I rather enjoy my few hours of grown-up time. Am I being selfish and unsupportive of my friend? If I went to the bar and had my drink instead of drinking at the table, would that be a reasonable compromise, or should I just not drink so he doesn't feel bad?

This is one of those questions that split both the Elder groups and the individual advice givers right down the middle. Several Elders who have had experience with substance abuse, either their own or that of a family member, believe that anyone struggling with an addiction must either learn to live with temptation, or take responsibility for avoiding it.

Elder Kenti, sixty-four, a retired psychotherapist who lives in suburban Chicago, says she chose to answer this letter "because I have a family member who is in recovery. She has made a decision that alcohol is lethal for her but does not want others to alter their lifestyle." She writes:

> It is admirable that your friend is in recovery. Recovery is his journey, yet it is thoughtful of you to support him by abstaining when visiting or at dinner. Still, you do have the right to decide for yourself if and when to have a drink. You cannot control whether he feels bad or whether he relapses. At the pool hall, he is surrounded by others who are drinking, and that is a slippery place for him to be. Fortunately, you do not have an addiction, so having a vodka and tonic is appropriate for you. Your friend will learn, as do others who are in recovery, how to deal with situations in which there is drinking.
>
> Another meaningful way to support your friend is to attend open Alcoholics Anonymous meetings to learn more about the disease and recovery. You may also benefit from attending Al-Anon meetings, where you will learn about the 12 Steps of recovery and how you can use them in your own life.

The WebWisdom group, aged eighty-two to ninety-four, is mainly made up of former homemakers who raised kids. They sympathize with the advice seeker:

> Our group of Elders believes there is nothing wrong with your having a social drink while out enjoying yourself. You do support your friend when he comes to your house and you don't drink. But we do not believe you are being selfish if you want to drink in front of him.
>
> He needs to stop having someone hold his hand. Your friend needs to concentrate on overcoming his addiction and not on blaming others if he fails because they are enjoying themselves.

The Rockymountain Owls do not share the opinion of WebWisdom. They believe strongly that the friend's request should be honored with no compromises or questions asked.

One of the Owls, eighty-three-year-old Elder Auntie B., agrees with the group consensus because of her own experiences with alcoholism in her family. "That hit home with me because my father was a terrible alcoholic," she says.

"I can remember back to when I was five or six years old—that's a pretty good memory. I remember the times my father came home drunk, and he would always want to hurt my mother," Auntie B. continues. "I had this great big beautiful machete that came from the Philippines; he came home one night and he was looking for it, and I hid it under my doll bed mattress in my playroom. My mother put up with it as long as she could, and finally they got a divorce." Ironically, when Auntie B.'s father died, it was not from alcohol-related illness, but of emphysema, from a longtime smoking habit.

Unlike her mother, Auntie B., who originally hails from Alabama, learned from her mother's experience to not put up with drinking. She has been married seven times. Being a proper southern lady, she isn't one to name names—but acknowledges that she had to jettison a husband or two for bad behavior. "If I married a man who had a drinking problem, or talked to me ugly, he just came home the next day and found the divorce papers facing him, that's just how I did it," she says. "Of course my family was always in a state of shock."

The Owls wrote:

Addiction of any kind is such a terrible tragedy that we strongly feel you should support your friend in any way you can. Basically, you are choosing between your friend and alcohol, and when looking at it in that context, it may make your choice clearer.

If you still would like to have a drink, stop on your way home and have a drink, or wait until he leaves the bar to have one. We understand you want your adult time, but being addicted is so devastating; try to support your friend in any way you can.

In all honesty, if he has a problem with alcohol, he shouldn't be in a bar to begin with. If you are on a diet, you don't hang around bakeries. But that is another question for another day.

◄O►

The Best Policy

LETTER: INTEGRITY / HONESTY / FAMILY DUTY / JACK RUSSELL GETS NEIGHBOR'S CAT

My six-year-old son was walking with our Jack Russell terrier; the dog attacked and killed the neighbor's cat. The cat had come over to our home at least twice a day for the past seven years and ate with our three cats. I was shocked and sad and angry; why kill now? Could the cat have been ill and the dog sensed its weakness? He would always chase the cat off our property, but he had never harmed it.

A) My son told the neighbor that the cat died, and who killed it. The neighbor called the dog catcher to have us cited for a dog roaming. Family loyalty is paramount. You don't snitch on a family member. Should I pass this along to my son and tell him there is a time to talk and a time to keep your mouth shut?

B) Does the fact that the neighbor called the humane society to get us in trouble mean our friendship is over? I called and spoke with the husband and offered my condolences.

C) Should we get a new kitten or offer to buy a new cat for them?

None of the groups chose to answer the cat and dog question. But while the individual Elders who addressed the problem offer varying advice as to what to do about continuing the friendship or replacing the neighbor's cat, all agreed that this six-year-old showed more wisdom than his parent.

Wrote Elder chr, seventy-three, of Bay City, Michigan:

I believe that your son is the real adult in this episode.

From Elder Ursula, seventy-seven, of Tujunga, California:

I'm sure your boy has already picked up the high emotions and tension created by this sorrowful problem. HE didn't kill the cat—the dog did. As to the neighbor's actions to get you cited for a roaming dog, the defense to that is that the cat roamed, too, into the dog's territory. If it satisfies the neighbor, pay the fine. No, don't get a new kitten; they are grieving the old one. You can offer, when the time comes and they are ready to have a new pet, to pay for one, but they can get a new pet free (except for paying for the necessary vaccinations) at their local animal shelter.

As to imposing the family value about snitching, please reconsider what you are suggesting. Right now, your son is honest. This must have been a shocking experience for him. Do you want to make it worse by accusing him of disloyalty to his family, too?

Elder Nancy, seventy-seven, of Malibu, California, answered this one "because I have a lot of experience in the pet department. All four of my kids were in the 4-H program and we've had many, many dogs, cats, rabbits, and horses. I've had a zoo in my house at times." Her current menagerie includes a parrot, three cats, and five dogs.

Your son did the right thing in being honest about the cat's death. You have taught him well. When a family has a problem to face, they should face it together and you did from the fact that you called the cat's owner and apologized.

When my kids were young, their German shepherd got out of the backyard. The dog got into a neighbor's yard and ripped open their rabbits' cage and killed the rabbits. Needless to say, we were shocked and the neighbors were highly upset. After a telephone call from them, my son, who was about twelve, went up to their house and repaired their cages and we bought new rabbits for them. After everyone cooled off, we all remained friends.

What I'm trying to say is that these things happen with kids and animals. Your neighbor shouldn't have let her cat out to come into your backyard and eat your cats' food. It was an accident waiting to happen.

Being a pet owner brings many responsibilities. I've had dogs bitten by rattlers and killed by passing cars. A Jack Russell I had years ago was killed by a coyote in the backyard. I used to feed my dogs outside and one evening I wasn't thinking and didn't bring them in early enough. All I found was my dog's hind leg. The coyote was running off down the canyon with the rest of him. That did it! Now everyone eats indoors and food dishes are picked up.

Accidents happen and your son's experience will teach him how to avoid others. If I were you, I'd pat my son on the back for having the moral courage to tell the truth in a difficult situation. Then offer to go with them to get a new kitty. I always feel that the new owner needs to pick out the pet.

Elder Kriko, seventy-five, of Tempe, Arizona, agrees that the key to an amicable resolution is greater responsibility on the part of both pet owners. And to his way of thinking, it's the dog, not the boy, who poses a threat to the neighborhood.

A dog that attacks and kills a cat can be considered dangerous to the community. It could conceivably attack a baby, not knowing any better. You need to get him trained and certified safe, or confine him with extra-secure ties in the yard. You can set up a running line so he can get the needed exercise, but it must be demonstrably secure. Your first responsibility is not to the dog but to the community.

I know what I have said to you sounds harsh, and it must be hard for you to read it. Console yourself that it was only a cat that was killed, and that you have a remarkably honorable, courageous, and responsible son.

Set in Stone

LETTER: NEW NEIGHBOR PILFERING FROM ME?

I recently put up a flagstone retaining wall at my house. It took several weeks to finish and there was stone lying all over my driveway during the process. Yesterday I went over to my new neighbor's house to return a shoe my dog had taken from their yard. On their back porch hidden from my view by a large bush was a large stack of stone that looked exactly like what I used to build my retaining wall. I believe they pilfered it from me while the wall was under construction.

What really aggravates me is that I had to purchase more stone about halfway through the building process because there wasn't enough. Now I think I wouldn't have had to buy more if they hadn't taken what they did.

I don't know whether to say anything to them because I can't be absolutely positive it is my stone. I took a piece from their stack the other night and compared it to mine, and they are identical. But they are brand-new neighbors and I hate to accuse them and then find out it was theirs from their old residence. What do you think?

After considering the unfortunate story of the Jack Russell terrier, some of the Elders may wonder why this dog was allowed to wander into the neighbor's yard in the first place. But wander it did, and the flagstone stash was discovered. The Elders hold a wide range of thoughts on what to do about it. A few charitable souls maintained the possibility that the neighbor *didn't* steal the stone, but most suspected the similarities were more than coincidental.

Between them, the Asbury Friends group, aged seventy-three to one hundred and five, have endured more than one thousand years of neighbor problems. This group, facilitated by Elder Dawn, could not agree among themselves. Writes Dawn on their behalf:

Thirteen ladies and three gentlemen are responding. We didn't come to a consensus, so here goes.

One member of the circle felt that you should let sleeping dogs lie. Don't pursue it; just ignore the behavior. Her reasoning was that you have to live alongside them, and why rock the boat?

Others in the group thought that you should go over and start up a conversation with them about what happened with the stones and how much extra the job cost because of that. We don't think that they'll fess up; however, it's an indirect way of making them believe that you know.

On the other hand, if they did indeed bring those stones with them from their last house, then you'd feel terrible and would start out with a huge neighbor problem.

The indirect approach seems best. Good luck.

Elder Jangela, sixty-six, of Detroit, Michigan, suggests a return visit.

You are in a quandary. Should you confront your new neighbor and risk having a "bad neighbor" for the long run? Should you not confront your new neighbor and stew over the issue?

It is likely your neighbor has pilfered your stone, probably thinking if it was lying around in the driveway you wouldn't need it. Whether or not you needed it, it is still pilfering.

Now, there are many ways you can handle this situation.

You could, of course, take it back. While that may be what you would like to do, it probably is not the best solution.

You can go over and talk to them and give them your reasons why you think the stone is yours. That's the best thing, but you probably wouldn't get any satisfaction because they probably would not admit to taking it and that would upset you.

You could ignore it and get on with your life. That may be the best thing to do.

I would, however, suggest an alternative. You said you saw it in the first place because you were returning a shoe your dog took. Well, you can either wait for your dog to take something else, or you can be neighborly and bring something over to them (like a street directory, the names of the local elected officials, or anything you think may be of interest) and go in through the back so you are obviously passing the stack. When they come out you can say something like "Gee, that looks like our stone" and see what they say. It could be they liked your stone and went and got some just like it or the previous owners may have "pilfered it." They may admit to taking it. In any event, the rule of thumb, whenever you feel someone is not being truthful, is to allow them a way to get out of the corner they have put themselves in. Be gracious. You probably will be living next to them for a long time. And resign yourself to the fact that if they did take it, you do not have good neighbors.

Other Elders advised similar nonaccusatory ways of trying to let the new neighbors know that their stone-snatching has not gone unnoticed:

Kenti: *Rather than accuse your neighbor, I suggest you simply inquire about the stone. You could say that you noticed the stone on their porch and wonder if it somehow got to them by mistake. If they say it is rightfully theirs, you could mention that you had to order more partway through the job and thought there could have been a mix-up with the delivery. Then the discussion is over.*

chr: *The next time you see them, ask, "Did you find the shoe that I returned to you? I'm sorry that my dog took it and I'll take steps to prevent him from doing it in the future. I did see the flagstone behind the bush on your back porch. If you're going to use them in a project, I suggest that you get your measurements just right, because I did the same thing and I came up very short of what I needed. I wouldn't want the same thing to happen to you, friend."*

Elder Ursula, however, does not see any point to beating around this particular bush. She spent fifty years as a legal secretary, and it shows in her advice.

It is a touchy situation, but your neighbors shouldn't get away with this theft. It is HIGHLY unlikely that they would bring stones from their old residence with them, showing no mortar, no chipping, no placement, and identical to what you had purchased. Write a letter and a bill for the stones you had to replace. The letter should welcome them to the neighborhood, state you hope that they will enjoy their new home, and that you're willing to share what you have, when possible. State that you found the missing stones on their property, and you hope whatever project they had in mind for using those stones will be beautiful and useful, but you expect payment in full for the extra stones you had to buy to complete your wall. Send the letter by certified mail, receipt requested, so you will have a record of their getting the letter, and wait a few days. If you get no response, take your copy of your letter and that signed receipt to your attorney, and let HIM or HER handle the next steps. I anticipate you'll find your stones on your front porch within a day or two.

◄○►

More Neighborly Advice

LETTER: NIGHTLY NAUGHTIES; NOISY NEIGHBORS

This may sound humorous (and in a way, it is), but my new neighbors are very noisy during sex. She screams, and I get woken in fright. (Yes, they are definitely enjoying themselves.) Sometimes this happens several times a night. I don't want to embarrass them, but how can I say something tactfully? I can't keep losing sleep over this. (Earplugs are not an option.) I have never seen them. What do I do, leave an anonymous note under the door?

Unlike the "pilferers" in the previous letter, this amorous duo is only robbing their neighbors of some shut-eye. Elder Grandma-Dan, sixty-one, of Troy, Michigan, and her husband faced this problem when they were in their twenties, living in a first-floor apartment.

This definitely hit my funny bone! Like you, my husband and I did not want to embarrass them, and quite frankly had a few chuckles lying there in the dark. For a long time, we kept our mouths shut, and just trained ourselves to cope in various ways—or made love ourselves!

In the end, I actually learned something from these two. What I learned was that being an uninhibited lover (I was on the inhibited side at the time) can be a good thing, an exciting thing. My husband was thrilled!

If it is really disturbing your sleep, you probably need to address this issue with the couple. Start by taking them a "welcome neighbor" gift—cake, cookies, your favorite recipe. Opportunities will open up whereby conversations will lead to being able to tactfully mention "how thin the walls/floors are" and how easy it is to hear them.

This is how we handled the situation with our neighbors upstairs; one evening when we were having dinner it just came up (no pun intended), and we all had a good laugh about it.

Says Elder Michelle, sixty-four, of Portland, Oregon, "My letter tells you why I answered this."

Years ago, our neighbors sent us a very funny card that alluded to just such a "naughty" situation. I do not know if they heard us through open windows or if they just sent a funny card to amuse us, but I can tell you that we were much more discreet after that. We laughed, but we never asked our neighbors about the card. They have been our great friends for thirty-five years. The U.S. mail will deliver your message for a stamp and it may just do the trick. Give it a try. You have nothing to lose but a restless night.

Father Figure

LETTER: BIOLOGICAL FATHER—OR HUSBAND?

I am thirty-four years old and until two years ago would categorize myself as someone who made good choices. However, I am now in a terrible position and have no idea what to do.

I was married two years ago to a man in the military. Shortly after we were married he left for a sixteen-month deployment. During that time I had an affair. When my husband returned home (knowing of the affair), I ended it. Several months later, I moved out of the house and into a small apartment. After I moved out the affair started again. My husband knew the affair started again and together we sought counseling to try to resolve the issues.

This last January, my husband and I began to reconcile and I ended the affair for good. In February, however, I began getting very sick and found out that I was pregnant. Due to the timing it became very clear that it was not my husband's child—both my husband and I knew it immediately and later the conception date was confirmed by the doctor. For some reason, I felt compelled to tell the birth father. My husband disagreed with telling him, but it just seemed too wrong not to do so.

The birth father would like to be involved in the child's life, but my husband will only stay with me if he is not. My husband says that to save our marriage I must convince the birth father not to be involved at all so we can tell our families I am pregnant and have them think the child is my husband's.

Should I save my marriage and hide the truth? Or do I simply accept the fact that I am paying for my mistakes through the end of a marriage and work with the birth father to create a life for this little girl? The birth father is also a good man who wants to love and support this child.

The Elders who answered this question saw it as an emotional decision, but one with profound legal ramifications as well. From both perspectives, they put the child's welfare above the mother's feelings.

Writes Elder Myra, seventy, of Providence, Rhode Island:

If your child's birth father truly wants to be involved, to "love and support" his child, there is no way either you or your husband can stop him. Conception dates are tricky, but a DNA test can be used to prove biological paternity. He can then go to court to assert his right to have connection and contact with his child, assuming he is willing to provide support. It is important for your husband to realize this so it won't seem as though you are making a choice between him and your former lover.

I agree with you that living with a significant lie can have devastating consequences for all parties. In addition, your child has the right to know the truth, if only from a medical, genetic perspective.

You state that for some reason you felt compelled to tell the birth father. I think that was the correct choice, but it also reflects the uncertainty you feel about your relationships with these two men. This is an issue you might want to explore in counseling so you can get back on the road of making good choices. Also, now that you are about to become a parent, your choices will need to be based on fulfilling the needs of your child.

Elder Aunt Vic, seventy-two, of Eugene, Oregon, chose to answer this letter because "I was the child involved in a situation similar to this."

"While my mother was married, she became pregnant by another man, who I was always told was my biological father. When I was born, she was still married to her first husband. I was later told that in order to protect me, my mother thought it best to put her legal husband's name on my birth certificate. She soon divorced her first husband and married the man that I was told was my biological father. For some reason her first husband always remained close to her family and relatives.

"My mother died when I was twelve. Then the problems started. My mother's first husband, after years of not paying much attention to me at all, came swooping down claiming to be my biological father. I was hounded for years by this man's family claiming to be my relatives. I was perfectly happy with the dad I had.

"These people (my mother's first husband's family) have been hounding me and tracking me down and forcing themselves on me for years. I am seventy-two years old and I still get mail from them wanting to get personal information about me to put in their family records. I have always wondered why they think I'm so important. I'm just one little insignificant person who doesn't even like them."

Yes, I agree, you are in a bad situation. However, I think your instincts are right on. I think you are aware of the negative consequences of trying to live a lie, and your gut feeling is telling you not to do it.

By far the worst part of keeping the secret is what it will do to the child. Even if you are able to keep the truth a secret for a long period of time, I guarantee that eventually it will come out and the child will find out. When she does, she will wonder why it was kept a secret. She immediately will think it was because it was something bad. It can't help but cause her to feel some shame in who she is. It will follow her all her life.

We all want to do the best we can for our children. I think your instinct is telling you what you must do. If your husband won't accept your decision, you will just have to move ahead on your own.

◄○►

People Like Me

LETTER: A NEW HOME FOR ME?

My grandma died suddenly on Christmas Eve. I was very close with her and I miss her very much.

She lived in a small house and naturally left the house to my momma and my uncle. My momma owns a house already and my uncle doesn't wish to live in the area. I live in the projects and my family worries about me because of the crime in the area, although I am used to it and it doesn't really bother me anymore. They decided I should have the house.

Initially I was so happy because I stayed there a lot when I was little and it feels like home already. But then I started thinking about my momma and my uncle and how it wasn't fair for them to give me the house and have nothing for themselves. I am from a poor family. Even though the house isn't worth much, my uncle could get a reliable car and my mom could have some retirement money if they sold the house and split the money.

I don't think I can live in the house. I was in the bedroom going through some things the other day and I looked at the doorknob. It is the kind that looks like a giant diamond. When I was little, I remember thinking that if we ever were really, really poor, my grandma would just give us one of her doorknobs to sell so we could get food. Memories like this made me realize—how can I take the house when my momma and uncle could finally have something nice for themselves instead?

I discussed this with them and they said that I am helping them because I can keep a lot of the furniture and they don't have to sell it, store it, or find places in their homes for it. They said that since my great-grandma had the house built, it is nice to keep it in the family. They said they want me to have it. But this isn't fair!

I was divorced by age twenty-four, my husband abused me terribly, and I have no money because of medical bills from repeated concussions and a brain injury. People like me live in the projects. That is where I should be. My momma and uncle should sell the house and split the money. I would be so selfish for deciding to live in the house. Right?

> THANK YOU for your help. This is tearing me up inside. My uncle really watched out for me when my father left us when I was three and my mom always put me first. I just don't know what to do.

This is a letter all of the Elders can agree on: People like this young woman don't "belong" in the projects—and, for that matter, neither does anybody else. "Your comment is really disturbing," says Elder Nelly, sixty-eight, a former librarian who lives in Atlanta, Georgia. "Just because your crumb of an ex-husband told you that you were worthless—or whatever he said—you're not obligated to believe it."

Elder Heart of Texas, eighty-one, of Salado, Texas, chooses to try to persuade this young woman to accept what her relatives have offered by telling a story of how much her own parents, and indeed the whole family, received by the act of giving to someone else.

Dear lady, please accept your mother and uncle's offer of your grand-mother's house. When people do a generous thing, they do not feel they need to be rewarded. Since your grandmother passed away, they felt it was too difficult to get rid of her possessions and home. They must have felt that you would take care of the house and by their love for you, wanted you to have it and her possessions.

Love is given in so many ways and I felt that my parents showed me how this could be done. They had eight children, but they adopted a child in need from Laos. They sent money to a Christian group that saw that the money was used for this girl's education. They contin-ued this until she graduated from college. None of their children were college educated, but they felt we lived in America and we had free-dom to make our own way. This girl became a doctor and emigrated to America and my sister had the privilege of visiting with her in Cali-fornia. Her gratitude to my parents was doubled when she heard that none of us eight children had a college education.

After my parents passed away we found many letters they had re-ceived from this girl. It was their love for another less fortunate person that made us all the more proud of them.

Writes Elder Michelle:

When you were a little girl, you thought your grandma could give you one of her "diamonds" so you could survive. Guess what, she just did.

Hindsight

LETTER: IF YOU COULD GO BACK?

> If you could go back to your early twenties and make only three changes what would they be? Why?

Although the Elders seem to share the ability to keep their eyes on the future, they also point out that they have learned from past choices as well.

From Elder Seeley:

1. *I would make certain that I visited my parents and my grandparents at least once a year in spite of the fact that they lived 1,200 miles away and my income was not exactly that of a robber baron.*
2. *I would have taken a five-year leave of absence after the birth of my daughter instead of just a six-week maternity leave; that way I would not have missed her first word, her first step, and her first real hug—her arms were around her caretaker's neck.*
3. *I would have not purchased all those "things" in an attempt to "keep up with the Joneses"; instead I would have socked that money away and invested it for the future.*

From Elder Digit, seventy-two, a forensic consultant in Willingboro, New Jersey:

Only three changes, eh? That's a challenge! But here they are:

1. *I bought a guitar in my early twenties (a Martin single O) for $50 in a pawn shop. I still have it. I would like to have learned to play it better than I did. I was good enough to be able to sing in coffee houses, but it would have been nice (while my hands were still supple) to have learned to play classical guitar.*
2. *In my early twenties I was still at university, getting a B.S. in physics. I wish I'd paid more attention, studied harder, and gotten better grades. I also wish I'd taken a few linguistic courses as electives, to please my polyglot father as well as myself.*
3. *I married when I was twenty, and was divorced when I was twenty-five. I was too young, and I wish that there were some way of undoing the harm that I caused her.*

Elder Sylvia, seventy-four, of Hillsboro, Oregon, a teacher and special projects coordinator for two companies, says she wanted to answer this letter because "I wish I had been wise enough when I was twenty to ask someone older the same question."

If I could go back to my early twenties and change three things they would be this:

I would try very hard to love and respect myself, to believe in myself and have compassion for myself, because only then could I truly love, respect, believe in, and have compassion for others.

I wouldn't be afraid to aim high, work hard, and take chances.

And I wouldn't be afraid to love, to give love with all my heart and being—not because I felt I wasn't whole or needed someone to complete me, but for the joy of sharing. It all starts with learning to love and accept ourselves.

Elder Kriko, seventy-five, of Tempe, Arizona, thought answering this letter was fun.

When I was twenty I was drafted into the Army during the Korean War. I hated it and resisted every minute. Only later did I realize how valuable the experience was and how foolish I had been not to take advantage of the wonderful opportunities presented to me. I should have learned Japanese and Korean, I should have taken the Army up on their offer to send me to officer's training school, maybe I should have reenlisted for at least several more years and made myself into a real man instead of a resistant snot.

After I was released from the Army, I found myself confused and aimless. Because of the G.I. Bill, I was able to go to college. I graduated with a degree in education and became a teacher. While I don't regret having been a teacher, I now wish I had pursued a more personally satisfying direction. I didn't know it then, but now I know I should have been an artist. That would have meant poverty and disappointment and maybe failure. But every day I would have had a sense of joy I didn't have in teaching.

Several times in my life I had the opportunity to be an actor. I think I would have loved that life and possibly could have become a film director. Once again, that would have meant sacrifice and probably failure, but it would have made me whole.

You asked for three, let me add a fourth: I would have liked to be a professional jazz musician. I have some talent and creativity but no stomach for the effort it takes. Plus, I can't stand a noisy, smoky club. But oh, the joy of making music!

Oh, By the Way . . .

LETTER: POSTPONE MY WEDDING OR NOT?

I have been engaged for almost two and half years. Throughout my relationship, my fiancé and I have always had arguments and disagreements; several have been very intense. When we decided on our wedding date we both felt it was perfect! Now that the date is coming closer, my fiancé says that we should postpone our wedding due to the fact that we argue and fight. I certainly don't want to postpone it. I feel that setting a date to be married is like meeting a deadline—we should do everything in our power to meet this date. What should I do? By the way, we have a one-year-old son.

Nancy thinks this couple should plow ahead on schedule. She recalls enjoying the 1950s TV series *The Bickersons*, based on the classic 1940s radio series starring Don Ameche and Frances Langford as the quarrelsome couple (for trivia buffs, Lew Parker replaced Ameche as the husband in the television series). "I answered this one because too many people think that marriage should be a bed of roses," Nancy says.

It sounds as if your fiancé has commitment issues. He is getting cold feet now that the day is approaching. If you have been together for two and a half years, even though you have argued and disagreed with each other, it sounds as if you were meant to be married.

Lots of married couples have their disagreements and arguments. (There used to be a TV show called The Bickersons. *It was really funny.) If you are both strong-minded, independent thinkers and stand up for your own opinions, it is bound to happen. I argued with my husband for thirty years. The important thing is to be able to admit when you are wrong.*

You need to think about your son. His birth needs to be made legal. As much as we would like to think that it doesn't matter, it does.

Marriages are not made in heaven, even though songs and movies say it's so.

Marriage was once described to me as two strong plow horses linked together plowing the field. We would like to think of it as two beautiful racehorses in a race toward success, but that isn't what lasts. The plow horses are building for the future. It takes two linked together to do the proper job.

You need to get married and create a loving home for yourself, your husband, and your son.

And now, back to St. Louis and the Garden Villa Elders, who resemble eighteen Bickersons as they discuss the choices faced by the eager bride and the reluctant groom. Some group members laugh derisively as Ben reads the final sentence of the letter, with the italics reflected in his voice: "*By the way*, we have a one-year-old son."

"She should get married, so her son has a father!" exclaims Elder "Ernie" triumphantly, as soon as Ben is finished reading.

Ernie apparently has been waiting for this question. He had also chimed in with this exact comment earlier, when the group was still discussing the decision facing the young woman whose relatives want to help her escape life in the projects. "We'll get there in a second," Ben had told him gently, in response to the baffled reaction of the rest of the crowd. But finally, the group has caught up with Ernie, and he isn't about to miss his opportunity.

Hilda echoes Ernie's sentiments. "I think if they want to get married, do it right away," she says. "She has known him long enough. Children need two parents, not only a mother or a father."

Ben nods. "The only thing I would say as a caution to that is, I don't know whether it's better to have a father and a mother who argue all the time, or one mother who doesn't have that conflict."

Hilda, however, sticks to her guns. "She has to know whether she's willing to take that all the time. It's up to her. She knows what she gets."

Elder Claudia jumps in: "*He* wants to postpone it—not her."

Hilda thinks this over. She folds her arms and announces, "Then cut it off! There is no future then."

A few members of the group suggest the less drastic option of a postponement. "If they break up, she might find another man who, even if he's not the natural father, would be a better father for the boy," offers Bob. "I don't think they should get married until they find out if they can live together amicably." Adds Elder "Bonnie": "I think they should wait and see if they can resolve their differences."

Hilda shakes her head. "It's not going to change. She can either take it or leave it."

There is a long pause. "Does anybody have anything else?" Ben asks.

All eyes turn to a gentleman who has entered the group late and has taken a seat in an unobtrusive spot in a line of chairs set up away from the folding tables.

The man looks startled—then grins apologetically. "I don't want to make any opinion," he says. "I'm just nosy to see what's going on."

Hilda never changed her mind—but the fact that most of the group members wanted to allow the couple some time to see if they could discover a way to benefit from their doubts led Ben to compose the following response:

In this matter we tend to agree with your husband-to-be. If the two of you don't feel comfortable getting married at the present time, then it would be better to wait. Any problem that you experience in an engagement that you cannot resolve will not go away in marriage. This isn't to say that you must resolve every single difference before getting married, but you must be confident that they eventually can be reconciled.

Your wedding date is only a deadline in the sense that you have all of the arrangements lined up for that day. If you aren't ready to get married, however, these things can—and should—be changed to a later date.

This approach will also be better for your young son as well. While there is no doubt that a stable, two-parent family would be the best environment to raise your son, he will get no benefit from having two parents living together if they are constantly fighting. This is not to suggest in the least that you and your fiancé have reached the point of parting ways! We are simply trying to say that the child should not be the primary reason to rush into a marriage you are not prepared for. He will be better off in the long run if you make a careful, considered decision about your and your fiancé's future.

In an ideal scenario, however, you and your husband-to-be would be able to work past your differences and be able to come to some sort of peace. Civil, constructive communication is key! Sit him down and, without letting the situation escalate into a fight, discuss what you feel are the most serious issues in your relationship and how these can be addressed through compromise. Perhaps consider seeing a relationship counselor in order to get a second opinion on the subject.

Don't be afraid to wait. Photographers and caterers and flowers can all be rescheduled. You can never reverse your choice to be married once you have made it.

Best regards,
The Garden Villa Elders

WORKING KNOWLEDGE
Wisdom for Career Satisfaction

I left my horrible job yesterday and was hired at a wonderful job with a great boss today, and she told me that if I do well (and I will) that I will be considered for an upcoming assistant manager position. I start tomorrow! Your advice gave me the courage to change my circumstances. Thank you so much!

"Audrey"

—From "Feedback & Kudos"
www.ElderWisdomCircle.org

The manager does things right. The leader does the right thing.

—*On Becoming a Leader*, Warren Bennis

Working Mom

I am writing to ask for some advice on balancing my career and being a mother. I have a four-month-old daughter whom I absolutely adore but I feel very guilty when I leave for work every day. I know it doesn't get any easier either. Do you have any advice on how I can stop feeling so guilty?

Elder Nancy, seventy-seven, of Malibu, California, went from homemaker and mother to career woman, but not by choice. In 1978, Nancy lost her husband to an accident—not out on the highway somewhere, but right outside her window, at the family home in a rustic canyon overlooking the Pacific. "That year we had tremendous rains, and a lot of the property fell away from the front of our house," she says. "He was doing some grading with a small tractor in the backyard there, and all of a sudden the whole area gave way underneath him, and down he went."

Nancy didn't have time for grief. She had already been obliged to return to work as a teacher while her husband was still alive because his business, producing sprinkler clocks, had failed. After his death, the family finances only got worse. "He left me sinking in debt—I didn't know how I was going to pay the gasoline bill, pay this person and that person," she recalls. "I had to write letters to everybody: 'I owe you $5,000; if I pay it off $5 a month, is that okay?' And not only was there a terrible financial mess, the house was a mess—the ground was a sea of mud. Everything was left undone when he died, and I had to deal with the builder he had hired, who was a crook of the first order.

"I felt like Scarlett O'Hara, saying, 'I'm going to live through this, and when it's all over, I'll never be hungry again!' "

Though Nancy's story is an extreme example of entering the career world out of necessity, many of the Elders, both men and women, come from a generation that did not have the luxury of broad-ranging educational and career choices that their own children and grandchildren have enjoyed. Those in their late seventies and eighties grew up during the Depression, so they accepted hardship as a fact of life. Because many of the Elders married young and started families right away, they did not have the time or the financial resources for an extended adolescence. Theirs was not a generation that spent a year abroad and then took a sweet summer bartending job in Baja with the goal of "finding themselves."

Like Nancy, many of the Elders tell stories of hard choices made in the name of money. But this group is not one that has become bitter or envious of the privileges that their offspring have had. If anything, the career advice that follows in this chapter paints a picture of a generation that celebrates their children's good fortune. And in spite of the fact that many of the Elders followed their heads and not their hearts when it came to their career choices—or perhaps because of it—with a few notable exceptions, most of them encourage young advice seekers to pursue their dreams. The message: Do as they say—not as they did.

Though her financial need was daunting, with a little careful planning, Nancy managed to pay her bills *and* gain personal satisfaction through her career.

With the help of her children, she managed to cover the household expenses while holding on to her husband's life insurance money. "I had three teenage kids at home, between sixteen and twenty, and they all went to work," Nancy says. "It was a cooperative venture in order to keep the house. I was working to pay the mortgage, and they were working to bring in money to keep us going. A lot of times we ate casserole after casserole, and made do."

Nancy acknowledges that her family was always a little different from her worldly and affluent neighbors in the canyon. Her kids were young in the 1960s, a decade that the West Coast embraced as an endless summer of love. Just down the road was what Nancy describes as a "hippie commune," where visitors, including children, could be found frolicking naked in the pool. When one of the youngsters from the commune wandered up to visit, he was welcomed—but only if he said "please" and "thank you," and always addressed Nancy and her husband as "Mr. and Mrs."

After her husband died, Nancy spent the next year or so teaching, and then worked for a pet rescue organization. But just as the pet rescue career was falling apart as a result of the company owner's legal problems, Nancy got an offer from a colleague who finally offered her just the right place to invest that carefully guarded life insurance money: "How would you like to buy a little school?"

By that point, Nancy had just about had it with the politics of the teacher's life; being a rebellious "sassy pants," Nancy says she never much cared for the way teachers always got caught between the parents and the principal. But, she adds, "I always had a hankering to run a school, and really take care of the teachers, be the liaison between the administration and the teachers, who often end up out in left field." She and her friend became coinvestors in the school.

The school became all that Nancy expected, affording her the opportunity to lead instead of follow. And now she can't imagine *not* having had a career outside the home. "I think it's boring," she exclaims. "I think that for a woman just to be a housewife is stifling. I grew up a lot when I went to work."

Nancy's letter:

The first thing you are going to have to do is to stop feeling guilty about your career.

I had to go to work when my husband's business failed. I had four children, the youngest being three years old, when I started working as a teacher. I ended up in education for thirty-five years. I loved my work and I really feel that the years spent balancing work, home, and kids was well worthwhile.

Yes, I used to come home in the evening and have to face my own kids' homework, a dirty house, and dinner yet to cook. But, in looking back, I wouldn't change it in one little way.

I've enjoyed taking care of the grandchildren, baking cookies, and reverting to the role of the "housewife." But if I were younger, I would still be working.

There is only one thing you need to watch out for, and that is the care you provide for your daughter in your absence. Whomever you leave your child with should be a person of the highest moral character. They should also feel free to correct her if she misbehaves.

Always remember when you come home to spend time with you daughter as you are making dinner or even just watching television. Then to bed with a story and hugs. Remember, no guilt on your side.

Elder Arianne, sixty-seven, of Wyncote, Pennsylvania, agrees with Nancy:

You are emotionally responding to old and narrow rules that insist a woman must be home with her children twenty-four hours a day to be a good mother. Now, logically speaking, you know that isn't true. In fact, my pediatrician urged me to go back to work when my last child was three years old. He knew my children and family would be much happier if I were a happier mom.

You have the right to have a life of your own outside your home if you wish. You are not required to give up everything except your family. No one faults a father for working, even if he works very long hours. Isn't it time you accepted your right to also lead a full and varied life?

Grandma-Dan, sixty-one, of Troy, Michigan, who works full time as a medical social worker in the hemophilia clinic at a children's hospital in nearby Detroit, believes the answer is not quite that simple.

I am thankful that both of my daughters grew up to be mentally healthy, mature women, but even today we continue to have discussions about all the "what ifs" regarding me having to work and them being cared for by others and also having to take care of themselves much of the time. They have told me how much they wished I could have been a stay-at-home mom and what that would have meant to them if I had.

My youngest, who is now the mother of two, is budget cutting and staying home with the firm support of her wonderful working husband. I know it is a hard choice for them financially, but I so admire them for sticking to it for the sake of my grandchildren.

My oldest, who is also married, is not planning to have children, period. She absolutely loves her career. I wonder if there is something inside of her saying, "No kids as long as your career comes first," and it does. I am proud of her, too, for knowing herself to be a career woman, and one who would not be able to compromise her career in order to raise children as a working mom.

Instead of focusing on whether it's good or bad to be a "career mom," Kriko offers a practical solution to the guilt issue:

Someone must be caring for your baby while you are at work. You must pay that person something. Maybe it is possible to compromise so that you can work less and pay less and spend more time with your daughter. Don't waste your resources trying to figure out how to feel less guilty; you will need them all to focus on making things better.

Dress for Success

LETTER: DRESS CODE

I run a small, successful ad agency. My media director, a male, is buying in as a partner. He is a great thinker, able to communicate well and a good soul. But he dresses like an extra in *Grease*. The guy is forty-five years old, wears short sleeve open collar shirts with the top two buttons undone, and when it's time for client meetings he wears business clothes that are twenty years out of date. And I have to tell him to get rid of his gum in meetings. How the heck do I get this guy to look like he is in a business that is supposed to be up on the popular culture, partner or not, without hurting his feelings or making him angry?

Nancy knows that clothes can make the man—or the woman.

At Nancy's school, the children wore uniforms, and teachers were asked to dress with similar respect for their school and their positions. In the first years of Nancy's involvement with the school, teachers were required to wear skirts. But for one young teacher, adhering to that dress code wasn't enough for the mothers of the students.

"She was probably twenty-two, blonde, and very pretty," Nancy says. "She was the kind of gal who would come in and sit down and all the men's heads would turn. She was a very solid teacher. But I tell you, that girl was persecuted that year by those women. It was just jealousy, I guess."

Despite the unfairness of the charge, it fell to Nancy to try to remedy the situation. She writes about how she handled it:

Being the owner of a business requires some difficult interviews with the people with whom you work. One big one is when you have to talk about personal care or dress. I was an administrator of a private school that had a dress code for their students. Therefore, some of our teachers were criticized for the way they dressed by our parents who didn't feel they gave the right image. On many occasions I had to tell the teachers that their skirts were too short. The teacher who taught fifth grade was well endowed with a large bust. Parents' complaints were that her blouses were too tight and they didn't think she was dressed appropriately for the classroom. Now, her blouses were not too tight, it was just that the mothers thought that she was too young and pretty to be teaching their children, even though she was well qualified academically and her students loved her. I went to her and explained the situation, so she modified her dress and the gossip died down.

All talks like the one above must be on a positive note. Since you are in the ad business, your partner must be aware of the importance of appearance and making a favorable first impression. Talk to him privately and sympathetically and tell him what you think he could wear that would zip up his appearance. Suggest something that you think would look terrific on him. He probably hasn't purchased anything new for himself in years. You could open the door to a new sense of fashion.

Elder Seeley, sixty-five, of Tucson, Arizona—retired from a long and varied career as an RN, a realtor, and a science teacher—was surprised by this letter because, she says, "it is almost a total role reversal. Usually it is the women who must adhere to a stated business code and the men who seem to instinctively know how to dress for business."

Seeley, who lived much of her life in the Washington, D.C., area, was married to a government employee who, after twenty-six years of marriage, "traded me in on a new, improved model." She responded by marrying an old school friend of her ex-husband's. "He was so mad when I married 'Johnny' that he refused to speak even to his own bimbo for a week," Seeley says, pleased. "Revenge is a dish best served cold, very cold."

Seeley did inherit one minor problem with her new husband, and it is one that served her well in answering this letter.

Husband number two, though a distinct improvement over husband number one, is somewhat fashion impaired.

It's not that he has bad taste, Seeley explains; he just doesn't have any at all. "I guess at a certain age, they don't care if they mix-match different plaids and stripes together," she says. "I think it's a function of age, I really do, because Johnny is eighty, but when he was in his twenties and thirties he was the Beau Brummell of Denver, Colorado."

Seeley solves this problem by buying his clothes, including silk boxers, which she says few men would ever buy for themselves. And he tells her he likes them. "They feel good!" she says, with a hearty laugh.

It is my understanding that creative types such as media directors tend to be given a lot of latitude when it comes to dress codes. However, since he is "buying in" as a partner, he does need to present a more businesslike persona.

So, what do you do? You take him out to a nice business lunch and then to a shopping trip at a good men's store to help him purchase at least two tailored business suits—one in dark gray or navy and one in deep brown or black pinstripe, six business shirts in current subdued colors—one to be kept at the office at all times in case of an "accident," two pair of shoes—oxfords or wing-tips—one pair in black and one pair in dark brown or cordovan, eight silk ties in a foulard or regimental stripe pattern or plain subdued colors, and one

*good wool winter overcoat. That should do it for a start. No, the
dress is not "hip," but it will serve for at least ten years and he can
add to this wardrobe some of the more fashion forward looks—
which will be fashion past next year. Tell him that the wardrobe is a
condition of his becoming a partner and is non-negotiable. If you
can, you should offer to split the cost of his new business attire with
him and consider it a bona fide business expense (check with your
accountant). If you really flatter him, he will consider himself the
luckiest man alive!*

Elder Web, sixty-four, of Farmington Hills, Michigan, has met
plenty of "dress slobs" during his forty-year business career, which most
recently has included ten years as a recruiter and employment counselor. He says, "Business can be lost over unshined shoes or a stain on
the tie."

*I feel the answer to your question is easy. Establish a dress code that
you and every other employee must adhere to. I understand you are in
a creative business and many creative people march to their own
drummer, but it is still a business, and the reaction of customers is
most important. Don't make it personal. Treat it as what it is: business.*

Elder Kriko, seventy-five, of Tempe, Arizona, is an artist in many
media: photography, sculpture, drawing, writing, jewelry, and even umbrella design. He advises more tolerance for the eccentricities of the
creative spirit.

*I can think of three scenarios: Do it your way, do it his way, or com-
promise.*

*My first thought is that you have a successful business. That is a
great achievement. Has he been your media director all this time? Has
he pleased your clients with his ideas and presentation? Are people
complaining about his lack of professionalism? Are you losing business
because of his appearance and gum chewing?*

*If his work is successful and your clients are happy, maybe what he
looks like and how he behaves is part of what makes them happy. It
may be unpleasant for you, but you might think of it as the kind of*

contrast that makes comedy teams work so well. Just think of Burns and Allen, Abbot and Costello, Martin and Lewis, Lucy and Ricky, Billy Crystal and Meg Ryan. Why do they succeed? Probably because they are opposites.

This difference between you two may be the very spark that makes your endeavor successful. No client wants to come to a meeting full of official seriousness or unkempt raggedness. But the two together are often delightful, especially if both bring wonderful ideas.

I think you might try letting him be himself for a year or two, bite the bullet and see how well things go. If it doesn't work out to be profitable, then you have plenty of reason to suggest that he change.

Wood I Bee a Good Teechur?

LETTER: ANSWERING THE QUESTION OF BEING FIRED

For the first time in my life, I was fired from a rather simple sounding job: pharmacy clerk. I was fired because of performance issues. I had worked for the organization for a year and had five discussions with my boss (initiated by me) about how to improve the process, and even though I reached each of the goals set, there was just too much work for me, but I kept working as hard as I could.

My background: a B.S. computers and management, 3.75 magna cum laud; after a management job of five years I have moved around to five jobs in the past five years.

I am going to apply for being a substitute teacher and possibly become a teacher if I like it (my older sister and here husband are teachers of twenty-plus years). I am uncomfortable about the two-sentence answer I created to answer why I was fired. Some people tell me I should say I was laid off, since I was paid severance pay. I am confused, hurt, and unsure of myself. Your opinion would be nice as to how you would answer why you were fired when applying for such a sensitive job as being a teacher and role model to young children.

Elder L. David, seventy-one, of Monterey Park, California, thinks this writer might want to run a spell-check before sending out his ré-sumé seeking a position in education.

Hi,
    I hope that I can help you a little bit. First of all, the people who tell you to use the term "laid off" as opposed to "fired" are absolutely right. You should always present yourself in the best light.
    Another suggestion for future jobs: Err on the side of caution when it comes to telling experienced people how to improve the procedures that they have instituted. They might resent being told by someone with less experience how things should be run unless they specifically have asked for your input.
    One other (I hope) helpful hint. When applying for any job, be careful not to make typos, misspell words, etc. You did that here. Ex-amples: It's magna cum laude, not laud, and there should be a period after laude and a new sentence should have started. You said "here" husband when you meant "her" husband. You changed tense incor-rectly; i.e. you said, "After a management job of five years I have moved . . ." It should have been "I moved." There are several more of these types of errors. I am only bringing them to your attention be-cause you say that you are applying for a job teaching. I'm sure that anyone reading your résumé and application would have a negative reaction to these types of errors.
    I hope that you will take this criticism in the manner it was in-tended, to help you put your best foot forward.

Take it from a retired high school principal—Elder Toni, sixty-four, of Folsom, California—teaching is not the career for someone finding too much challenge in a job as a pharmacy clerk.

Five jobs in five years tells me two things: You haven't found your niche and you haven't been very happy. If this is the case, please don't rush off to become a teacher because your older sister and brother-in-law are in this field. Second, if your job as a pharmacy clerk was too much work to do and you had difficulty pacing yourself, you should know that teaching is all about pacing and trying to "do it all."

Teaching is one of the most difficult career choices for anyone. You teach students of all abilities; you teach to the state standards; you teach students who care and those who don't. You deal with parents who support you, and those who want to lay blame on you. A teacher must learn to deal with the unexpected: a threat to the school and a lockdown; a student telling you information that must be reported; a case of lice throughout the school; an angry parent visiting your class-room; a happy parent bringing cupcakes to the class . . . I could go on.

At this point in your life, you might find more success in a field that is less demanding than teaching. Look into community college courses or extension courses for areas of interest. Become a student for a while and learn more about what you want and like. Good luck and have fun searching.

Elder Ruthie, sixty-four, of Swanton, Ohio, acknowledges a check-ered career path of her own. She also admits to having been fired on more than one occasion.

Born the ninth of eleven children in a post-Depression farm family, Ruthie did not find such a direct career path as did some of her siblings. "All seven of my brothers were older than I—one became a doctor, and two others engineers," she says. In high school, Ruthie did well in math and science, but the subjects bored her. She had some natural talent in art, but the school offered no art department.

Ruthie's mother died in a car accident when Ruthie was five. "This led to me learn many household skills early on," she says. Feeling lost after high school, Ruthie took a year off before college and channeled those housekeeping skills into providing home care for families while the mother was delivering a new baby. She was fired from one of those jobs. "The bottom line is that I was doing too good a job of caring for the house and the children. The mom felt threatened by me, and used my tardiness—the one time I was tardy—to dismiss me."

Ruthie went on to college, and during her last semester was invited to start an art department at the college. "It was a glorious time of turn-ing an old basement room into a place to create art," she says. But after a year, and following the death of her father, Ruthie felt the call to be-come a nun. "After two and a half years at a Carmelite monastery, I was fired again," she says. "They sent me home before I made my [final profession,] as they felt it was not my calling."

Ruthie returned to teaching art, then moved on to a position teaching religion at a parochial school—from which she was fired "for no other reason except that there was a different person they wanted for the position." She then held a parish position as director of religious education, where she was not fired, but clashed with the new pastor and left "less than willingly."

But Ruthie eventually did find her way to the right job, and wants the advice seeker to know it's possible to do the same.

It is no crime to be fired. When applying for new positions I never found it necessary to write or say anything less than the truth. My record of job changes was seven in ten years, so I sort of know where you are coming from.

Don't be afraid to keep searching for the right job, community, or relationship. These are things that form you and you help form and when it all comes together it is truly wonderful. I was fortunate to be able to do that at age thirty-eight. I have been in the same place, same job, and same community for twenty-six rewarding years. It could happen for you as well.

Look up "Euphemism" in the Dictionary . . .

LETTER: ESCORTING?

Next week I'm taking a flight to Scotland to marry my partner of six years. We have a very strong relationship. However, I feel I have very little on the level of practical support to offer in the relationship—such as a finished education, a job, general income, etc. This relationship is my priority and I will not compromise it for anything.

Recently I was looking through job offers in a local paper and found an ad for escorts, offering daily cash, a safe environment, and training. According to the person running this service, an escort can make $10,000 a week—with such an income, I could not only prepare MYSELF for travel, but I could help my incapacitated father get a $1,000 root canal on his last working tooth (his dentures don't work for chewing), I could pay off ALL my college debts, and I could move on with my life.

However, I know that there are many negative aspects to consider: disease, stigma, relationship integrity, and legality, as well as personal spiritual health and self-image.

If I lived in a world that had none of the above negative factors, I'd be all over the opportunity! Unfortunately, such a world doesn't exist. I'm stuck between my debts, my desire to contribute and not be dependent, my sense of responsibility, my feelings of inadequacy and desperation, and a general feeling that escorting is not something I should do because of the risks.

One can't be sure from the letter whether the writer is a man or a woman, but the Elders seem fairly confident that the advice seeker is the bride-to-be, not the groom.

Writes Elder Frank, seventy-two, of Greensboro, North Carolina:

Dear Stuck Between,

Congratulations on your pending wedding and the strong relationship that precipitated the union. You did not mention how your fiancé responded when you told him you are considering a job as an escort. I would like to share with you the dictionary definition of escort:

A. One or more persons accompanying another to guide, protect, or show honor.

B. A man who is the companion of a woman, especially on a social occasion.

C. A person, often a prostitute, who is hired to spend time with another as a companion.

The association of the title escort with sexual favors is not just a whisper but is listed in paragraph C.

This advice seeker reminds Elder Karethleen, sixty-four, of Littleton, Colorado—author of several children's books and one book of adult fiction—just a bit too much of her flighty granddaughter. "She has a pixielike approach to decisions, always hoping for a happy ending," Karethleen says of her young relative. "The young woman who wrote this letter strikes me as someone who has her head in the clouds and needs to be able to come down to earth."

> You have this lovely romantic notion that somewhere there is a rainbow and a fairy godmother who will wave a magic wand and all your fears and doubts will disappear. And there will be enough money to cover your college debts, and even take care of your dad's root canal.
>
> Be practical. It seems to me that you have some self-doubts about your ability to carry your full share in this marriage. Your education and your aptitude for generating an income are all problems that you will have to face, and I am afraid that you do not have a realistic solution to them. An "escort service" is hardly the place to make a living, even though they promise you $10,000 a week! Girl, what are you thinking! An escort service is a euphemism for prostitution.
>
> Find out what your qualifications for employment are and consult somebody in career guidance. Or go back to school and finish your degree. But the best idea would be to talk frankly and openly to your future husband about your feelings and concerns. There is no obstacle that cannot be surmounted if you have love and total trust in each other.

Grandma Dee, sixty-four, of Grand Rapids, Michigan, has a question of her own on this one:

> Have you asked Dad if he would rather have a root canal or an honest, morally secure daughter?

Writes Elder Michelle, sixty-four, of Portland, Oregon:

> The first question you need to ask yourself is "How would I feel if I became an '(full service) escort'?" The second question is "How would my partner and/or children feel?" The third question is "How would my father feel if he knew that money I earned as an escort paid for his dental bills?"
>
> You have heard the quote "Integrity is what you do when no one is looking." But if you do not have a strong moral compass, perhaps you

will need to heed what others think. I say this because I was struck that your letter did not indicate that you thought about "the escort business" in moral terms, which indicates to me that you do not consider it to be immoral but dangerous in other ways.

If your moral compass tells you that it is wrong to offer your services to "lonely gentlemen," you will feel ashamed for doing it. That is important to know.

After six years together, I imagine you know each other well and he has many reasons to want to marry you. If he knows what he is getting into, then that is his choice and you need to trust that he is strong enough to make it and to deal with it.

"When in doubt, do nothing." When you know what is right for you, do it and have a fulfilling and righteous life.

Passion or Practicality

LETTER: THE ACTING BUG

I love acting; it's my true passion. But I'm caught between pursuing my dreams as an actress and choosing a conventional, more secure job and giving up my passion. It's hard to know what to do with my family telling me all their opinions (which are all different!). I don't want to be fifty years old and regretting not being an actress my whole life. But I also don't want to be a deadbeat, without a job. My aunt knows a talent scout in Hollywood. And I've gotten leads in all my school plays. People tell me I should be famous, and I don't care so much about being famous, but I want to be happy with what I'm doing. What should I do?

Elder Marble Rye, eighty-eight, of Studio City, California, can't imagine doing anything other than acting. She believes there are way too many people out there who consider acting to be a lark, something anyone can do. "Being famous is *not* a profession," she exclaims. "If she's not talented enough, then forget it!"

But if the letter writer has that spark of talent and doesn't care about the spotlight, Marble Rye believes she should go for it. She believes that it's possible to combine passion with common sense. And she encourages the young aspirant not to see fifty as an arbitrary cut-off point to an acting career.

My vision, being an old lady, is: It's never over. Here I am, a one-legged person, and very old, and I'd still like to act. Not everyone has to play an ingénue. I got some of my best work when I was in my seventies— moms and grandmas.

My recommendation is work at a practical job if you have to, but keep doing plays—that's how I got an agent; he'd seen me in a play. And if you can't earn a living acting, you can do it for fun, as an avocation. Tenacity is the operative word.

Elder Elizabeth, eighty-six, a teacher and author in Mission Viejo, California, writes:

You don't know how lucky you are! You have the option of making choices.

I was a young girl during the Great Depression, and my dream was to become a doctor. Unfortunately, at that time money was as scarce as hens' teeth, and when I graduated from high school I had to get a job as an office worker and be glad to take home $15 a week. College at that time was virtually free, and I went to night school to continue my education. This almost came to a halt when World War II began, when my choice was to take part in the war effort by working for an aircraft company. The war ended, and I married my soldier sweetheart. Life went on, I had two children, but the dream was still there.

With the help of a very supportive husband, I completed my education, but now I was confronted with another choice: Very few medical schools were open to women, but teachers were in great demand. I chose the practical option, and devoted myself to being the best teacher I could be. Did I regret this choice? No, because I loved the work I was doing. But now to answer your question: It's a no-brainer. Of course we know the percentage of actors who

fall by the wayside, but that should not discourage you in the slight-
est. You have the choice of making your dream come true. Go
for it!

Elder L. David, seventy-one, of Monterey Park, a Los Angeles sub-
urb, is not so confident in the advice seeker. He says, in essence, "Don't
quit your day job."

I think that it is great to have a passion. I also think that it is impor-
tant to temper one's passion with a dose of reality.

I live in the Los Angeles area, and often go out to dinner in or near
the Hollywood area. In talking with people who work in restaurants,
as well as retail establishments, I've discovered that many of them are
holding their jobs just to survive until they get a break in show busi-
ness. In a few of these restaurants, the waitpersons provide entertain-
ment. Many of them are very talented singers, comedians, magicians,
etc., but almost none of them ever get any sort of break in show busi-
ness. My wife and I also happen to be personally acquainted with a
number of lounge entertainers in Las Vegas. Some very talented
entertainers find they are employed only a few nights a week at their
chosen profession.

I know that this sounds like a pretty negative reply, but what I am
leading up to is that I think that you should get the education and ex-
perience you need to make a living, then you will have something to
fall back on.

I'll summarize by paraphrasing a college professor I once had: "It's
great to have long-term plans, but make sure you can survive the short
term, too."

The succinct reply from Elder Horatio Victor of Regina, Saskatchewan:

Follow your star. I am now in my eighties, pursued money instead of
the stage, and failed in both.

◄O►

Name-Calling

I have recently been forced to compile a generic list of common errors that coworkers on my project teams have made. This list was created as a compromise that I negotiated with my manager, instead of another assignment that I found abhorrent, which was listing coworkers by name with the errors they have made.

Management has now insisted that I associate the errors I reported in this compromise document with the specific people. I need the trust and friendship of these people. I am afraid that people may lose their jobs over this. I am afraid of having recalled incorrectly and naming the wrong name. At this point, I feel complying would be against my moral principles. I cannot afford to risk my job over this. Again, these are coworkers that I am to report on, not subordinates. Do you have any suggestions for me?

Elder Walk-On, seventy-two, of Bethesda, Maryland, does indeed have suggestions on how to handle a delicate situation:

I would think you are completely justified in saying that you cannot name names because you did not compile the list with names. You had an agreement with management that names would not be used, and therefore you did not save names. To include names now leaves you open to the possibility of harmful errors.

However, there is still the question of the future. If your managers persist in their demand for names, you will need to decide whether to stay or leave.

One thought is that you level with your coworkers and let them know that this is being demanded of you and that you will have to comply. You can tell them that you are reluctant to cite anyone by name, but management leaves you no choice. Exhort them to check and recheck their work to avoid mistakes. I see no other way out for you. In the final analysis, management is justified in trying to weed out the chronic sources of error, and it is your duty to follow their instructions. It is not a pleasant task to be sure and may not suit your personality, but it is a reasonable request for the future.

Offers Elder Digit, seventy-two, a forensic consultant from Willingboro, New Jersey:

It seems to me that it's probable that "all" of the people you're being asked to "snitch" on have made "all" of the mistakes you've listed—not necessarily recently. So you might be able to argue that everyone, including yourself, can be tasked with having made mistakes. Then you could add your manager's name to the list, tasking her with the mistake of not keeping her word to you.

Your company has already lied to you about the compromise and is asking you, requiring you, to betray your friends. How much is your paycheck worth compared to your self-esteem?

A Problem with "Senior" Management

LETTER: PASSED OVER BECAUSE OF AGE?

I am a young, vivacious, attractive sixty-one-year-old who has worked at the same facility for five-plus years. They have moved up three younger employees into the executive director position. The newest is a mere thirty-one years old and has been here three years. My opinion always seems to be sought for these appointments; most recently I was asked, "Besides yourself, who here do you think is qualified to be the next E.D.? We thought about you, but you're so good at what you do, we didn't want to burden you with this position." This same upper level management individual made comments to me about face-lifts. All this sounds like a veiled excuse to pass me over. I need this job or my pride would have me walking.

"I never fail to be angered at the plight of older women in our youth-oriented society, where older men are a force to be reckoned with but older women should be hidden in the nearest cubicle," fumes Elder Seeley. "A sixty-year-old man is still 'sexy,' but a sixty-year-old woman—unless she looks like Jane Fonda—is past ready for the shelf!"

I agree that, in all probability, you are the victim of age discrimination; what is worse, there is no way you can prove it and there is little you can do about it.

The next time they ask, answer them honestly and without feeling that you are being unduly "pushy." Tell them that there is no one other than yourself who has the experience, maturity, and many varied qualifications for the position.

That condescending comment about not wanting to burden you with the position is the big clue that they just don't feel that your aged, creaking shoulders could possibly handle such weighty problems and decisions; please do set them straight next time! The comment about facelifts probably was to suggest that the company is trying to project a younger, more vital image—so get a wardrobe and hairdo change and project it!

My pride would definitely have me walking, but then I am not in your position and since you do need the job, stick it out until you choose to retire, but at least recommend yourself and only yourself for the next promotion for which you are qualified when your advice is sought.

Moving Up

LETTER: OPPORTUNITY KNOCKS!

It seems that an opportunity of a lifetime has come up for me. I have been offered a permanent career position in county government. Great pay, excellent benefits, and a chance to begin the second phase of my life in a new career. I am forty-five years old. My daughter just recently graduated from high school and is beginning her new life as a young adult. I look at it also as a new start for myself and my wife.

I am excited about this new opportunity, but my wife is not, and is telling me not to take the job. She does not like the area where the job is located, the cost of living is higher, we are away from her family, and she is reluctant to cut the umbilical cord to our daughter. I have both my and my wife's long-term interests at heart, but she is telling me NO! Does she, as my spouse, have the right to tell me not to do this? She also says the timing isn't right. Opportunity doesn't care about timing. I am afraid that I am damned if I do, and damned if I don't.

Collectively the Elders have made a lot of "career moves"—geographical and otherwise. While they offer varying suggestions on how best to handle his wife's objections, all of those who answered this letter agree that the husband must follow the job.

Elder Ursula, seventy-seven, of Tujunga, California—a legal secretary who also holds the distinction of being named Poet Laureate of Sunland-Tujunga, 2006–2008—says bluntly, "I was rather disgusted with this wife's attitude, and I wanted to give the husband some support in making changes in his life to suit his passions. She needs to be reminded what marriage is about."

Your wife does NOT have the right to tell you not to do this or else she will leave you—it is just such family decisions that need to be talked about fully and with all the facts on the table.

If she remains set in her opinion, then you have the very difficult decision of taking the new job and waiting to see if she will follow after you've been gone for a while. A separation will not be as harmful to your daughter at this point, since she is commencing her own adult life.

None of this will be easy—and I just hope your wife will realize that your choice of work remains primary in this family, and you are NOT obligated to continue working in one field if a better choice is available to you.

Elder Heart of Texas, eighty-one, of Salado, Texas, holds a traditional view of the expectations of a wife regarding her husband's career.

My husband changed jobs several times in our marriage because we felt it was a step forward to his career. We moved five times within ten years as better opportunities came his way. For my part in this I always agreed, as I looked forward to meeting new people, finding a new home for our family, and helping in any way I could to make it a successful move. My husband's career came first; I was a stay-at-home mom with five children, and every advantage he earned benefited us all. We both had left our families after high school with World War II—this seemed the way with many young people during those days. We could only afford a college education for him, not me, so I learned to adapt and grow with every move we made.

I would suggest you take her to visit this area, look for the interesting things that are available and things she could become involved in. If she is interested in church activities, check out churches in the area. If she is into art, music, drama, library, or community services, check out these things also. Many communities are always looking for new people to volunteer with these services.

You ask if your wife has a right to oppose you in this move. Yes, she has a right, but you have to look at all the reasons she is saying no, and discuss them together. You may need an outside counselor. If you are close to your church, a discussion with your pastor could be an answer. I really think you need to work hard to change her mind, as it could be a beginning for the two of you. If she still insists that you stay, I am afraid a big division in your marriage may occur as you regret the opportunity that was lost.

From the Wizeones group of Albuquerque, New Mexico, aged seventy-eight to ninety-three:

We believe that it is the responsibility of the wife/husband to accompany their partner whenever a good job opportunity presents itself. If she gives you a definite NO, it means that she is choosing her family, and a daughter who will be living her own life, over you. Go for it. If you don't take the job, you will always resent her for it. Good luck!

◄○►

Earning or Learning

I've wanted to teach college full time since I was in high school. In-stead I went into the "real world" and did quite well, working my way up to a six-figure salary. The job is good, but it has a lot of pressure.

Now I've been presented with the opportunity to teach college near where I live. The list of advantages is very long. There is only one disadvantage, an over 50 percent pay cut. I'd go from "upper class" to "normal."

We've been doing a lot of saving, so we can afford the pay cut without a drastic lifestyle change. The question is, from someone with experience looking back, would you take a job you love, or a whole lot of money? Is there any wisdom that a guy in his mid-thirties needs to know?

Elder Gpa, eighty-five, of Rochester Hills, Michigan, chose a practical career in sales and marketing. He and Gma, eighty-one, offer this advice:

To us wisdom is choosing to enrich and fulfill your life over scrabbling for money and possessions I was in my first year of college when World War II came to America and I volunteered my services. After the war I could have continued my law studies under the G.I. Bill, but I chose instead to get married and go to work. I chose the materialistic world and hardly a day went by that I did not regret my choice.

From our experience we would recommend you base your choice of career on quality instead of quantity. You have our best wishes for a long, happy, and joyous life.

Elder Ruthie did not make the same "sensible" choice as Gpa, but her circuitous career path leads her to a similar conclusion.

Looking back, I have no hesitation recommending you do your dream job. If you can be happy and fulfilled in a job, there is no crime in getting paid well for it. However, if you are doing a job that does not satisfy your real need to feel whole, creative, and of use, if the pressure of it keeps you from enjoying what you have worked for, then no amount of money can compensate for what you are losing.

You may find that your dream job is a nightmare in reality, but that learning experience is also worth whatever you will have sacrificed to learn it.

I am a firm believer that each of us is here to fill a need in this world. There is a place that no one else fits but you. When you find that place, your rewards will be priceless. You need to understand this advice comes from a person who has lived at or below the poverty level most of her life with no regrets and much joy.

And How Was Your Day?

LETTER: WHY CAN'T MY HUSBAND LEAVE WORK AT WORK?

My husband can't seem to forget about his job when he comes home. He gets home around 7 p.m. and it seems all he can do is talk about the hassles he went through until we go to bed. If he isn't talking about that, he is falling asleep. I'll interject things about what the kids did that day; he'll make a small comment, then go right back into all the stress he has had to endure that day. It feels like my husband's whole life is consumed now by his job. But I can't tell him to suffer through it all by himself and not to share anything with me. What can I do? It seems there should be a way to balance things better than this.

The Chelsea Elders—a twelve-member circle, aged sixty-five to ninety-one, at an assisted living community in Warren, New Jersey—write:

Our elder group is about 92 percent widows whose husbands lived with the stress of their work and, because of that, we are alone today.

You indicate that "things are not balanced," and that tells us the situation is affecting family life. Certainly, you must share his problems occasionally, but it is quite self-indulgent of him to always have the family involved with his difficulties at work.

You have "gently" told him to forget the hassles and keep his job separate, but that has not helped. We suggest you be forthright and tell your husband exactly how you feel. Remind him that this is his family and it is not reasonable for them to always be absorbed with his battles on the job. We suggest you, your husband, and the kids select evenings during which you share planned family activities such as card games, movies, or bowling, activities that will allow your husband to take his mind off the job and bring you together in things you all enjoy.

Your happiness may be well served by taking time away from the kids and the job to talk of the problems you have with his never being free of the job.

Elder Web suggests that talking about work may simply be an excuse for not talking about the real problem.

The fact that he is consumed by his work may indicate he doesn't feel the two of you have anything left in common. Rather than initially talking about it, or possibly starting an argument, start making efforts to make his evenings more interesting. Prepare a candlelight dinner, have hors d'oeuvres, and maybe a predinner drink (if you two indulge), a little wine afterward, and see where it leads.

In the canyons of Malibu, Elder Nancy has experienced more than her share of loss. She and her husband lost a son to cancer when he was only nine months old. A grandson died of cancer at age thirteen. And, like some of the women in the Chelsea Elders Circle, now she is alone except for her menagerie of animals, including a blind pug dog who has figured out how to find his way around by relying on touch and hearing.

However, Nancy never wanted to remarry: "thirty years was sufficient, thank you!" she asserts. Her adult children have remained close, even though they have struggled with problems of their own. A daughter is a recovering alcoholic, and a son has struggled to find himself; at one point, he lived in a tent on the lower level of Nancy's property. He has also spent a tour of duty with the Hare Krishnas. *"That* was a thrill,"

Nancy says, rolling her eyes. "When my youngest daughter was in Los Angeles International Airport, getting ready to fly to Colorado for her honeymoon, all of a sudden she and her new husband hear bells, and the usual singing and leaping around. And my daughter says to herself; "Oh my God, I hope it isn't 'Henry.' And it was! He was leading the pack, with his wife bringing up the rear. It's just so *embarrassing*."

However, she laughs as she says it—to Nancy, tolerating her children's rocky road to self-realization is part of the definition of family. And for this resilient widow, thinking about how annoying and self-centered her husband sometimes could be about his job also made her recognize the same qualities in herself—and to recall how nice it was to make up after the fight.

> *For years, I felt the same way as you. I was home with four children from dawn to dusk and was ready for any adult conversation when my husband came home. He would come in, eat his dinner, and fall asleep in front of the television. If we did talk, it was all about his work and coworkers.*
>
> *Then I went to work when my youngest was in kindergarten. The minute my husband walked in the door, I would regale him with MY day. It finally came to a head one night when he yelled at me and told me he didn't want to hear about my class. I was hurt, but in thinking about it, I found that both of us were venting.*
>
> *Venting is very important to each and every one of us. We can't really tell our coworkers how we feel, but we can tell our nearest and dearest—sometimes much to their boredom. Now, years later, I look back at some of those intense conversations I had with my husband. He didn't know it at the time, but he gave me a logical way of looking at life and work.*
>
> *Now for a suggestion to help you solve your problem: Why not suggest a short day trip on a weekend? We used to go to auto races and air shows. Sometimes we went apple picking with the kids. The ride to wherever you are going will offer plenty of time for talk. I used to like visiting antique shops, and although my husband grumbled at first, he got so he liked visiting with some of the characters who ran the shops.*
>
> *Venting is useful, but he does need new interests, and so do you. It will make you both happier over all.*

CHAPTER 8

New Tricks from Old Dogs

Wisdom for Aging Gracefully

Orchids to ALL the Elders. It was a great comfort to talk to someone who's had a few more spins around the block than I have. In exactly twenty more years, I'll be eligible to be an Elder. Perhaps someday I'LL get to be one of you. What a great thing to aspire to! You are all heroes!

—From "Feedback & Kudos"
www.ElderWisdomCircle.org

"You are old, Father William," the young man said,
"And your hair has become very white;
And yet you incessantly stand on your head—
Do you think, at your age, it is right?"

—Lewis Carroll,
from *Alice in Wonderland*

Tell Me About It

Chapter 3, "Sibling Stories: Wisdom for Brothers and Sisters," introduced Elder Horatio Victor, eighty-five, the bullying big brother of Elder Jacobus, eighty-one, of Saskatoon, Saskatchewan. Horatio Victor, a long-time member of the EWC, answered this brief letter online when he was a sprightly eighty-two-year-old. At that time, he was living alone, as he had for some thirty years, in a twelfth-floor apartment in Victoria, British Columbia, surrounded by his own artwork and the many souvenirs of his exotic travels.

More than fifteen years earlier, Horatio Victor had suffered a heart attack, followed by a quadruple bypass. Thus warned by the universe of his own mortality, he sold his car and traveled the world, solo, for seven months, visiting China, Hong Kong, Japan, India, Rome, and Paris. He refers to that trip as Around the World at sixty-six.

At the time he responded to the letter, Horatio Victor was plagued with some physical problems, but preferred his own cooking and was getting around quite well with the aid of his distinguished collection of walking canes. One, hand-painted, came home with him from India; another, picked up in Thailand, was topped with a hand-carved dragon that looped around to bite its own tail.

Horatio Victor has always exhibited a brave sense of humor about the aging process. At one point, he e-mailed the Elder Wisdom Circle a photo of himself sporting a neatly cropped white beard and a snowy handlebar moustache, wearing a jaunty fisherman's cap adorned with a large pin bearing the slogan "In the end, old age and treachery will out-smart youth and vigor."

Along with this photo, Horatio Victor also e-mailed a copy of a paper a college student had written about him, circa 2004. In the paper, the student wrote that Horatio Victor had asked her whether she worried he would pass away before the paper was completed. He suggested that, should this occur, the young woman might end her term paper with this sentence: "And then he, inconveniently, died."

As things turned out, Horatio Victor—conveniently—lived. However, before the paper was completed, he had another scare, which, like his heart attack, reminded him that forever might not be quite as long as it once seemed. He found himself in the emergency room at Victoria General Hospital with an injured shoulder, a cut on his head, blood in his hat, and no idea how he'd gotten there. "Maybe I passed out, maybe I was mugged," he said later, sounding determinedly nonchalant. The emergency room staff patched him up, called him a cab, and sent him home.

While living in Victoria, Horatio Victor was already beginning to wonder whether he should consider moving to the same senior community in Saskatoon where his brother Jacobus was already living, quite contentedly. But Horatio Victor, always the rebel and the loner, was less accepting of the concept of assisted living. "I say to myself, 'I hope I die before they have a vacancy,' " he said then.

As it happened, increasing short-term memory problems led Horatio Victor, at age eighty-four, to decide to move in to a multilevel care facility in Regina, Saskatchewan, just a few hour's drive from Jacobus's residence in Saskatoon.

The move did not go smoothly. Upon his arrival in Saskatoon, Horatio Victor lived for several months with cousins in Regina who had picked him up and driven him there from Victoria. During his stay, the cousins had to make an extended trip out of the country, so they arranged to have Horatio Victor stay with friends. On one unnerving occasion, as brother Jacobus tells it, Horatio Victor "took it upon himself to leave the friends' house in the middle of the night. He was picked up by the local police." He was admitted to a local hospital for extended care until arrangements could be made to move him to his new assisted-living home.

Still, he made an effort to adjust. In a telephone conversation not too long after making the move into assisted living, Horatio Victor spoke with pleasure of being one of few residents given a private room with a view; he also confided that he was in the market for a female companion. At this stage of life, he said he was less interested in physical than spiritual companionship. For practical reasons, he also sought a woman with better hearing than his.

And, despite struggles with his memory, this highly intelligent former Mensa member had adopted an informal "student," one of the other residents, and was excited by their daily discussions. "He's older than I am—and he needs to organize his thoughts; in that way I help him a lot," Horatio Victor said. "And, of course, as a consequence, I organize *my* thoughts."

He added that every morning, he would start his day at the computer, checking on current events and amassing general knowledge. To Horatio Victor, who worked as a computer software specialist pre-Internet, surfing the Web was nothing short of magic.

In this same conversation, Horatio Victor was almost apologetic in pointing out that he had stopped using the computer to answer letters online for the Elder Wisdom Circle. Not because, at eighty-four, he felt his abilities to offer good advice had begun slipping away; rather because, at eighty-four, he felt compelled to devote his considerable brainpower to analyzing the challenges facing people his own age instead of working on the issues of the young. "Only a fraction of people ever arrive at this stage, and there are problems that arise that you can share only with people who have reached that stage," he said.

Though he fought to avoid moving into a facility for the aged, upon arriving, Horatio Victor turned this life change into a positive by using his neighbors as case studies for his generation. Among his observations: There is a marked difference in the way men and women in his eighty-plus age group adjust to aging.

During their youth, he said, the women had directed much of their energy to nurturing their families. Now, in their widowhood and old age, they could still look to their children, and grandchildren, to give their lives purpose. The men, however, had defined themselves by two ephemeral things, career and virility—and, in their eighties and nineties, could no longer rely on either one. "It makes for a lot of lost men," Horatio Victor observed.

Because of his keen awareness of the human condition, it would be hard to consider Horatio Victor a lost man, at any age. And one thing that will never be lost is the help he has given to others through the Elder Wisdom Circle. No matter that Horatio Victor's mind may grow more isolated from the world as his memory deteriorates; the legacy of his wise letters survives. He remains a connective segment of the Circle. His story, and others like it, represent the best argument for the continued existence of the EWC.

Naturally, Horatio Victor and his Elder Wisdom Circle colleagues can address questions of aging gracefully better than those who have not yet reached sixty—or eighty, or one hundred. Whether tortured by fears of aging or simply curious about what lies ahead, many advice seekers come to the Web site with questions about the aging process. And when it comes to exploring the inevitable through a question as open-ended and intriguing as "What is it like to be old?"—well, nobody does it better than Horatio Victor.

> *I am eighty-two. Most people my age are dead.*
>
> *Old age is both fun and sad. It's carefree because no one expects anything from you. But if you have no family, no one cares.*
>
> *I have always been lazy, and now I don't have to work.*
>
> *Old age has its advantages and disadvantages. My memory is failing, so I forget the bad things, but also the good things. And now I can smile at pretty girls and they smile back because they know I'm harmless. I walk with a cane and when I drop it, a pretty girl will pick it up for me.*
>
> *My teeth are falling out.*
>
> *I'm deaf in one ear and wear an aid in the other. I don't hear all the trashy noise around me, but I miss the sound of music.*
>
> *People don't tell you this, but death doesn't scare me anymore.*
>
> *I'm a man and, for the first time in my life, I love babies and they love me. They smile at me. I wonder, is it because I am losing my teeth, and will soon be like a baby?*

If they had had a chance to meet, Horatio Victor and Elder Kriko, seventy-five, of Tempe, Arizona, probably would have become great friends. Kriko, a retired teacher-turned-artist, is, like Horatio Victor, an intellectual and something of a Renaissance man. Kriko is an artist, writer, and student of Esperanto, the artificial language introduced in 1887 and intended by its inventor, Dr. Ludwik Lejzer Zamenhof, a

Polish oculist and linguist, to foster communication between speakers of different languages. Unfortunately, the universal language never really caught on.

And how did Kriko discover Esperanto? Unlike many Arizona retirees, Kriko sees no point in devoting the golden years to playing golf. "Why would anybody go out in the 112-degree heat and knock a ball around?" he reasons. Instead, he thought he might study a language, maybe French, but he didn't want to pay the steep tuition at the local university. The idea of teaching himself Esperanto, he says, "just popped into my head." He went to the library and hunted up books on the subject. In one of those books was the address of a local teacher of the language; he wrote to the teacher and was soon immersed in learning a language that few will ever speak or understand.

Kriko says that sometimes he has a hard time finding people who want to discuss life's deeper questions. He delights in the challenge of answering them for the Elder Wisdom Circle.

I am an American. My country is young and brash and favors its youth. Some countries and cultures consider their old people to be treasuries of wisdom and knowledge and love, and treat them accordingly. As America matures, it seems to be giving more respect to its older citizens. It is a slow process.

Old people have lost some of their vitality, some of their muscle, some of their mind power, and some of their influence. Whether an old person lives in a culture that honors and respects him or one that discards him, he still suffers from loss of strength.

Old people differ dramatically one from the other. Many become depressed, many are upbeat and enthusiastic. Many give up and sit in front of the TV and become isolated, others are full of ideas and goals and action and participate fully in society.

One of the things an old person notices is that everyone is younger than he. It is true that you get a dollar off at the movies, but the movies are all about teenagers looking for sex.

So, to answer your question, what is it like to be old? It is like everything else, but a bit slower.

Kriko is not the only Elder who views old age not as a radical change but as the slowing down of a previous reality.

This feeling of life in slow motion has its pros and cons, the Elders say. One stops to smell the roses not only because one now has the time, but also because one can't walk as fast as one used to. It's a benefit, but one born of necessity.

Elder Jacobus says that old age has forced him to devise a mental checklist he uses before leaving his apartment. He also keeps a small notebook in his pocket filled with reminders of bills to be paid, appointments to be kept. "I want to be sure I don't forget to switch off the stove; I don't want to forget to pull up my zipper before I get out into public," he says. "I have to say to myself, 'Do not forget.'"

But Jacobus calls this not an inconvenience, but a "learning opportunity." And in his reply to this question, he writes:

I move a lot slower than I used to, but that doesn't really matter all that much. I have more time than I used to have.

Elder Ursula, seventy-seven, of Tujunga, California, writes:

It's just like being young, but slower and more interesting because of the many things I've learned during my seventy-seven years on Earth. My parents, fortunately, believed we were put here for several purposes, one of which was to be able to understand the questions being asked in the fields of astronomy, physics, mathematics, chemistry, history, archeology, geographical history, linguistics, music, art, religion, and other areas of human inquiry. My thirty-nine-year marriage (so far) to a professional astronomer continued those interests and is a loving, amazing relationship, and my own professional career as a certified legal secretary for fifty years (I'm still helping two attorneys now) continued those interests.

I am very thankful that so far I have no symptoms of mental deterioration; on the contrary, I continue to find out new and wonderful things about our Earth and the people who have made knowing it well possible. I've been named Poet Laureate for our small community of about 72,000 people for the next two years, and I write regularly.

Although I use a cane to stand up and walk for any distance in territory that is unfamiliar to me, and I can't seem to lose an ounce of weight, I'm pretty healthy and capable. I won't be able to ride horseback anymore—I weigh over the maximum two hundred pounds allowed—and I won't be going swimming any longer because of the back injury that requires me to use a cane in the first place, but those are small losses for me. I get along well with other people; I do what I am physically able to do; and I try to help others as much as possible. Not bad, for seventy-seven!

When it comes to her thoughts on accepting the limitations of old age, the pen name of Elder-Student, eighty, of Dallas, Texas, says it all. She writes:

What is old? I believe that old is a state of mind that can be positive or negative, and I have chosen to be positive. My education was interrupted during World War II, and I worked all of my life. I have returned to university and I am now a junior and maintain a 3.866 GPA. I ski in the winter, and golf in the spring and autumn, and dance when I have a partner. Through my church I am able to do some things to help others not as fortunate as some of the rest of us. Except for a cranky knee, I enjoy good health because I take care of myself. For me, being old is the reward for outlasting all the big and little problems that happen to all of us along life's pathway. Each day is a blessing that allows me to enjoy my family, especially my eight grandchildren. I can read, study, travel, play cards, work the crossword puzzle, exercise, walk the dog, practice my French, volunteer at the library, work at the computer, go to the symphony and the art museum; good grief, there are so many things to do, I do not have time to have negative thoughts about being old. Thanks for your question. May you be blessed, also, by being old someday.

Elder Michelle, sixty-four, of Portland, Oregon, is one of several members of the group who isn't so willing to define herself as "old." She began her response, "I suppose it would be smart-alecky to say that I will tell you what it feels like to be old when I *am* old . . ."

Elder Digit, seventy-two, of Willingboro, New Jersey, is another:

I think one of the best answers to this is T. S. Eliot's "The Love Song of J. Alfred Prufrock," which I invite you to read.

  But you're asking the question of a bunch of people who, while we may use the title "Elder," don't particularly think of ourselves as "old."

That's a state of mind, and we wouldn't be here if we were "old." Me personally? I'm only seventy-two. I run my own full-time consulting business, volunteer about twenty hours a week driving an ambulance as an emergency medical technician, am treasurer of several volunteer organizations, and my long-suffering wife (who is forty years old) is convinced that my dictionary does not have a definition of "retired" in it that matches anything the rest of the world would recognize.

If this response from Elder Ruthie, sixty-four, of Swanton, Ohio, is any indication, people become funnier with age. "Some people fear being old," she says. "It's something that I embrace."

Smear some oil on a pair of glasses to blur your eyesight. Put a nylon stocking on your head and pull just some of your hair through the top of the stocking (about 40 percent of your present head of hair). Put a cotton ball in each ear to diminish your hearing.

Tightly wrap a ten-pound sandbag around each ankle. This will simulate how much harder it is to walk. Wake yourself up at least every three hours at night and stay awake at least one full night each week.

No matter what ravages age will do to your body (and it will), it is a choice worth making to keep a sense of humor. Growing old has been great fun for me; I hope it will be for you as well.

Oldophobia?

LETTER: OLD PEOPLE

> I sort of have a phobia of old folks. They scare me and I just can't get those ugly wrinkles out of my head! No offense or anything, but you're scary and disturbing.

Quite a few Elders chose to respond to this in-your-face observation. Several suggested that the phobic advice seeker read Oscar Wilde's novel *The Picture of Dorian Gray*. The nineteenth-century fantasy tells the story of a vain, impossibly handsome young man who gets his wish when he asks that his painted portrait rather than his own face suffer the ravages of time. Gray's misguided obsession with exterior beauty leads to his tragic demise.

Some viewed the advice seeker's problem as a legitimate concern; others decided that this letter writer should lighten up and therefore approached the question with a little humor. And almost all reminded the writer to be aware that young people are just old people in training. Writes Michelle:

You could very well be afraid not of old people but of getting old your-self. And of death.

From Kriko:

Your case does not seem like a medical condition, just an aversion. Everyone loves young, smooth skin full of vitality and glowing with health. Old, wrinkled skin is certainly wrinkly.

I don't hear you saying that you want to get over this feeling, but you did write to us, so I'll guess you would like to feel more comfort-able around geezers and grandmas. Probably the simplest thing would be for you to learn some relaxation techniques. Self-hypnosis is great for that purpose.

Once you have some control over your tension, start to get a little closer. Don't jump in to visiting ninety year-olds. Try spending time with people who are just beginning to get wrinkled, like your mom. Then move up to a medium wrinkle, oh, say about age fifty. Hang out with people as they age for a while, then gradually work up to people who look like hound dogs without fur. By the time you start to get wrinkles yourself, you no longer will be afraid of them.

Elder Nancy, seventy-seven, of Malibu, California, a retired teacher, says she observed similar feelings in her students.

I remember we had a group of sixth graders that we wanted to take over to an old folks' home to sing Christmas songs. Things went well until the day arrived. All of a sudden I had three girls weeping and screaming that they were afraid to go over. They said that they were afraid of old people. Nothing I could say or the other adults present could do would make them see that they were giving joy to others who didn't get out often. The long and the short of it was I stayed back at school with the three girls and the other children went.

We did an art project while we were waiting for them to return. In talking to the girls as we did our project, I was surprised to find that none of them had older grandparents or elderly relatives that they were in contact with. They really had never known an older person, so they were afraid.

The class returned from their trip, and they all had had lots of fun. One of the boys had met a fellow who had worked for the FBI. Another child met a lady who had been a dancer on the New York stage.

The next time we planned an afternoon at the old folks' home, everyone went. The girls who had been afraid made some friends with the elderly gentlemen and ladies.

If you continue to be afraid of old people, try talking to one sometime and find out about them and what they have done in the past. It could be quite an interesting adventure for you.

Digit sees the problem as an "irrational fear" and suggests that the writer seek counseling to figure out what past experience may have triggered it. He also offers that the youth of America can be a little frightening sometimes, too.

When I watch some . . . not all . . . "young folks," they scare me! Driving too fast, with a cell phone glued to one ear, cutting in and out of traffic as though they were immortal? Yup, that scares me . . . but not "all" young folks do that, just some. So, once again, I wonder why "all" old folks scare you.

I don't take offense, but I do invite you to find a way of exploring the root of your phobia.

Elders Gpa-and-Gma, eighty-five and eighty-one, of Rochester Hills, Michigan, suggest that it may not be some long-ago trauma, but American pop culture, that lies at the root of this writer's fear.

We are somewhat closer to old people than you are, and we under-
stand your concerns about those scary ones. Ugly wrinkles are only a
small part of it. How about bald heads? Unmentionable odors? Un-
mentionable noises? Drooling lips? False teeth? Runny noses? It is no
wonder you have a phobia about old folks. But there is good news;
you will grow out of it.

You may have another phobia that is an outgrowth of modern
American culture, where style and appearance take precedence over
substance and wisdom. Movies, television, slick advertising, fashion,
and celebrities have combined to create unreal images that some of us
want so desperately to be.

Elder Holiday, eighty-six, of Tarzana, California, however, has no
patience with this "phobia."

Child, wake up and smell the roses. Have you ever tried approaching
an older person and just started a conversation with him or her?
AFRAID OF WRINKLES? What nonsense! You, too, will be old
one day and will develop wrinkles.

Don't look at the outward appearance of an elder. See what's in his
heart and mind and find wisdom and understanding there. Try volun-
teering your services in an adult community and learn more about ag-
ing. Unless you plan to die at a young age, know that you have getting
old to look forward to and be happy with it.

From "Your Grandparents" of Pleasant Hill, California, a group in
an assisted living residence whose age averages mid–eighties but includes some members in their nineties:

It is important to get over this fear now, while you are young, because
you don't want to be afraid of yourself when you are older.

Because of his fascination with the aging process, it comes as no surprise that Elder Horatio Victor opted to do battle with this question
online. And, knowing Horatio Victor, it also comes as no surprise that
he chose satire as his weapon.

At last, I have found somebody who hates wrinkles like I do, and I'm
only in my eighties. Nobody pays any attention to me, and now

*there's someone who is afraid of me. You make me feel very impor-
tant. And, you know, I don't talk to old people either, because if they
talk to me, I can't hear them. I'm almost deaf. I think you and I
would really become friends, because I don't like them either.*

*I just had a thought. The only way to avoid getting old is to die
young.*

Unmentionables

LETTER: MARKETING IDEA FOR FEMALE UNDERGARMENT SALES

I was wondering if you could give me some advice on a marketing
idea for female undergarments. I've noticed that in the stores undergarments for the elderly are not very attractive, and the attractive undergarments that are available in stores do not offer the
support needed, or come in the sizes needed.

My group and I are trying to enhance Victoria's Secret products
so that they fit and fully support the baby boomer era and beyond.
This product line will offer high-quality sensual undergarments and
sleepwear. Our slogan: "Sexy never goes out of style." We want
women of age to have a choice in stylish and sexy underwear.
They haven't lost their appeal, so why should their clothes?

One word from Elder Marnie, seventy-seven, of Philadelphia,
Pennsylvania: "YAYYY!!!"

*First off, "elderly" is a word somebody made up that a lot of us can't
relate to. We don't dig numbers. I'm seventy-seven, my gorgeous husband (of twenty-five years) is fifty-six, and we still turn each other
on. I, like many women of my age, still feel "beautiful" and attractive
to our mates. We want to look adorable, whether dressed, undressed,
or in our underwear.*

*It is disheartening and frustrating to walk into a Victoria's Secret
and know that all those pretty, satiny, ruffled, lacy, silky things are*

there for young "Cosmo" types, and we will just end up buying something in the fragrance line. If Victoria's Secret starts catering to older women, it'll be the wisest decision they've ever made.

To Michelle, however, at any age, underwear is underwear.

I am not disappointed in the lack of style in female undergarments for older women. Truly, I wear basically the same undergarments I have always worn. I have never found a problem finding pretty, supportive garments.

It will be noted, though, that the first thing I do when I get home is remove them. That has not always been the case, but lately I prefer to be without them.

Putting on the Brakes

LETTER: DRIVING ISSUE

My father refuses to get new tires and brakes on his old car. He also loses his car once in a while. He should not be driving, according to my doctors. He also refuses medical help. How can we approach this issue? He just passed his driving test. We think he is unsafe and his car is unsafe. He used to be a motorcycle cop, so he has a huge ego and thinks he is safe. Help!

Never mind those wrinkles; for some drivers, the elderly are never more terrifying than when they are behind the wheel.

Several Elders responded by suggesting that family members take legal action to get this driver off the road immediately, regardless of the fact that he had passed his driving test. In Holiday's view, the fact that the driver refuses to service his car and occasionally loses the vehicle is a sure sign of early dementia. Elder Seeley, sixty-five, of Tucson, Arizona, who's had more than her share of experience with elderly relatives who stayed at the wheel too long, also suspects dementia, and advises the family to write a letter to the state driver's licensing authority.

Digit, who volunteers with a local emergency medical squad, insists that the best thing to do is to appeal for intervention to the police department, the father's auto insurance agent, or an emergency unit such as his own.

> I'm one of the people who would be called to deal with the accident that your father may cause. Sadly, in many cases it is the person who caused the accident that is relatively uninjured, and the innocent victims who are dead or damaged. Is there some similar organization in your area that you might appeal to for local help?
>
> Finally, if you're willing to run the risk of doing something illegal, is there any way of confiscating his car keys? Or perhaps the next time he loses his car, can you arrange to have it vanish so it can't be found?

Others, however, came up with solutions that while acknowledging that the father might be experiencing early signs of memory loss or dementia, give this driver the benefit of the doubt. This personal story comes from Gpa (with, as always, the aid of Gma):

> I was in your shoes in July 1970 when I had to ask my dad for his car keys. I am now eighty-five and still driving my car, so I can look at your question from both sides. There are ninety-year-old people driving cars safely and cautiously. There are ninety-year-old people driving cars who are blind and deaf. There are twenty-year-old people who drive carefully and there are twenty-year-old people who drive recklessly while deafened by roaring boom boxes. Age alone cannot be the determining factor. If your doctor's opinion that he should not be driving is based on age alone, he is being unfair to your father.
>
> There is pain and anguish for old and young when the moment of restricting mobility and freedom must be faced. The resolution was somewhat easier for me because Dad was running his car into objects and people. He was getting traffic tickets for violations and accidents. Your ex-policeman father probably never received a traffic citation. I had to act quickly or someone was going to get badly hurt or be killed.
>
> In your father's case, if the state renewed his driver's license with a perfunctory eye test and questionnaire that anyone can prestudy and

*memorize, I would be concerned, but if the state renewed his license
based on a driving test, there may be no cause for alarm about his
driving ability.*

*As for the brakes and tires on his old car, you could approach this
in several ways. Tell him he should recap or get new tires and fix the
brakes to relieve his family of stress and worry about his safety. Or he
could trade in for a new car. Offer to pay for upgrading the car.*

*You did not indicate your father's age, but time is relentless and has
no respect for retired motorcycle cops with or without big egos. You
will want to keep a close eye on your father's driving, and at the first
indications of trouble, such as fender-bender damage to the car or failing health, confront him again and gently, gently, request his car keys.*

Elder Elizabeth, eighty-six, of Mission Viejo, California, was recently
denied a driver's license renewal because her eyesight had weakened
without her being aware of it. "A trip to the eye doctor, and a cataract
removal, cleared everything up," she says. "But the few months I was
without my car and dependent on friends, family, and taxi service made
me realize how important driving is to a senior." She writes:

*"I can't hear and I don't see well, but thank God I can still drive."
This little joke sums up the feelings many elderly have about giving up
their right to drive. I can understand your concern about your father,
but look at it from his point of view. The DMV in your state has already certified him as fit to drive. Therefore, his eyesight is still good,
and his mind is sound enough to answer the written questions. Never-
theless, he does have a problem with his car. It might be nice of you to
offer to buy him a set of tires as a gift, and cajole him enough to get his
brakes fixed. Flattery sometimes works better than threats. Saying
"Dad, I can't believe how well you're driving at your age. But I would
feel better if you took better care of your car," could be a way of soft-
ening him up.*

*Driving is his way of keeping his independence. Take that away
and he has very little left. However, there is another side of the coin.
He should have a medical checkup to make sure everything is in order.
And then if you are still convinced that your dad is a threat to himself
and others, report him to the DMV, which will make the final determination.*

In order to ensure that she doesn't keep driving after she can no longer do so safely, Elder Nancy periodically enlists a family member to ride with her while she negotiates heavy Malibu beach traffic in order to keep tabs on her driving reflexes. But she is not the only Elder to point out that you don't have to be old to misplace your car.

I ran into a young woman who had lost her car in the parking lot, and I had to help her find it. Nowadays that can happen to anyone.

"Organ Recital"

LETTER: GROWING OLDER GRACEFULLY

> I just turned sixty and have always been in great health. However, it seems like my body has taken on a mind of its own. I've recently been diagnosed with degeneration in my right shoulder related to arthritis. My knee hurts; I'm stiff in the morning. I can't seem to stay on a diet and lose the weight I need to!
>
> How do I maintain a positive attitude and not become a complaining little old lady with too many aches and pains? I have vowed not to give an "organ recital" when someone asks "How are you?" but I also don't like my decreased physical capacities. I am active mentally and physically, with five volunteer jobs, gardening, traveling, etc. I want to maintain these abilities for another thirty years or so!

Nancy's response: Beware the loaded question "How are you?"

How does a person maintain a positive attitude? I think you just have to ignore most of the little things and for major ones talk to your doctor.

One thing you can't do when you're asked how you are is tell the truth. Tell your friends you feel great even if you took a pill to kill the pain that morning. Then go on and talk about the most recent thing you did that was fun.

I recently had two friends whom I hadn't seen in twenty years visit me. We had a wonderful visit about old times and what each of them was doing now. All of a sudden one of them said, "Gee, we have been talking for two hours and none of us has mentioned anything about the prescriptions we take." The three of us laughed and went on talking.

The Rockymountain Owls of Montrose, Colorado, aged sixty to ninety-five, don't give a hoot about chronological age.

Norman Vincent Peale said, "Live your life, not your age." We agree wholeheartedly!

Eviction Notice

LETTER: DAUGHTER DOESN'T WANT TO TAKE CARE OF ME

My eldest daughter and I were always firm friends. Four years ago she encouraged me to live with her. She offered me a rent-free apartment that used to be an office. It has a separate entrance. All went well until two years ago when she changed jobs, and my health deteriorated at the same time. I tried not to impose on her and did pretty well on my own. Then she began treating me like a child, and she was becoming very nasty. I approached her to have a talk, which she refused to do. Two weeks ago she came to my apartment and told me she will be putting her house up for sale in three years and that she wants me out of here a year prior. I will be eighty by then. I have no income except Social Security. Two years ago I was diagnosed with dementia or early Alzheimer's. My doctors disagree with that diagnosis. My question now is, my son in another state wants me to live with him, but his wife is punitive and he is afraid I will get hurt emotionally. She does not work outside the home. I have to make good decisions for my future, and I am stymied.

The Elders who answered this letter were unanimous in encouraging the letter writer to explore options other than living with one of her children.

"I nursed both of my parents through dying, and I know how hard it can be," says Elder Michelle. "I answered the way I did to help the mother realize that maybe the daughter *does* want to care for her, but the burden has become too much, and she does not know how to talk about it."

Your eldest daughter and you were firm friends. She loved you enough to take you in, but she did not know what that would require of her. My guess is that she does not know how to talk about this with you, and so she avoids you. She probably wants to take care of you, but she has found that she has to give up too much of her life to do so. So she feels guilty.

You are both in a difficult position, and because of this have forgotten how much you love each other. It is time for you to let her off the hook. Let her know that you know she has done her share and now it is time to figure out what you should do. You have a son, but that does not sound like a nurturing situation. Are there other siblings who could share the responsibility? Is it possible to find a "group home" near your children where you could be independent but still get care?

This is the time for the family to join together and talk, not about you but with you. You have clearly raised children who respect and love you. Remember that. Give them the chance to treat you with respect. Asking more than is possible from any of them will only cause pain for all of you.

The Chelsea Elders of Warren, New Jersey, aged sixty-five to ninety-one, believe the advice seeker may not be considering the many possible reasons her daughter might want her to move out. "It is our feeling that there is much more to this situation than we are made aware of in the letter," they say. "Children often cannot support elderly family members and they must find the best alternatives."

It is unfortunate that your daughter finds that she no longer wishes to take care of you. It would be good if you could talk this out with her, but you indicate she is avoiding that possibility. Apparently your son feels you would not be happy living with his wife and him. We suggest you might arrange to have your son, daughter, and you get together to discuss your situation, with one objective in mind: to determine your future now that your daughter wants you out of the house. Questions that should be asked are:

1. *Do they feel you should live alone or seek other possibilities?*
2. *Do they recognize that you have to live on Social Security with rent payments, food, clothing, and essentials expenses? Will they help with the incidental expenses?*

If your situation becomes one of facing the future alone, there is some help available in facilities for the elderly. State, as well as some local communities, offer this sort of support, but you may have to have both family and, in some cases doctor, approval to get into these facilities. You probably will have to sign over your Social Security payment to them as well. Further, you may be able to find support groups, such as church organizations, that will offer guidance and help.

You will be joining a large group of elderly who have chosen not to live with their children. Our suggestion is that you look toward the future and move on with confidence to a new experience.

No Pets Allowed

LETTER: ELDERLY GETTING RID OF A PET

We just found out that my grandmother, who just turned ninety-two, will no longer be able to live alone. Because they don't want to place her in a nursing home, my mother and father have decided to take her in with them, but because of my father's allergies and their constant travels, they do not want to take my grandmother's dog. My grandmother has had her dog for years and he is her constant companion. It is going to break her heart to part with him, and we were wondering if you had any advice as to how to break the news that she can't take the dog with her.

Unlike the situation presented in the previous letter, this grand-mother is welcome in her offspring's home—the problem is her furry companion. The Elders, many of whom also rely on pets for compan-ionship, agree it would be cruel to ask the ninety-two-year-old to give up her beloved dog. Some suggested allergy medication for the father of the letter writer. Others pointed out that the parents' "constant trav-els" should not be an issue, because whoever is engaged to care for the grandmother during their absence could also take care of the dog.

Elder Ursula was a little more sympathetic to the father's needs. It would be unreasonable, she thinks, to expect the writer's father not only to be willing to care for the grandmother, but to risk uncomfort-able allergy symptoms as well. She offered an alternative suggestion for the advice seeker:

What would happen if you were to take the dog? You didn't say whether that would be possible. Your grandmother might be able to visit you, or you could take the dog for a visit to your parents'.

Getting Up There

LETTER: HOW TO DEAL WITH AGING?

I am thirty-three years old and I do not know how to deal with ag-ing. I am married, and my husband and I do not have children. We want some, eventually but not anytime soon. We both are like two big kids, and we like it that way. The fact that three years ago I moved to the United States from the Czech Republic makes me feel even younger because of all these new experiences. I also started going to college again. So I would say that my spirit is very young and I do not want to lose it, ever. I know I cannot stop time and so I would like advice about questions that worry me about aging:

1. If my husband and I do not have any children, do you think we are going to regret it later?
2. Would you like to be forever young or stop aging?

3. How do you keep your spirit young?
4. Would you have advice about how to keep in shape and healthy even after sixty?
5. What is the thing you miss about being young? What is the thing you do not miss?

I hope my questions are not too overwhelming, and I will be looking forward to your answers.

This chapter opens with a letter from someone who wants to know what it's like to be old; this young adult wants to know how to prepare for old age along the way.

Most of the Elders took this multifaceted question as an opportunity for self-examination. Elder Ruthie, however, is annoyed by what she seems to perceive as the writer's immaturity, and offers this terse answer:

It is a shame that you don't think you have to grow up before you grow old.

But after getting that off her chest by writing it down, Ruthie admits, "I am using this opportunity to vent a little. I think I might respond differently if I were answering the person face to face."

Like the advice seeker, most Elders who responded to this letter put the question of children at the top of the list. Writes Kriko:

Will you regret not having had children? I hear a lot of older people complaining that their forty-year-old children have come back home to live and the parents are sick of them. I hear complaints that grown children don't pay any attention to their parents, don't even call.

However, I do not hear anyone complaining about their grandchildren.

Nancy—who in high school ran with a pack of "bad girls" called the Sinful Six—says she doesn't miss the constant emotional drama that seems to plague the young. "I don't understand what the fascination is about youth; I have found it to be highly overrated," she says. "If you talk to someone about their teenage years, they tell you they were miserable with mean girls, cheating boyfriends, etc. Thank God people *do* grow old." On the child-bearing question, this mother of four adult children writes:

> I don't think you will regret not having children. This is of course assuming that both of you agree. If you changed your mind at a later date, you could adopt children, thereby giving a home to the homeless.

Elder Frank, seventy-two, of Greensboro, North Carolina, and Largo, Florida, heartily disagrees.

> The biological clock is ticking, plus it is nice to be able to keep up with those who run wild. Even adoption is gratifying. Be young with your kids. Do it NOW!

The Gold and Wise group of Sussex County, New Jersey, comprised of three women aged seventy-four to eighty-two, cast their vote with Frank's.

> The first item that grabbed our attention was regarding having children. First of all, we want to make it clear that we do believe that you will regret not having children, especially if you have the choice to do so. We know of nobody at our age who regrets having children and we know of several people who regret not having children. None of us knows of anyone who is happy that they never had children.

In answer to one of the advice seeker's other questions, they add:

> Would we stop aging? Of course! Who would not? Would we stop time? Absolutely not!
> We would like to suggest that you worry too much about keeping in shape, keeping a young spirit, and the future in general. Nobody can predict the future. One of us was diagnosed with MS at age forty-eight and is now dependent upon others for everything. One of us is in a nursing home at the young age of seventy-five because a physician

prescribed an overdose of medication. Plan for the future without neglecting today. In other words, make every day count!

When Elder Jacobus files his responses to letters for this book, he almost invariably writes at the top of the page, "I hope this is in order." That's the way Jacobus likes things—in order. That's the way he answers this letter.

You ask some very good questions, and I shall try to answer them to the best of my ability. Allow me to tackle them one at a time.

1. *My wife and I did not hesitate very long before we decided to have our first child. We took a little longer deciding about having a second child. That is why our daughters are six years apart. We never regretted having them. My wife died more than seven years ago. I consider myself lucky to have daughters and grandchildren.*

    Children can be a great joy. They can also bring a lot of sorrow. This depends upon what kind of people they become. Some children are selfish and try to get as much from their parents as they can. Others are loving and caring. One of my daughters is very concerned about me. She and her husband have me over for supper once a week since my wife died. The other daughter and her husband occasionally pick me up to attend a symphony concert where my grandson plays the viola. If my wife and I had decided not to have children, I would not have that support today.

2. *I can definitely say that I would NOT want to be forever young. I have always looked forward to the next stage in life. Now that I have been retired for twenty-four years, I enjoy the freedom that comes with it.*

3. *I motorcycled for thirty years [Jacobus's former biker's club was called The Retreads]. I gave that up ten years ago. I have discovered that every time I give up one activity, I have time to pursue something new that I could not do before. When I quit motorcycling, I built and flew model airplanes and joined a bowling team. I do not fly airplanes or bowl anymore. I don't*

have time to do that because now I do a lot of writing and photography.

4. *Exercise, eat well, keep active with things you enjoy, keep making new friends, do volunteer work where you are helping people. You need to feel needed and accepted.*

5. *When I was young, I didn't forget like I do today. It was also easier to do things like drive my car. I don't miss having all the responsibilities I had when I was young.*

Keep enjoying life and learn to accept aging as it occurs. I am sure you will.

Jacobus takes comfort in order. But it is getting harder and harder for him to find order in his relationship with his brother Horatio Victor. Try as he might to trigger Horatio Victor's memory with childhood reminiscences, he doesn't have the power to repair his brother's memory. For the first time in his life, Jacobus finds himself taking care of the former bully.

Jacobus says there is no official diagnosis for his brother's memory loss. In the first months after the move to his current residence, the gaping holes in Horatio Victor's ability to recall sometimes would send him into a state of agitated frustration. "At that stage, he got very angry sometimes, and has had to be sedated," Jacobus says.

On other days, he's the old Horatio Victor, filled with quirky humor and curiosity about the world. "He has his good moments and his bad moments," Jacobus says. "The way I see it, he tries to remember the right term or word to use. By the time he remembers it, he has forgotten what he wanted to say. He used to be very upset when this happened. Now he is much more at peace with accepting his limitations and making the best of it.

"What is happening to my big brother makes me very much aware that I am fast approaching my departure from this world," Jacobus says. But Jacobus says he is willing to accept old age and death as part of the natural order of life—and as yet another learning experience. For Jacobus, *this* is what it's like to be old.

"I cannot predict for sure what I would do if I had only twenty-four hours to live," Jacobus muses. "I know I would do a lot of thinking. I also know that I wouldn't do much grocery shopping. I certainly wouldn't buy any green bananas. I could see myself trying to remember anybody with whom I've had some unfinished business and attempting to arrive at an amicable closure.

"I am presently at peace with the thought of dying. If I can be as at peace as my wife was when she died on November 3, 1999, at age sixty-eight, I'll be okay. When she died, I realized there was no take it or leave it. I had to take it. There was no alternative.

"I asked myself at the time, 'Okay, what are you going to do now?' I made a firm vow to myself that from this day forth, I will make a real effort to make sure every person whom I meet shall have a better day because he or she met me, whether it is the cashier or another motorist at a four-way intersection. That vow has made a huge difference."

Jacobus also says he has no reservations about telling the story of his brother's memory loss in the pages of this book. "I am sure he would feel the same way," Jacobus observes. "Whatever you say is likely to help other people appreciate the good life."

CHAPTER

9

SUCH SWEET SORROW
Wisdom for Letting Go

I'm sitting here with tears in my eyes, so forgive me if my typing gets all garbled. My grandparents died when I was very young. The only one I remember lived until I was twelve, which wasn't long enough. I am thirty now and I still miss her and I wish so much that I could ask her about my problems. I am so touched that your group is using its collective wisdom to give good advice to people who need it. It's about the kindest thing I've ever heard of.

Sincerely,
"Jasmine"

—From "Feedback & Kudos"
www.ElderWisdomCircle.org

Only in the agony of parting do we look into the depths of love.

—George Eliot

Unspeakable

LETTER: SPEAKING AT A SMALL CHILD'S MEMORIAL SERVICE

My grandnephew, three years old, was accidentally smothered in his sleep by my nephew rolling on top of him. I have been asked to speak at the memorial service and feel compelled to speak to my nephew and his family and give them hope and reasons to live a full life. It is also my desire to honor and memorialize my grand-nephew. Any suggestions for readings, comments, other? I have searched high and low but nothing has touched my heart or felt right.

Elder Treefrog, sixty-five, of West Bloomfield, Michigan, chose this pen name for his work for the Elder Wisdom Circle because he likes the sound of the little guys outside his window on a summer evening. His house in suburban Detroit is surrounded by lakes and wetlands, and that means frogs—and they can get pretty loud sometimes. No matter how hard he's trying to concentrate on his writing, however, Treefrog never wants to silence the frog choir; it's a comforting sound of nature.

Sometimes, Treefrog admits, he'd rather listen to the frogs than all those confused and frightened voices clamoring for answers from the Elder Wisdom Circle. Letters like this one: What do you say when there are no words?

There are times when letters like this one send Treefrog running back to the EWC Web site to find a query about automobile engines, home repair, or gardening—or maybe a question about pet care. After all, who without a heart of stone could resist this plaintive plea that came in from one desperate pet owner: "My ferret needs help"?

Sometimes Treefrog latches on to these practical questions for the same reason he turns to his favorite hobbies, cooking, painting, and fishing: to get away from it all. You've got to take a break, he thinks, to apply your wisdom to something that can be repaired with a screwdriver or a hammer, a clog that can be flushed or a plant that has a shot of blooming again in the spring, or else you'd just crawl off into a corner, curl up into a fetal position, and suck your thumb until doomsday.

Besides, Treefrog has plenty of hands-on experience with nuts-and-bolts matters. Once he'd decided to give up the priesthood in favor of becoming a husband and father, Treefrog made his living in construction and contracting, a career that paid the bills raising a family but never brought him much in the way of enjoyment or satisfaction.

And in his retirement, Treefrog finally put his building skills to work on something *really* important: adding a garden room onto the family home. Inside these glass walls, Treefrog has nurtured a paradise of plants from all climates, some of them souvenirs of his travels. Bougainvillea, delicate orchids, pink-blossomed tillandsia (a member of the pineapple family), fuku-bonsai, the good-luck *ti* plant of Hawaii, Song of India, African violets, and pungent rosemary, transplanted to the snowy Midwest from sunny California. Want to know how to keep those pesky aphids off your roses? Treefrog's your man.

But much as he tries to resist them, Treefrog finds himself drawn back again and again to stunned, aching letters like the one from the grief-stricken great-uncle—the kind of letters that form the basis of this chapter. They are not always about such a confronting matter as the death of a child, but each one, in its own way, is about something important that must be given up—either against one's will or by choice.

"These letters can be summed up with just one word: *loss*," Treefrog muses. "It's about the loss of life, the loss of love and trust, the loss of companionship, the loss of innocence. I think they are a sample culmination of how frail we are, how fearful we are of the wide variety of losses and 'endings' that life thrusts upon us, right from birth to our last breath."

Adds Treefrog: "Individuals lose love, jobs, marriages, children, health, friendships, confidence, money, pets, and, finally, life itself. My tattered old *Webster's Collegiate* mentions the following under the definition of *lose*: 'destruction, dissolve, destroy, loosen, deprivation, separation, defeat.' Any or all of these words can bring a person to their knees."

Questions about loss are bound to find their way to the Elder Wisdom Circle, if only because the longevity of its members serves as testament to the fact that loss *can* be survived. You can't make it for sixty to one-hundred-plus years without losing someone, something, or some part of yourself that feels irreplaceable, and all of the Elders are quick to offer encouragement, and to let the advice seeker know that he or she will make it through.

Some in the group, however, have been given a particularly sharp and life-altering jolt. Treefrog is one of those people.

Even the peaceful garden room reminds Treefrog of his family's tragedy. All he has to do is smell the rosemary. It will always remind him of "Clara."

Along the coastline of Encinitas, California, decades of natural erosion have resulted in massive overhangs, cavelike indentations carved out at the bottom of the coastal bluffs. These overhangs are beautiful but fragile—a constant threat to both the expensive bluff-top homes and oblivious beach-goers who spread towels or set up beach chairs below for protection from wind or sun. It's hard to think about danger on a placid beach like this.

Treefrog and his wife's oldest boy, "Michael," then thirty-two, celebrated the new year by marrying "Clara" in California on New Year's Eve 1998. Michael was a good-looking kid, an athletic six-foot-three. In high school he was a star football player, basketball player, and class valedictorian. He graduated from the University of Colorado at Boulder, and, after graduation, took off on a sabbatical to travel the world. He wandered through England and Europe, ran with the bulls in Pamplona. Michael trekked the Himalayas, slept on park benches in Jakarta, sojourned through opium fields in the Golden Triangle of Southeast Asia. He spent time in New Zealand and a month in Australia playing volleyball. He finally ended up in Hawaii, broke, and got a job waiting tables. As soon as he earned enough money to get there, he headed for California, and earned his Master's degree in environmental sciences at UCLA.

In 1997, Michael met Clara at a party in northern California. She was a mechanical engineer for a large biotech company. After searching the world, Michael found his soul mate right here in the United States. About the same time, Michael received a Fulbright scholarship that would take him to Norway, and being apart was painful for both of them. Ultimately Clara quit her job and joined Michael in Norway, but when his study was completed they returned to southern California. It was the perfect location for these two, as both loved surfing and the ocean. Michael took a desk job that never excited him, and Clara was no longer particularly enchanted with her position either. She dreamed of opening a seaside surf shop and of publishing a magazine that would cater to women surfers.

Michael brought Clara home to Michigan to meet Treefrog and his wife, "Mary," in the summer of 1998, and they all went camping in the northern woods. Both parents were taken with Clara's raven-haired beauty, her intelligence, and, most of all, her love for their son.

They were married at a friend's home in Encinitas, a beautiful place by the ocean near the Scripps Research Institute of biomedical science. After their marriage, Michael kept his uninspiring desk job, but Clara quit and started working to establish her surf shop and magazine. They rented a small flat in Encinitas, about a block from the ocean.

On January 16, 2000, the event that changed all of their lives became a terse news story in the *San Diego Union-Tribune* and the *Los Angeles Times*. But on January 15, all Treefrog and Mary knew was what they learned from two phone calls: the first a frantic, garbled cell phone message from a stranger whose phone went dead before they could figure out what the caller was trying to say, the next a call from Michael: "Clara is dead. Mom, Dad—please come."

Landslide Kills Woman as She Watches Husband Surf

ENCINITAS—A woman sitting on the beach was killed Saturday when part of a bluff suddenly collapsed and sent tons of dirt and rocks tumbling down on her, officials said. Horrified sunbathers tried desperately to dig through the moist red dirt that covered the woman while she was watching her husband surf. The victim was identified by the San Diego County medical examiner as "Clara Carpenter," of Encinitas.

Michael had wanted to surf; Clara decided to stand on the beach and watch. It was a warm, dry winter day. About a dozen surfers rode the waves, families were having picnics, and young skateboarders flashed their bravado moves on the concrete paths. As Michael headed into the water with his board, there was a loud noise and he felt the ground shake like an earthquake. He turned and saw that a length of the beach was covered with large boulders.

Michael ran toward the spot where he last saw Clara. He saw her sunglasses in the sand. Michael was among those who helped find and uncover her body, crushed by fallen rock.

The accident occurred on a Saturday that was also Martin Luther King Day, so the coroner's office was poorly staffed through the weekend. Clara's body, they said, could not be released until Tuesday at the earliest because "the cause of death had to be determined." By then, Treefrog was too furious to contain himself. "*Look* at her, for God's sake!" he exploded.

On Monday, Mary, Treefrog, and Treefrog's mother and brother-in-law worked up the courage to visit Moonlight Beach. They were stunned at the vast expanse of cliff that had collapsed.

There were many flowers scattered on the sand. On the concrete steps leading down to the sand was an alcove where people were leaving flowers and bits of things they thought were important: dolls, pictures, poems, tiny surfboards. At the bottom of the steps was a very rusty old sign, barely readable, that read BEWARE OF FALLING ROCK.

There were also a couple of paramedics there, just standing and watching. Treefrog introduced himself and the paramedics said they were among those who dug for Clara alongside Michael. They found themselves hugging each other; the paramedics cried, too. They wanted to know how Michael was doing. They'd done all they could—what good would it have done for Treefrog to tell them that Michael, as well as Treefrog and Mary, would never be the same again?

Mary tried therapy to get her through the tragedy, and it seemed to work for her. Treefrog went to one session and walked out. Talking to a shrink who presented him with a laundry list of her academic degrees, her personal experiences with grief, and a hefty bill wasn't doing anything to help him cope with living in a world in which a beachside cliff can fall on a laughing newlywed bride.

While he and his family tried to recover from the death of Clara, Treefrog decided to try to get involved in teaching and volunteering, doing something that would help other people, to take his mind off his own problems. He started noodling around on the Web, looking for opportunities. He doesn't remember exactly how he found the Elder Wisdom Circle, but he did. Or maybe it found him. So, eventually, did the letter about the three-year-old.

Treefrog writes:

One does not settle into a "ripe old age" without having experienced the loss of loved ones, and I want you and your family to know that you have our heartfelt prayers that peace and acceptance be found and nourished by all who knew this young person.

"Acceptance" . . . that's the hard part, isn't it? Three years old, a life just beginning, surely a bright future in store. It is difficult to believe or accept that it was not meant to be. And somehow the notion that it was "God's will" just doesn't help to lighten the heart either, does it? In this case, all I can do is to pass on some thoughts and hope that you will find something worth sharing with others at the memorial service.

It is my belief that God doesn't "will" bad things to happen. His Divine Plan often permits things to happen in the hope that we will put our busy lives on "pause" long enough to recognize and share with each other the precious nature of life and love, even in the midst of tears and sorrow. We have a choice; we can either become bitter and hard hearted with the loss of one so young, or this child can lead us all to thoughts of life and its meaning, thoughts that no other event possibly could have triggered. Birth and death are two of life's events that I believe surpass all others in terms of their ability to allow us to speak of, share, and experience love. From this standpoint, the loss has a purpose, a Divine one, one that all hearts and souls who knew this little boy must come to realize and hold on to.

Your grandnephew, young as he was, has provided a wonderful opportunity to contemplate and share with one another all the mysteries of life and love, being and purpose. Did this young child have a purpose? Did he accomplish anything in his short life? I believe that this little young angel is looking down at you and your family right now and asking those very questions of you! Can you hold each other close and precious? Can you live each of today's moments knowing that some measure of meaning and love has been added to your life because you knew and experienced him? If you can, then there is a little angel at God's side smiling very much, and so is God.

God bless and keep you and your family in His arms.

The Elders participating in this book collectively seem to have recognized this letter as one of the most difficult ever received by the Elder Wisdom Circle; instead of answering it, most of them opted for a respectful silence. Only one other group member, Elder Kriko, seventy-five, of Tempe, Arizona, tried to come up with some words of comfort. "I selected this letter because I was deeply touched by the tragedy," Kriko says.

For the memorial service, Kriko suggests some readings that might be soothing at such a stressful time: The Robert Louis Stevenson poem "My Shadow" or the lyrics to the Beatles song "Golden Slumbers." He also suggested music: Gabriel Faure's "Pavane," "Over the Rainbow" from *The Wizard of Oz*, Brahms's "Lullaby" or the popular song written in 1940 "When You Wish Upon a Star."

But, along with being a visual artist, Kriko is a writer, and he decided to include with his advice a poem he composed himself. In his letter, he modestly credits the poem to "Anonymous," but gave us permission to reveal the identity of the man behind the words.

Please accept my deepest condolences at your overwhelming loss.

People at funerals are numb and scared. I've noticed after a funeral there is a lot of laughing, clearly a release from the tension and stress. No funeral is as stressful as one for a young child.

You can create a lighter mood if you suggest that people send new stuffed toys instead of flowers, saying that they will be donated to an orphanage after the funeral. Some people have liked having a balloon release. Those kinds of things help create a lasting image to comfort the family and friends.

Here is a poem that is respectful but lighthearted:

From a Dead Child to His Mourners

Thank you for coming to say goodbyes,
And showing me the tears in your eyes,
I can't tell you where I am right now,
But I can say that I'm not yet a sacred cow.
Like the cow contentedly munching grass,
And a bit like Alice through the looking glass,
I feel good and happy and very much at peace,
Like Mary's little lamb whose soft fleece
Keeps it warm and snug.
I'm like a little bug
Hiding underneath the rug until the people leave.
Then I'll blossom out and you can go ahead and grieve,
But not me. I do believe I'll just finish up this poem
And then go play till the lambs and cows come home.

"Sad and a Little Mad"

LETTER: MY PAPA

> Hi. I am nine years old. I need help. My papa died and I am very sad. I don't know what to do. I can't keep my mind off of it. I am very sad and a little mad. I can't control it. Can you give me ways how to? I miss him and I didn't even get to say good-bye.

While most of the Elders may have been shocked into silence by the letter about the lost three-year-old, this one that came from a child not too much older who had experienced a loss of his own brought a flood of empathetic responses from these "cyber-grandparents." Not that it wasn't tough to come up with the right words; says Elder Myra, seventy, of Providence, Rhode Island, "You can just feel the anguish. I had to read his letter and wait a few days before I answered it."

Myra's father died when Myra was a child. "When he died, we had an aunt we were very close to, and my mother sent my sister and me to stay with her," Myra says. "That's the way it was then—she thought she was protecting us. She was a 'stiff upper lip' kind of person. I never saw my mother cry. She didn't do it intentionally to hurt me, but it was devastating not to be able to say good-bye." Her letter:

I am so sorry that your papa died. Of course you are sad and sometimes mad or angry. Those are normal feelings to have when we experience a terrible loss of someone we love. My father died when I was ten years old, and I still miss him sixty years later. The terrible pain you are feeling now will gradually get easier, but it takes a long time, so be patient with yourself.

I am so glad you wrote to us because it is important for you to reach out to people and share your feelings. Please try to find someone you can talk to and cry with, and don't be afraid to express your anger, even your anger at your papa for leaving you. It is also normal to forget about him sometimes and enjoy what you are doing. This is not a betrayal of your papa, but a way that you will recover, which is what he would want you to do.

Sometimes people die and we don't get a chance to tell them good-bye. But you can have your own good-bye ceremony for your papa. Do you have a photograph of him? You can sit with the photo and "talk" to him, and do it whenever you feel like it. Maybe someone can take you to his grave or a place like that, and you can bring the photo there and a special item that reminds you of him. And remember it isn't just the good-bye that matters. It's the love you and papa shared for nine years and the love you still hold in your heart. Part of him will always be with you.

Elder Barbara, sixty-two, of Greene, New York, lost her husband when her sons were eight and ten years old. She remembers how unsympathetic the other children could sometimes be.

The first thing I want to tell you is that it is normal to feel sad and to not be able to keep your mind off your father's death. I know that some of my sons' friends were really cruel, not at all understanding the grief my children were feeling.

No one forgets a loss like that completely, but you will learn to go on with your life and have fun again. It takes a while, though, to get through all of your grieving. Do you have a picture of your father? I came home and found my younger son crying about a year after his father died; he told me he was having trouble remembering him. So we looked through all of the photos and he picked two and we framed them and put them in his room where he could look at them whenever he wanted to.

Elder Seeley, sixty-five, of Tucson, Arizona, lost her father at age thirty-three and still feels the loss. She borrows her advice from a very young neighbor:

I asked a wonderful little girl who lives down the street from me what you should do; she was only nine when her father died very suddenly. "Bella," my little friend, kept a work jacket of her father's and actually slept with it for a while. My father made me a special necklace that I used to wear all the time; now I wear it often. Perhaps there is something of your father's you could keep for comfort.

Elders Gpa-and-Gma of Rochester Hills, Michigan, aged eighty-five and eighty-one, believe that "this cry for help echoes those of the multitude of children in a tempest-tossed, war-torn world." And, they add, "We tried to hold this child in our arms for a brief moment, and assure him that his feelings are normal and he can have his papa with him in his heart, always."

With Gma's input, Gpa writes about his own dad:

My pop died many years ago. Anytime I want to visit with him, I bring to mind the fun times we had. I remember when I was nine or ten years old we were on a beach in Atlantic City. Pop was very strong and he would walk on his hands in the sand. I was so proud of him. Or I would think about him cheering wildly and noisily for me when I came in third in the running broad jump at my high-school track meet. Many times when I did something really good, I would

*take a minute to ask, "How was that Pop?" And in my heart I would
hear him say, "You did good, son."*

This is another letter Treefrog could not ignore; he has an eight-
year-old grandson. In trying to figure out how to respond, Treefrog tried
to think about how he would explain it to an eight-year-old if his other
son, "John," the boy's father, died.

*My young friend, you are a very gifted person, did you know that?
There are two reasons I think you are very smart. First, you wrote
a good letter about being sad and mad, and second, you are wise to
see you need some help and are brave enough to ask for it. Good for
you! I have a grandson just about your age. I think if his father
were to die, I would really hope my grandson would come and talk
to me.*

*You are sad and mad because someone you loved was taken away
from you and you could not stop it, you could not be there to say
good-bye. I can understand those feelings because I have felt them
many times. I remember those losses, but you want to know something? They no longer make me feel sad or mad. I'll tell you why.*

*I believe that your papa is not so very far away from you at all.
Remember, you are part of him and he is part of you! This will
ALWAYS be so. I wonder if you look a little like him? That would be
nice! Maybe you are smart because he was smart! How can you
really say "good-bye" to someone who is part of you?*

*Don't be sad; smile when you think of your papa. I am ab-
solutely sure he is smiling at you and wanting you to be strong and
grow up to be a man he will be proud of. And don't forget, if Papa
is part of you and you are part of him, you can talk to him anytime.
Trust me, he is listening and may talk back to you in ways that
someday you will understand. Meanwhile, right now, go on over to
the person who is closest to you who you love and give them a big
hug. Smile and just say, "I LOVE YOU!" Bet you will feel better
already. Don't forget to let them hug you back! I do that a lot and it
works every time.*

◄o►

Something Missing

LETTER: EMPTY NEST

> My only child, a daughter, will be going off to college next fall. The two of us spent most of the summer looking at schools and now that she has made her top choices she is going through the process of preparing applications.
>
> We have always been extremely close on every level. She is loving, caring, and great fun to be around. I will miss her so very much. My husband is often aloof, cold, and self-involved. It has been my daughter's love, affection, and companionship that has sustained me and brought me comfort and joy for most of the last seventeen years. What can I expect to feel and how can I cope with the enormous changes I'll be facing?

Luckily, not all of the letters about loss that come to the Elder Wisdom Circle deal with something as traumatic as the death of a loved one. In fact, in this case, the daughter may very well be home for Thanksgiving—or, depending on the geography of her college acceptances, even on weekends, and probably bearing a pile of dirty laundry.

For this letter, the Elders were quick to recognize that the problem is not that the daughter is leaving her mother, but that the mother appears to be trapped in a troubled marriage. The WebWisdom group, of Royersford, Pennsylvania, aged eighty-two to ninety-four, noticed right off that only one parent seemed to be involved in helping the daughter with her college plans.

Elder Anita, seventy-four, of Brewster, New York, says of her advice: "I chose to respond this way because I think sometimes people need a little 'shock therapy.' This is *not*, nor should it be seen as, a crisis."

I will not be able to say what I need to say in a way that will sugar coat it, so I shall just go ahead and say it. I am sorry that your daughter's leaving will create such a void in your life, but I hope that you will see that you should have been preparing for this for the past seventeen years. If your relationship with your husband was not what you needed, and you did everything you could to change that, then you should have found friends to fill your need for companionship. We should not be using our children as the excuse to keep our marriage together, and we should not be using them to fill the role of a partner or best friend. We should enjoy them, share with them, and help them to separate and become independent from the time they start school.

I really hope you will begin to do some of the things you put aside doing over the years. Join a club, a gym, a book group, do a social activity with others, whether your husband wants to join or not. You might try to rekindle some romance with your husband. Has he felt left out all these years, or did he prefer that you left him alone? Did he perhaps feel jealous of what you and your daughter had? Ask him, talk with him and, if necessary, go with him to a marriage counselor to help him learn how to communicate.

The Heavensviewsages of Delta, Colorado, aged seventy to ninety-three, also see the mother-daughter issue as a distraction from a faulty marriage. "It sounds to me like the husband has been cut out of the whole situation," says one member of the group, an eighty-five-year-old retired telephone operator who asked to be called "Elder Giggles" because of her ability to laugh at life—even though she now relies on a wheelchair as a result of the lasting effects of a childhood bout with typhoid fever. Her group's response:

There are a number of things that jump out at us immediately from your letter. From the way you describe your relationship with your daughter, maybe your husband had no choice but to keep to himself and find his own life. Your most important commitment should be to your spouse in a marriage, not to the product of the marriage, i.e., the children. It is a shame that your primary relationship was neglected to this extreme. If your daughter and your husband had this relationship and excluded you, would it hurt your feelings?

It sounds like your daughter is healthy and ready to go out into the world and make her way. You must let her go and test her wings, as the saying goes.

This will be a wonderful opportunity for you to rekindle your relationship with your husband. Relationships take work, and you and your husband have not put in the effort for this garden to grow anything but weeds. You could awaken a sleeping giant!

In her letter, Myra advises the worried parent not to tell her daughter how much Mom will miss her—tough advice, perhaps, for a mother to understand. Isn't saying "I'll miss you" a pure and natural expression of parental love?

Not for these two, Myra says.

Myra holds master's degrees in special education and counseling, but bases her advice on her own relationship with her mother after her father passed away. Two years after her father died, Myra lost a sister and, once again, her mother shed no tears. Though her mother did not weep, Myra was a bright, sensitive girl who could not help but feel guilty knowing her mother would be alone when Myra left for school.

Myra explains that for a parent with a healthy mother-daughter relationship, to say "I'll miss you" might indeed be exactly the thing to make a daughter feel loved and secure. But in the advice seeker's case, she believes the daughter can't help but sense that her mother is too attached, as well as that her mother and father have a poor relationship. "If the mother says, 'Oh, I'm going to miss you so much,' it's sort of a reproach, on an unconscious level," Myra says. "It's not a normal situation; there are layers of meaning. It would just add to the guilt that this young woman is feeling."

Myra does give the Mom credit for not trying to coax her daughter to stay at home and attend a community college. She encourages her to continue in that healthy direction.

It is wonderful to have a loving and happy relationship with our children, but it is also important that they separate from us and become independent adults with lives of their own. Going away to college will help your daughter accomplish this critical life task. As her mother, you will need to support her by distancing yourself from her everyday life and not letting her know how much you will miss her. She is probably aware of the dynamics of your relationship with your husband and may feel guilty about leaving you. This will impede her development, and it is not appropriate to burden her with your unhappiness and loneliness.

—◄○►—

Full Nest Syndrome

LETTER: ADULT SON MOVING BACK HOME

> After much struggle (and failure) at living on his own, my twenty-two-year-old son is moving back home soon. I am encouraging him to seek career counseling that is available free through my employer. I am wrestling with how much help beyond this to give him when he does come. He has tried junior college and flight training, and never seems to be able to sustain any effort (including jobs) for any length of time. He is in good health, although he smokes (outside), and is handsome and very sociable, which may be part of the problem.

Here is a parent with the opposite problem: Instead of trying perhaps too hard to keep a young adult at home, this advice seeks a creative suggestion on how to get one to move out permanently. The Elders all agreed that this young man needs to be pushed from the nest—although opinions varied on how hard to nudge.

Elder Tina, seventy-three, of Greensboro, North Carolina, says, "I chose this one because I have friends who are dealing with the same situation. Also, I struggle with how much to help my adult children even though they are living on their own. I hoped to convey that there is a delicate balance between helping out someone in need versus enabling dependency."

Tina writes:

Your son is apparently one of what are called the "boomerang kids" who return to the family nest. This is very common nowadays. You're just one of many parents going through the same thing. Twentysomethings are moving back home with such frequency that this has become the new "normal." Sociologists say it is taking young people longer than ever to make the transition to full adulthood.

You state that you are encouraging him to seek counseling, which is available free through your employer. I think you should insist that he take advantage of this because it will help him find direction.

It is important that you and your husband sit down with your son and set some goals and boundaries before he moves in. You should have some understanding as to how long he thinks he will be staying with you. You should encourage him to send out résumés, find a job, and then to save as much money as he can so that he can become independent.

You should all discuss his doing some chores around the house while he is living under your roof. He can choose certain chores, such as mowing the lawn, painting the house, cleaning out the garage, vacuuming, loading the dishwasher, and doing his own laundry. He shouldn't expect to sit around all day. Hopefully, you will all stick with whatever "plan" you have worked out so that his stay will be pleasant for all of you.

From the Rockymountain Owls group of Montrose, Colorado, aged sixty to ninety-five:

We think that it is okay to allow your son to move back home, but only with limits set around his behavior and specific goals for the future. Limits would include being up in the morning, working toward a goal of finding a job, working, or getting training in a career. Have this conversation with him BEFORE he moves back in, and let him know this is not an endless vacation living off mom and sleeping till noon every day and partying all night. If he won't agree, pat him on the back and tell him good luck.

Elder-Student, eighty, of Dallas, Texas, tells the advice seeker that rules or no rules, the son should stay out of the nest. Her letter:

You apparently have a healthy twenty-two-year-old son who simply cannot seem to accept the responsibilities of growing up. He does not need to be enabled in his efforts to depend on his good looks and personality any longer. The sooner he learns that life is a serious matter and, through his own efforts, he either succeeds or fails on his journey to becoming a responsible adult, the sooner he will no longer need to use your home and your employment to sustain his current lifestyle. Because your letter does not mention the possibility of any health or

mental problems or addiction of any kind, this is a pretty straightfor-
ward answer. Tell him lovingly that you care about him and his fu-
ture, but he needs to grow up; he doesn't need to move back in with
Mom.

Barbara was the only Elder to suggest that the advice seeker may be
partly to blame for her son's difficulty in moving on by inadvertently
providing the wrong subliminal message. "I answered this because of
her choice of words," Barbara says. "It reminds me of the many years I
spent thinking my wonderful son would be a 'failure'."

Kids have built-in radars as to what their parents are thinking and feel-
ing. That is why I was so upset to notice the words that you used in
your letter, most particularly "failure." If you feel that he is a failure,
he will pick that up and will judge himself the same way.

The trick is to help your son become eager to find a job and live on
his own again. You write that your son is social and you think that
may be part of the problem. Does that mean that you don't trust him
to pay attention to finding a career because he is having so much fun
with his friends? If you really think that this is his problem, then I sug-
gest that you give him a short vacation where he gets his room and
board rent-free. And then you can inform him that you need for him
to either pay rent or do some work around the house to pay for his rent
and meals. It will teach him responsibility and he will most likely either
become so tired of doing menial work that he wants to train for a real
profession or he will be so tired of not having much money that he'll
start doing some of the same work for your neighbors. Either way, he
will become self-motivated if he needs to do something to support
himself.

I wish you luck. I know that it is hard to live through this time. But
I urge you not to even let yourself think that your son is a failure. If
you understand that he is detouring, then you can help him find his
way. He needs your trust even though he has not yet earned it. It is
easy to trust your children when they are doing "the right thing"; the
real challenge is to trust them when it looks like they are screwing up.

◄○►

The (Very) Long Good-bye

> We're retiring out of state (some four hundred miles) in three years. Any ideas on how to prepare our five, seven, and nine-year-old grandchildren to make it easier for them? We have been very close to them since they were born.

The Elders recognize that these concerned grandparents seem to be projecting their own separation anxiety onto the grandkids. Who, they ask, will *really* be missing whom?

Myra admits to having "a good laugh" when she read the letter. "The idea of this grandparent thinking about preparing her young grandchildren for a move *three years* ahead of time seemed so absurd that I thought it was a joke," she says. "But of course I didn't respond that way. I tried to give some perspective on the issue, as well as suggestions for staying connected when the time comes."

My first suggestion is that you don't even think about preparing your grandchildren now for your move. While three years seems like a short time to us, for children ages five, seven, and nine, it is a very long time, more than half of the youngest one's life! Also, four hundred miles is not a huge distance in today's milieu, so I'm sure you will be seeing them fairly often. Many of my contemporaries have grandchildren living on the opposite side of the country or even abroad.

A couple of months before you move, you can tell them about your plans and show photos of your new home and the area where you will be living. Of course you'll reassure them that you will be visiting and keeping in touch by telephone and audiovisual technology. Videos are a great way for grandparents to stay connected with their long-distance grandchildren. You can also plan intergenerational vacations together through organizations like Elderhostel or on your own.

My guess is that if you are already worrying about what will happen when you move three years from now, you are feeling very anxious about it. Try not to convey that anxiety to your children or grandchildren. Since you are moving because of retirement, I assume this is your choice, so why not look forward to the adventure and the comforts of your new home?

Elder Frank, seventy-two, of Greensboro, North Carolina and Largo, Florida, writes from the perspective of a grandfather who lives not four hundred, but three thousand miles away from his grandchildren.

I am not sure which is the stronger of the two emotions involved in your move: Your loss, or theirs?

A good idea, for the children's sake, is to make them part of the move. For example, we have a small bedroom that contains a picture of each grandchild. We refer to it as the "grandkids' room."

Locate the local zoo, water park, and other youth amusement areas for their visits. The main issue is maintaining a communication line. Have a specific phone time weekly. An inexpensive way is to obtain a cell phone that has free evening calls after 7:00 p.m. or a phone card and give it to them as their very own Grandma/Grandpa Happy Card.

Four hundred miles is a day trip, and I recommend a quarterly visit minimum at first. It will soothe both you and the kids. As they age, their personal activities will help them cope. As for me, I still miss mine after four years and two visits per year. But every Sunday morning my cell phone rings and a little two-and-a-half-year-old says, "Hi Pop-Pop!" Sure makes my day!

Being There

LETTER: SHOULD CHILDREN BE THERE WHEN GRANDPARENT DIES?

My mother has been raising my niece and nephew since they were two and three. Their mother died when they were three and four. The children are six and seven now. My mother has colon cancer and can no longer care for the children. I moved to her place and have taken on the responsibility of caring for her and the children and am pursuing legal guardianship of the children. My brother, their father, seldom comes around.

Today we were told that the cancer has spread to the lymph nodes. The children know that Grandma is sick, but they do not know that her diagnosis is terminal. What do I tell the children? Do I wait until my mother is actually dying? She wants to die at home. Is it okay for the children to be around during her final hours? When she takes her final breath, should I let the children see her before the coroner takes her body?

This advice seeker probably would feel lucky to have a grandparent problem as easy as the one in the previous letter. Even though many of the Elders are now grandparents themselves, quite a few of those who answered this question relied upon their personal experiences as children when they lost a parent or grandparent many years ago. Myra is not the only Elder who suffered in the long run because well-meaning adults tried to protect her as a child from the harsh realities of death. All seemed to agree that nothing would be more damaging than to deny the children the chance to say good-bye to their grandmother.

Writes Elder Jacobus, eighty-one, of Saskatoon, Saskatchewan:

You don't want to hide the fact that Grandma is not expected to live. It is better if the children know the truth than for them to be shocked later on. There are many people who have lost a loved one and regret so much that they never had an opportunity to say good-bye. Give your children that opportunity. They will miss her dearly when she is gone, but they will never regret that they had the opportunity to say good-bye. It will be a precious memory that will help them with their grief of losing her.

Elder Walk-On, seventy-two, of Bethesda, Maryland, agrees. She also believes that the adults should not hide their grief from the children because it may help them to understand that their own sadness is normal, and is shared by the rest of the family. But she reminds the advice seeker that the children's father has a right to some input into the decision.

I believe that death is a part of life and that it is unwise to shelter people, young or old, from this reality. However, since your brother is still around, even though he makes himself scarce, you should start by talking with him to learn how he feels on this subject. Unless you get legal guardianship before she worsens, his feelings should be considered.

While the Elders agree that good-byes should be encouraged, they hold sharply differing opinions as to whether the children should be present at the moment of death—although they did seem to agree that the kids should be spared from watching the body being removed after death, whether it is from a home, hospice, or hospital room. Even as an adult, Elder Jangela, sixty-six, of Detroit, Michigan, writes that her bittersweet memory of holding a friend's hand as the woman died remains clouded by the image of later watching that friend's body being loaded into a hearse.

When it comes to watching life leave the body, some felt that such an experience is difficult enough for adults to comprehend, let alone children, and should not be allowed. Others felt that the children should only be barred from the room if the grandmother is visibly suffering or hooked up to medical equipment that could frighten a child.

Writes Elder Ursula, seventy-seven, of Tujunga, California:

I would strongly suggest that the children NOT be present in the room as Grandma dies; that's hard enough for grown-ups to understand and deal with. But do ask the kids if they want to say good-bye to Grandma or see that Grandma's presence has really gone away and she is no longer breathing. They may well say no; honor that decision. If they say yes, then AFTER the layout preparations have been completed, and BEFORE the coroner moves the body, lead them by the hand to the bedside and perhaps if you have any religious inclinations, say a prayer with them. The main idea is to indicate to the children that death, although sad and permanent, is not evil or frightening.

Elder Ruthie, sixty-four, of Swanton, Ohio, however, thinks that the children would be lucky to have the opportunity to be with their grandmother at the end. For nine years, Ruthie and a friend ran a residence for homeless women, and during that time they provided hospice care for three dying residents. "There were children in my home during these times, and I believe the experience of being present during the end of life was helpful to them," she says.

I would say definitely yes, especially if your mother is blessed to be able to die at home. These children are as much her children as her grandchildren. You did not mention the circumstances of their mother's death, but this will be like going through the whole thing all over again. But this time they will be older and more able to understand and deal with the loss. Children need to feel they are in the loop. At their age they can do so much to help your mother in her final hours. They can read to her, draw pictures for her, help her get a sip to drink, hold her hand, listen to her stories.

I wish I could find the words to tell you the effects of watching a person die. My experience has been that it has completely removed the fear of death from me. I was privileged to be present as my brother went through the dying process. His children were present and part of his care. That whole house became a sacred place and all of us felt it. Death is a part of life, and when one is able to better understand death, life has more meaning.

Several Elders thought that the advice seeker had neglected to consider the wishes of one very important person: the grandmother. The Chelsea Elders group of Warren, New Jersey, aged sixty-five to ninety-one, think that this dying grandmother might share their opinion because their response is "the collective thinking of a group of grandparents."

Our elder group, all of whom are grandparents, agreed that it would be best not to have children six and seven years of age present when Grandma dies. Death is a mystery to children and the experience can be frightening. There have been instances when young children are traumatized for months after seeing someone as they die. If you choose to have their grandmother die at home, it might be well to plan for the children to visit with other family members or friends during that time. Perhaps you might explain that Grandma has gone to visit their mother. The death of family members is always difficult, and it is wise to relieve children of the burden as much as possible.

Elder Aunt Vic, seventy-two, of Eugene, Oregon, thinks the best way to make the decision is to ask the children.

Let them know that if they want to be with her, it's okay; if they don't, it's okay, too. Each child is different in the way they handle these things. The same principle applies regarding viewing the body after she is gone. What is therapeutic for one child may be a nightmare for another.

The Right Time

LETTER: PET EUTHANASIA

I have to have my cat put to sleep, and I am feeling very guilty. No, I'm feeling like a murderer, even though he has started peeing and pooping all over the house and I can't continue cleaning up after him. I've tried many things, including the vet, but he won't go out, nor will he use his litter box. He is fourteen years old and has had a wonderful life, but I can't even look at him anymore, and it's not fair to him. I won't be able to adopt him out, knowing that he will be mean to anyone but me and that he will not use the litter box. I don't know whether to tell my son first (who's twenty-five but loves our cat to death) or just do it and put up with my son's anger toward me. My mom sent my dog to the pound when I was eleven, and I still get angry when I think about it (and I'm forty-four now!). I don't know what to do. My best friend's dad offered to take him to the vet, but I can't imagine him being gone after tomorrow.

This letter is about the loss of a different kind of family member. The Elders are all aware that a cat or dog's life span is shorter than a human's, but also realize that fact does nothing to ease the pain for the owner. They also know that having to make the choice for a pet makes losing the faithful companion that much tougher.

All of the Elders who answered this letter advised the writer to go ahead and feel the sadness, but to let go of the guilt. In his reply, Treefrog speaks for all of them:

> It's my belief that as God is in charge of releasing us from the "travail of the earth," we, in turn, are in charge of releasing our pets from the same travail. Murder? Hardly! It's called "altruistic love," love of the highest form, love that is unselfish and caring for the welfare of the other. In all honesty, if you ignore the pain and suffering of your pet, if you ignore the advice of your veterinarian, if you choose to look away from the signs that your pet's life has no quality, you are being very selfish and cruel.
>
> My friend, it is not "premeditated murder," it's "premeditated kindness." Our pets have no way to tell us of their pain; we have to see it and feel it enough to help them get well, or to help them pass on in peace.
>
> Your cat trusts that when the time comes, you will do what is best, not for yourself, but for him.

The Elders did, however, have various views on how the parent should handle the issue with the son. From Seeley:

> Of course it hurts; I am crying while typing this, thinking of my own beloved pets who were euthanized to relieve their suffering. When you explain to your adult son the need to put your pet to sleep, explain that he was suffering and you chose to send him to a better place where he can be young again. I cannot imagine why an act of mercy should make your son angry at you! I definitely would not tell him until after you have sent your wonderful old cat to kitty cat heaven. You are committing the ultimate act of love; please understand that and be content with your decision.

Elder Grandma Dee, seventy-four, a "snow bird" who spends summers in Grand Rapids, Michigan, and winters in Tucson, Arizona, says the advice seeker should evaluate her son's possible reactions before making the decision on whether to advise him in advance:

> *I have taken more than one pet for euthanization. I have helped them and petted them as they slipped away from this life. I felt that they would have been at my side if the tables were turned. I understand if you can't actually drive them to the vet yourself, since the emotional result could make it unsafe. As for telling your son, if you think he would cause a scene or interfere with your decision, tell him after it is done. If you think he will understand, ask him to help you say good-bye.*

From the Wizeones group of Albuquerque, New Mexico, aged seventy-eight to ninety-three:

> *Hopefully you will allow your best friend to take the cat to be euthanized on Monday. If you prefer to tell your son in advance, he will understand, because he saw how unhappy the cat was and he will be relieved, as will you.*
>
> *As an aside, it was a very interesting experience to discuss your letter with our Circle because there were two completely differing points of view: Most said, "He is only a cat," while others said, "He is a family member and living being." Clearly some of us believe there are "skin people" and "fur people," while most believe he is only a cat. All, however, believe he should be put out of his misery.*

Kriko, a devoted cat owner, believes that this parent's own experience should provide guidance on how to discuss the decision with the son.

> *You are still angry with your mother because she excluded you, not because she did a necessary thing. Sit with him and make him understand that the cat is not enjoying life; it doesn't even have control over its body anymore and doesn't know how to function. Many people create ceremonies to mark the passage of their pets. He could be the designer of such a ceremony.*

◄○►

The Ex

LETTER: TEN YEARS LATER AND IT STILL HURTS

My problem is that it has been ten years since my husband and I divorced and I still get a pain in my gut when I hear of him having a relationship with another woman. He was unkind and manipulative during our marriage, and it finally ended when I caught him cheating on me with one of our employees. I have to keep in contact with him because of our son.

My question is: How can I make it stop hurting? It is not continuous pain, just stabs of pain every six months or so. Do I just accept it? I know if I had a new man it would go away, but I have been unsuccessful in that area—maybe some trust issues?

Elder Helen, sixty-seven, of Sierra Vista, Arizona, tends not to mince words:

Your marriage ended because your ex was an unfaithful cheat. You should have had a party. You didn't do anything wrong, so why should you continue to punish yourself? Don't cry because it is over; smile because it happened. You have a son from this marriage.

Your ex is probably still unkind and manipulative. Only now he's making someone else miserable. Isn't that good news?

Elder Barbara, sixty-two, of Greene, New York, was a little more empathetic; she's been on both sides of this question. "It took me twelve years to start dating again after my husband died," she says. And, when Barbara finally remarried, she had problems with the clinging ex-wife. She writes:

Lots of girls and young women are obsessed with not being single. After a woman gets married, some of that tension goes away. She's done it, got a man. If she becomes single again, that is really hard to bear, so she often holds on to her last relationship to prove that she is not one of those failures, a spinster. When I used to go into a restaurant with my two sons, the greeter would ask if we were ONLY three people. Never would he ask a couple if they were only two. For that reason and many others, there was always a fourth seat at my table, always the ghost of my missing husband.

I had problems with my present husband's ex-wife. She wanted to keep a connection with him, ostensibly because of their son. She has admitted she always hoped they'd end up back together. If she had developed a friendship with my husband based on reality, she could have stayed a part of his life. But she wanted to be his "ex-wife" even though it had been thirty years since they'd been married and he'd had another marriage before ours. She believed that "ex-wife" was a position instead of an historical fact. If in your heart you haven't let go of your ex-husband, then you still will be hurt by what he does. You really do not want this unreliable man back in your romantic life. So my advice is to remind yourself of that fact. And get ready to open up to other people.

Elder Web, sixty-four, of Farmington Hills, Michigan, chose this letter because "I have gone through a divorce and the grieving process but was able to handle it a lot better than this person. Many people, including her, want to play the 'if only,' game, and that will never make you happy because it keeps you from ever doing anything."

It's interesting that you only feel pain when you hear about his new relationships. That "pain" is most likely jealousy, and not toward the ex or the new girlfriend, but just that he has someone and you don't.

Remember that we are not professional counselors but only provide advice based on life experience. In this case, the "experience" came from a divorce after a thirty-eight-year marriage. It was mutual and generally amicable but painful nonetheless. We kept a friendly relationship, then one day my ex stopped talking to me. Why? She had a "new man" and apparently didn't feel comfortable having me in her life any longer. Was I jealous? Yes, for about a day! Remember, we divorced for a number of reasons; I'm sure the two of you did as well. I recently started dating new ladies and am finding the experience both interesting and enjoyable.

First, you need to try to determine why you feel the way you do (the fact that you have had to keep in contact with your ex because of your son is not the reason). Since you have not been able to deal with it up to this point, you might want to consider professional counseling. You say you have "trust" issues, which is understandable, but at the same time it does not make for fun dating or relationships. Believe me, the last thing that most men want is a needy or distrustful companion, and I find most women feel the same way.

There are a lot of nice people in the world, many having gone through the same things as you, and you need to learn to put yourself out there and try. It's not going to be easy, or always successful, but if you never try, I can assure you nothing will EVER change.

The Heavensviewsages—including Giggles—agreed that the advice seeker must give herself a little push in the right direction. And they suggest one more key ingredient in the recipe for success:

Sometimes if you can find a way, forgiving someone who has wronged you opens a pathway to set yourself free. If you do not forgive him, we are afraid it may be impossible for you to move forward.

Understand that you don't have to take him back, or even be buddies, in order to forgive him. Seek out other activities, and don't dwell on the negative past; replace those negative thoughts with a picture of a bright, new future.

A Photographic Memory

LETTER: IS WIDOWER BOYFRIEND READY TO MOVE ON?

My boyfriend is a widower. His wife died a little over two years ago and he has a four-year-old son. Our relationship is good, but I was disturbed when I was over to his house for dinner and saw a large picture of his dead wife in the dining room. Am I just insecure, or is this a sign that he is really not ready to move on? Would it be wrong of me to suggest moving the picture into the boy's bedroom? I don't want him to forget his biological mother, but I also don't want her "watching" me try to build a relationship with her husband and son at the dinner table.

While the Elders were unanimous in their belief that the divorcée in the previous letter needs to let go of her cheating husband, they hold a wide range of opinions on whether it is appropriate for a widower of two years who has begun dating again to remember his late wife by keeping her photo above the dinner table.

Equally wide-ranging were their opinions on whether this new girl-friend—not yet a new wife—should have any say in what this man chooses to display in his own home.

The Rockymountain Owls group of Montrose, Colorado, aged sixty to ninety-five, think that the girlfriend might help the widower move on by making her feelings known.

It may be that your boyfriend is ready to move forward but doesn't know how to do so. He may feel the child needs to remain close to the biological mother and isn't sure how to accomplish that and move forward with another woman. He may need for you to suggest that he should make the home more receptive for a new woman to be able to come into.

Explain how hard it is for you, how confusing it must be to the boy, and how difficult it must be for him to continue to live in this state of suspended animation. It would make sense for the child to have a smaller photo of his mom to keep in his room if he wanted to. But, for the best for everyone involved, there has to be a clean break from the past to the present if there is going to be a future.

Elder Kriko also thinks that the photo might better be moved to the child's bedroom, but for a different reason.

Moving the picture to the boy's bedroom might be a good idea. If your boyfriend approves, it probably should be brought up casually at the dinner table. You might ask the child to tell you about the picture, how it came to be, what it means to him, etc. Ask him if he likes the picture. If so, ask him if he would like to have it in his room. If he doesn't like it, ask him if he would like to have it moved to a less prominent place in the house.

If he wants the picture to stay, it would be unwise to go any fur-ther, especially since his mother died so recently. He is very likely still feeling guilt and anger. The picture may have much more importance to him than you know. A stepmother, if that's what you will be, has to walk on eggshells when it comes to the biological mother. The boy probably will come to love you, but he may feel that in doing so he is being unfaithful to his mother's memory. You have to be the one to make it okay by honoring his mother in every possible way and respecting his relationship with her.

That big picture may be troublesome to you, but it is only A big picture, not THE big picture. That is all about warmth and love and a powerful relationship that includes your boyfriend, yourself and his son and what is best for all of you together.

Barbara, however, offers a different perspective from one who has experienced a similar loss. She says, "I still have pictures of my late husband on my walls, twenty-plus years after he died, even though I am very happily remarried."

Hopefully your boyfriend had a good relationship with his late wife, so that if she is watching you with her husband and son, she is wishing you well. I love my current husband very much and seldom think about my late husband, but he was an important part of my life.

One of the places where we missed my late husband the most was at the dinner table. No one sat in what had been his seat; we were all aware of his not being there, and it was sad. If your boyfriend put that picture up in the dining room, it might have been to help him and his son get through their meals. Just because you have entered the father's life doesn't mean that the son does not still need to see his mother when he eats.

I hope that you can enjoy this relationship while respecting that your boyfriend and his son have gone through some traumatic times. If things work out, your love will help both of them completely recover and will enrich your life. That doesn't mean that if you were to live with them that your predecessor's image still needs to be displayed in prominent places. But it does mean that you do not rush to get her out of the way.

Treefrog also believes that the late wife will always have a place in the hearts of the widower and his son—and for them, the photo is the symbol of that love.

My son, who is now forty, lost his wife of just one year. Her death was a very, very tragic one. They were just planning to start a family. It's only now that he seems to have reestablished some equilibrium in his life.

I'm bringing this up because different people recover from the loss of a soul mate in different ways, in different time frames, and to different degrees.

Your boyfriend, as with my son, will NEVER forget. If or when they encounter another possible "soul mate," that individual will have to accept the fact that there was, indeed, "someone very special" who came before them.

I think it would be wrong to suggest that he move the picture. Maybe someday he will move it. I am thinking that it will be a day when he falls so much in love that his heart expands enough to make room for another. If you can come to understand and accept this and not be disturbed, I think it will make more of a difference than suggesting that the picture be moved. He is still cherishing a memory, for both himself and his son.

Treefrog reports that Michael has landed back in California, where he is devoting himself to the art of wine-making at a small winery. Michael enjoys the work, but has told Treefrog that he doesn't know where he'll be by next year.

"Michael is doing well crushing grapes in Santa Ynez Valley," Treefrog says. "He is happy, but even though he has many friends, I believe he is very lonely and uses work and fatigue to cope. It's been quite some time since Clara's death, and he has yet to find another to love. I am not sure if he wants to.

"Meanwhile, time, and to a great extent, the Elder Wisdom Circle, has eased the pain in my heart and somewhat filled the void," Treefrog adds. "It is curious how, in reading of other people's losses and in trying to offer empathy and advice, one comes to discover what strength resides within."

The rosemary in Treefrog's garden room came from Clara's garden in California. After her death, Treefrog asked Michael if he could keep the plant. That rosemary is difficult, though. Its natural habitat is the Mediterranean, so while it grows like a weed in the West Coast's similar climate, its tastes are not easily satisfied indoors during the long winter.

Still, Treefrog carefully tends the rosemary, and probably always will. He just seems to be able to make things grow. Neighbors, he says, are always leaving bedraggled plants at his doorstep, confident that Treefrog can nurse them back to health. The solarium has become a regular plant emergency room.

Treefrog once answered a letter from an advice seeker who lamented the lack of a green thumb. "Know what I think a green thumb means?" he wrote back. "I think it means somebody who actually checks out what a plant 'wants' and what will affect it." Treefrog did not write this in his response, but he knows from experience that plants will only speak their minds if you are willing to hear what they have to say.

The writer of the letter that opened this chapter, seeking guidance in composing a eulogy for a child, later wrote back:

Dear Treefrog,
    Thank you so much for the time, love, and caring you sent my way. Your words were truly inspiring and I incorporated them into the memorial service for my three-year-old grandnephew. God bless you!

Meanwhile, a cooking tip from Chef Treefrog: A sprig or two of fresh rosemary on some New Zealand lamb chops, sautéed in olive oil, can make all the difference.

"WORDS" OF WISDOM

HuMOr

curiosity

love

ACTION

PERSEVERANCE

LISTEN

GOALS

patience

tolerance

family

spirituality

hope

charity

ATTITUDE

Knowledge speaks, but wisdom listens.

—Jimi Hendrix

◄○►

The Elder Wisdom Circle has answered more than 100,000 requests for advice. The letter below is Number 64,679:

> I love wisdom. I want to be wise. Please can you tell me how I can acquire wisdom. Thanks.

One order of wisdom to go; you want fries with that?

This impatient and rather demanding advice seeker is clearly in a rush down the path to wisdom. But one conclusion that may be easily drawn from the advice that the Elders have offered in these pages: Getting there is a slow process.

The Elders who volunteered to participate in this project have applied their wealth of knowledge—most of it born of personal experience—to many provocative letters from the Elder Wisdom Circle files. For this final chapter, we decided to pose to them a question of our own. And, as it happens, the one we dreamed up is not too far removed from the one asked above.

Question 1 (part I): *What all of you seem to have in common is that you are survivors. In your many years on this planet, have you developed any words to live by, or a philosophy of life that gets you through difficult times? Please try to sum it up in one paragraph or less.*

We realize that the phrase "One Paragraph or Less" might suggest the same sort of impatience found in the letter from the individual who "loves wisdom." We deny the charge. Rather, over the course of putting together this book, we have become aware that our participating Elders have *lots and lots* of wisdom—in fact, there is currently enough leftover advice for several more books lying on the cutting room floor. The idea of imposing a length limitation was simply to try to get the Elders to distill their thoughts so we could include as many as possible. Besides, one-paragraph wisdom will fit better on the T-shirts (just kidding, Elders).

And, in honor of the Elders' vast experience and knowledge, this question has a second part that allows our team to speak at more length—and not surprisingly, they have (so much for the T-shirt plan).

Question 1 (part II): *Feel free to take not more than a page (okay, maybe two) to elaborate on your philosophy. What life experiences led you to this conclusion? In what situations has it been helpful?*

What stands out most in the Elders' responses are the words—specific words that recur throughout their collective answers. Their stories may be different, but the Elders' "words" of wisdom are strikingly similar.

So, instead of using real letters from advice seekers as in the previous chapters, this chapter's "wisdom" takes shape around an alphabetical list of selected words that turn up frequently in the Elders' answers to this open-ended question.

Naturally, there is a great deal of overlap within the responses, since our Elders are wise enough to know there is no such thing as a simple answer. But we've tried our best to sort out, in a meaningful way, the results of our unscientific poll.

The word: ACTION
The wisdom: Take it

The members of the Webwisdom group of Royersford, Pennsylvania, aged eighty-two to ninety-four, came to a consensus on five "bullet points" that have served them well throughout their lives. This thought was on the list: "Don't wait for things to happen. Take the initiative."

Like WebWisdom, Elder Anita, seventy-four, of Brewster, New York, a retired clinical social worker, thinks that doing nothing always leads precisely nowhere. It took her a few decades to figure that out. She writes:

> When I was young, I was taught the Golden Rule ("treat others as you want to be treated"); that made sense to me and still does.
>
> In my late thirties, I learned "Do not expect rational behavior from irrational people." (That knowledge, she explains, came from trying to make sense of the erratic actions of a spouse who suffered from mental illness and alcoholism.)
>
> In my forties, I learned what Eleanor Roosevelt said: "No one can make you feel inferior without your consent."
>
> In my fifties, I learned that people ALWAYS have three choices, no matter what the situation:
>
> 1. Do nothing and keep complaining; being a victim is your choice.
> 2. Do nothing but STOP complaining; learn how to accept your situation.
> 3. Do something different.
>
> If you choose 2 or 3, I or someone else can help you. If you choose 1, you don't want help.

Throughout her life, Anita has chosen to live according to Rule Number 3: "Do something different." Her active approach became especially apparent in her early forties, when, after her failed marriage, she decided to become a social worker, and at that advanced age she began the education her family had not been able to afford for her after high school.

As an older student, Anita took a creative shortcut to amassing college credits.

> In all the years of being there for my children, I had put in a lot of volunteer time—so much so that if I made a list now, it would use up all my available space. One of the things I did was to co-edit a weekly newspaper called Africa Weekly, the only weekly newspaper in this country about Africa. When Ghana celebrated independence, I was invited to a luncheon at the UN, and I sat next to Eleanor Roosevelt.
>
> All of the activities I had participated in became a part of my "book" for independent study at a local college, and that eighty-five-page book

was the reason I was awarded eighty credits toward my undergraduate degree.

Anita continues to surround herself with people who take charge of their lives, at every age. "I have three children, four grandchildren, and I like to travel, by car when I can afford the gas, and especially with one special friend who like me believes that it is never too late to further one's education," Anita says. "She will get her nursing degree just a couple of months before she reaches her sixtieth birthday."

The word: ATTITUDE
The wisdom: Keep it positive

Adversity, suffering, pain, hardship—these words recur with heartbreaking regularity. But almost never do such terms appear as mere complaints; rather, the Elders tend to follow their personal tales of adversity with examples of how, through hard times, they've developed the strength to make their lives, and the lives of others, better.

It's all a matter, they say, of maintaining a positive attitude. Attitude is by far the factor most cited by the Elders as being crucial to their guiding philosophy. Writes Elder Ken, seventy-four, a retired Air Force officer and school administrator of Royersford, Pennsylvania:

Happiness is a decision you make.

The WebWisdom group came up with two bullet points that might fit under this particular umbrella (for those keeping score, WebWisdom now has two bullet points left; stay tuned):

Look for tomorrow to be better than the day before.
Don't dwell on your problems.

Elder Rose, sixty-four, a retired teacher of Calgary, Canada, employs emphatic capital letters as she writes:

I Am A Stubborn Optimist. That sums up my philosophy.
The most common mottos I chant are:

There's gotta be a way
I am blessed
God is Good, so all is unfolding as it should.

Nobody died here. Let's not sweat the small stuff. (See our later
category: PERSPECTIVE)

Unlike Anita, Rose does not cite Eleanor Roosevelt as a role model.
Rather, she chooses that cheerful cherub of children's fiction Pollyanna.
In Eleanor H. Porter's 1913 novel, Pollyanna's wealthy sourpuss Aunt
Polly is transformed by the girl's sunny presence. As a "tweenie," Rose
read the Glad Books, a series of sequels featuring the character that were
later published by Elizabeth Borton, and discovered "girl power." Rose
writes:

I was converted by Pollyanna's "the glass is half full" attitude. No
matter what happened, Pollyanna was NOT defeated because she re-
fused to give in to despair. In the end, of course, adults were humbled
by her powerful spirit. At that age, I needed SOME kind of power;
Pollyanna modeled power I could use.

In her response, Elder Jangela, sixty-six, of Detroit, Michigan, does
not choose to hide her past problems and challenges, but, through her
childhood recollections, enumerates the disillusionments that led to
personal growth:

Suffering is one of life's great learning tools, if used the right way.
In the fourth grade I told someone a secret and asked them not to
tell anyone. I don't remember what the secret was, but I remember
that the person immediately told everyone what I had said. I was hu-
miliated and hurt. I vowed then that I would be the kind of person
everyone could trust because I would never pass on secrets.
In the eighth grade, I, along with other classmates, was selected
to put on a mock radio show for the entire school. Over and over
and over, my teacher told me I wasn't projecting my voice enough or
my inflection wasn't good enough. He pushed me so hard I cried and
cried, but he was relentless. It worked. The show was a success

and, to this day, I am very comfortable doing public speaking of any kind.

In my workplace, I was removed, unfairly, from my position as manager of a large department. I filed a lawsuit that went to trial, to the Court of Appeals in my state and to the Supreme Court in my state. I lost the trial, won the appeal, and the Supreme Court declined to hear it, sending it back to the trial court for a new trial. We agreed to settle rather than go to trial. This process took seven years. I took an early retirement and have been able to volunteer my time for several organizations I support. In addition, I assist the law firm (whose partners have become my friends) with clients who go to trial by meeting with them and sharing my experience and how I got through it. The most important lesson of this whole experience was to love and forgive my enemy. It also taught me patience and enhanced my belief in the value of friendship. As I talk to people who are in similar circumstances regarding lawsuits and trials, I know I am sharing the fruits of my pain.

Elder Web, sixty-four, of Farmington Hills, Michigan, attributes his positive attitude to the appreciation of small pleasures.

Many of life's joys are simple, like a beautiful day, a beautiful flower, or in my case, a beautiful woman. But I also look for beauty in people beyond their exterior. It doesn't cost you a thing other than a few very enjoyable moments of your existence. How could you spend your time on this Earth any better?

Elder Dawn, seventy-four, of Rockville, Maryland, relies on the quote below to get her through hard times. She writes of the life experiences that led her, at an early age, to take those words to heart:

> "Each day there is set before us a choice between life and death, vitality and sterility. Somehow we have to get ourselves into the habit of saying 'yes' to life."
>
> —Anonymous

I won't say that was my level of sophistication at age twelve; however, that was the age of my first major crisis. My parents divorced, and in that day it was unheard of. You know how children like to be one with their peers; well, I was no longer in their league. My coping skills then were to read every book on psychology that I could, and this was my mantra and comfort.

Fast forward eight years: I married my childhood sweetheart after finishing my nursing degree. We had good years, but it turned out that he was an alcoholic. After having two wonderful boys, his problem became too much for them to witness, and I left him. This time my coping mechanisms were of a spiritual nature. The guys and I immersed ourselves in church life, and I was elected to the vestry. Out of chaos invariably comes growth. Those were good years.

There have been challenges since then; however, the early years have helped me to put most things in perspective and utilize my early methods, i.e., psychology and spirituality. With each issue that is thrown at us we build strength.

Writes Elder JeanMc, seventy-nine, of Sterling Heights, Michigan:

When things get tough, I just assume that tomorrow will be better. And it usually is. When it is worse, I take a deep breath and tell myself, "JeanMc, old girl, you'll get through this." And, so far, I have.

Elder-Student, eighty, a full-time university student in Dallas, Texas, calls faith and optimism her strongholds. In her response, she concentrates on the latter.

Regardless of the number and kinds of setbacks, roadblocks, detours, and pitfalls you will encounter in your lifetime, you must remember that nothing lasts forever, not even your troubles. Stand strong and tall, read all signals clearly and without prejudice, and be true to yourself at all times. Be ready to deal realistically with whatever issues must be managed today and go on to tomorrow with confidence and optimism.

My childhood prepared me for difficult experiences with which I would be confronted in later life. I was raised during the Great Depression and when my parents separated, my mother kept my younger sister and brother and I was sent to live with her parents in Indiana. They lived in a large home at the edge of town with lots of acreage and a fruit orchard, vegetable garden, hunting dogs, and a stability I had never known with my parents.

The experiences of my childhood allowed me to develop an attitude of acceptance of the present and optimism for a better future, always knowing that I must prepare to be independent and to rely on my own resources, not those of others.

Some of the things that I was prepared to face:

My first child was born with a malignancy, a tumor that started in the adrenal gland above the left kidney and had metastasized to the liver and aorta. At five months of age, they gave him six weeks to live. However, with prayer, great doctors, and a new treatment called X-ray therapy, he is now a prominent litigation specialist and the father of three beautiful children.

My husband was stricken with bulbar polio in the year before the vaccine was released for adults. He lived for sixteen years and did his best to provide for his family, even though he slept every night in a portable iron lung.

My middle son was murdered when two men on drugs followed him home from his work and killed him in his driveway; the thieves wanted his Mercedes and his Rolex watch. He left a wife and two small sons, three and four years old.

When my husband died, I had a man's responsibilities and I needed a man's income, so I started a small sales company. I was very fortunate to find manufacturers and importers who respected my intelligence and work ethic, and over the period of the next seventeen years I was able to support and educate my three sons.

In 2004 my youngest son offered me the opportunity to return to university to complete my bachelor's degree. I am now a junior at the University of Texas at Dallas with a 3.866 GPA.

Elder Heart of Texas, eighty-one, of Salado, Texas, has led an eclectic life. Formerly active in the Girl Scouts, she has been a librarian, an artist, and now devotes herself to writing. She has self-published several books, including a cookbook featuring low-fat, low-carbohydrate recipes; a collection of her architecture photos; and one book that seems particularly apropos to this chapter: a compendium of her favorite sayings, adages, and proverbs.

Heart of Texas has not let widowhood dampen her zest for life. As an example of her positive approach to tough experiences, she recalls how her family celebrated her late husband's life after he passed away following a long illness.

I tried to keep my positive attitude during my husband's illnesses. I continued trying to keep his spirits up even though he became worse. He reached the point where he did not want to be a burden to me and he was ready to let go. I knew what he wanted me to do and I made it as easy as I could for our children and grandchildren. He wanted me to take them somewhere special and just remember the good times. This is just what we did and it was a closure for us all.

For years he had let us know where he wanted his ashes spread. We had our memorial for him on the green of a special golf hole at 11:30 p.m. With my five children with me, I took his ashes to the bridge and let them flow into the creek below, while a CD of Bette Midler played "Wind Beneath My Wings." Then the grandchildren let balloons float into the dark sky.

I am now by myself, having moved two years ago to this special place in Texas. I live right on the golf course and am finding a great group of ladies to play golf with. This is a very active community, and I have become involved in many groups and clubs. I still feel there are things for me to learn; I may want to write another book or two when I find the time. Life has been good to me and my positive attitude is still going strong.

Elder Holiday, eighty-six, of Tarzana, California, served as office manager at an elementary school for disabled children until her retirement in 1981. Her cheerful pen name fits her personality. She writes:

No one goes through this life unscathed. No matter what one sees in other people's lives that might seem better than one's own, that's only on the surface. No one knows what goes on beneath. Envy is an exercise in futility, since not one person gets out of this life alive.

I have had several tragic events in my life that might have left me suicidal, but after the initial shock wore off, I decided that life is a gift from God and we have to make the most of this gift.

In 1956, I was severely burned in a barbecue explosion and hospitalized for seven weeks, with doctors not knowing if I'd survive. I had three small children and a loving husband, so I was determined that I was still needed and did survive, living with my scars and not allowing myself to feel disabled.

On December 25, 1975, my husband and I gave a dinner party in our home, including eight guests and the eldest of our three sons, who was visiting from another city. My husband was laughing, talking, enjoying the evening, and the next morning he was dead of a massive heart attack. He was fifty-six years old. At first, I felt I had nothing left to live for, but I was still working, had many supportive friends, and with their help overcame my grief in the determination that since I couldn't bring him back, I would have to enjoy life for both of us. I did that in retirement with unusual travels and continued interest in community service, to the point where everyone I knew looked upon me as a role model. In the early '80s, the youngest of my three sons finally came out to me that he was gay. I had suspected it for many years, denied it at first, but then accepted it by joining PFLAG, an international organization of parents, family, and friends who support their gay children.

My son became the first physician in New York to treat AIDS, and was instrumental in getting the treatment drug AZT legalized. He was loved and revered by everyone with whom he came in contact. He died of AIDS in 1989 at age thirty-seven. No emotion in the world is more devastating to a parent than the loss of a child. However, I have remained very proud of him and have continued working in the gay community for many years by cooking meals with a large volunteer group and having them delivered to people with HIV/AIDS and by getting involved with other gay rights causes.

Today, at eighty-six, I am grateful to still enjoy good health, still drive, and can continue working with energy that others, much younger, wonder at and admire.

The word: CHANGE
The wisdom: Embrace it

From Grandma-Dan, sixty-one, of Troy, Michigan, a medical social worker in a children's hemophilia clinic at a Detroit area hospital:

There is only one certainty in life that is for sure: THINGS ARE GOING TO CHANGE! So I had better accept this fact of life and stop trying to change things I have no control over!

Writes Elder Seeley, sixty-five, of Tucson, Arizona:

If I had one philosophy of life to express, it would be that everything in life is in a constant state of change, and I must adapt to survive. So many people seem determined to remain mired in "what was." Divorce hurts, but also offers new opportunities; physical infirmities lead to learning new skills; with age should come a new perspective on "what was." Who knows what the future will bring, but I am certain that is will take all of my intellect and acquired skills to survive it intact.

In my brief life (I'm only sixty-five, for Pete's sake) I have had thirteen major surgeries (my horse planted her two front feet in my abdomen and stood up, using me for leverage—it's a long story), been back to college three times, had at least four careers, had to suffer the deaths of one baby, four grandparents, two parents—and a divorce so my husband could have his eye candy on his aging arm. I have ridden the "upward mobility escalator" both up pretty high and had a remarkably fast ride down it! Now I suffer from severe arthritis and am pretty much immobile.

As I said, everything changes and we must adapt or lose. Like those trite comments: "things change" and "shit happens."

Other Elders add that the key is not only to adapt to change, but to look forward to it. Gpa-and-Gma of Rochester Hills, Michigan, ages eighty-five and eighty-one, remain dazzled and excited by progress.

Our generation has lived in and observed society evolving from horse and buggy to spaceships. From hand-cranked party-line telephones to cell phones in the pockets of hundreds of millions of people. From crystal radio sets to television. From the farm to the industrial age to the space age to "information economies." We see society savaged by drugs, liquor, tobacco, and AIDS. In our lifetimes we have seen political, racial, and religious wars and genocides, in which millions of people are killed and cities and countries are devastated. Looming ominously are environmental disasters, killer pandemics, and a deadly East-West confrontation. We elders are the living proof of the remarkable resiliency of the human race. Civilizations will progress, fall back, move on, develop new and exciting technologies, get smarter, get dumber, find joy and despair, but will always move forward to a better, saner planet.

The word: CURIOSITY
The wisdom: Don't lose it

"I'll shock you," said Elder Marble Rye, eighty-eight, a Studio City actress, widening her eyes behind her magnifying lenses during a recent conversation in her sunny living room. "I'm enjoying *right now*, being with you, and there are a lot of other times that I enjoy. But I don't mind dying. I don't mind at all, because it's such a *bother* to even go to the bathroom!"

Marble Rye, who lost a leg several years ago after being run down by a teenage driver, is just so tired of the *wheelchair*. Yes, it gets her down sometimes.

But, being a thoroughly social animal, Marble Rye's eyes light up at the chance to spend time with colleagues and friends; she belongs to a circle of actors who get together to do play readings, as well as to a book group. Despite the obstacle of the chair, with the aid of a caregiver she manages to get to the Friday night jazz concerts on the plaza at the Los Angeles County Museum of Art. "I used to be great dancer; I don't dance anymore," she says, with a straight face—but that doesn't stop her from appreciating the music.

And, after recounting the things that she enjoys, even Marble Rye herself begins to notice that the list is pretty long. When that fact is pointed out to her, she reluctantly acknowledges that she may not be allowing herself enough credit for not giving up. Maybe the film and theater community don't want to hire a—"what's the other word for cripple?"—disabled actress, she says, but Marble Rye has made a nice chunk of money during her career and, you know what, she just might use it to produce a play or a film herself.

How does she keep going? "Tenacity!" she exclaims, her former dark mood forgotten. "But the big thing is interest, and curiosity. My brother was a very famous sociologist—I sound like I'm bragging; he died some years ago—and he was a very curious person. And my husband was a very curious person. I didn't know that I was curious, but I'm finding out that I am."

Elder Web, sixty-four, of Farmington Hills, Michigan, believes that the key to maintaining that curiosity is to spend time with the youngest generation.

I enjoy being with my grandchildren; it is a constant reminder of how children look at the world, usually through eyes of wonder and curiosity. This helps keep me young, and I try to view the world through the same eyes.

The word: FAIRNESS
The wisdom: Offer it, but don't expect it

Elder Emme, sixty-three, of Bel Air, Maryland, a retired high school teacher, tries to live by three guiding principles: 1) Life isn't fair. 2) This too shall pass. 3) Fight injustice and intolerance whenever possible. On the topic of fairness, she writes:

When our children were young, most of our (and their) friends were considerably more well off financially than we were, and there were times I resented that and felt sorry for myself ("it's not fair"). It slowly dawned on me that we had one thing to give our children that many of our friends didn't: lots of time. Since we weren't "house poor," we didn't have to work extra-long hours, and since our house and yard were small, upkeep was relatively easy. That left us with lots of time to spend with the kids. By looking at things in a different way, I realized that fairness isn't necessarily important.

It is, however, important to Emme to treat others fairly, whether or not the world has done the same for her.

Both of my parents taught me that it's important to treat everyone as worthwhile individuals, my mother by her words and my father by his actions. He was the only executive in the small manufacturing company where he was employed to arrive at work at 7 a.m., when the men and women who worked on the line had to report. He felt that since he was in charge of production, it was important for him to let the workers know he was interested in how and what they did. As I went out into the real world, the lesson stuck with me and broadened naturally to wanting to fight intolerance and injustice.

The word: HELP
The wisdom: Give it

For a group of people who have joined the Elder Wisdom Circle with the express goal of helping others, this "word of wisdom" almost goes without saying. But the Elders also remind us that a word that is this important cannot be said enough.

Bullet point Number 3 from WebWisdom (four down, one to go):

Charity—give of yourself.

Elder Michelle, sixty-four, a retired high school counselor of Portland, Oregon, recalls a brief conversation with a friend that made her rededicate herself to helping others.

As I was agonizing over a picture of a baby, dead because of a war hardly anyone understood, the wise woman I was venting to exclaimed, "Look, beautiful flowers." Taken aback for a moment, I looked where she pointed and was struck by the exquisite beauty of the flowers before us. For a moment, I forgot the picture, the horror of man's inhumanity to man, but then I wanted to know how I could overcome the feeling of anger and helplessness that caused me such intense frustration with the way of the world. She said, "You do what you can to change what can be changed." And that is what I do, as much as I can. That baby a thousand miles away is my baby, too. I cannot help her, but I can help.

Gpa-and-Gma see retirement as a grand opportunity to help oneself by helping others.

When the business of business is over, and the burden of responsibilities is lifted, you have a choice. You can choose to sit in a rocking chair and rock yourself to death, or you can live and grow by investing yourself in voluntary but unobtrusive acts and words of caring and helping people.

From the three women of the Gold and Wise group of northern New Jersey, aged seventy-four to eighty-two:

Simple but true: Some words to live by have been "A little kindness goes a long way." It makes a difference in how you feel about yourself and others.

The word: HUMOR
The wisdom: Laugh

Elder Frank, seventy-two, of Greensboro, North Carolina, and Largo, Florida, recommends laughter, but knows how hard it can be sometimes.

Being positive is extremely difficult at times. My wife of twenty-six years experienced a pain in her right arm on one April 18th, and when the oncologist told me that I should just hook her up with an intravenous pain medication pump, I refused. Even though I found the leading cancer center in the area, she succumbed.

This was the most trying time of my life, but I knew I must go on and be strong for our children. Needless to say, we made it. A good sense of humor came in handy when asked "What happened?" I'd say, "Oh, she shopped till she dropped and wanted me to be left with the bills," or "I like nice accommodations, so she went to check out Heaven," but I was crying on the inside.

When one is able to make fun of themselves it shows confidence, but not to the extent of being a smarty-pants. Finding a smile during adversity makes fewer wrinkles than a frown.

The Wizeones group of Albuquerque, New Mexico, aged seventy-eight to ninety-three and led by seventy-eight-year-old Elder Rinchu, might be stiff competition for WebWisdom in the Wise Words Wars; this team came up with ten points on their list of guiding principles. Although the points from their list could fit in almost anywhere, we place this one here because humor tops their list.

Develop a good sense of humor. Take one day at a time. Don't take yourself too seriously. Relax. Say what you think. Make and meet priorities. Be a good listener. Think survival. Think positively, and turn it over to God.

Elder Elizabeth, eight-six, a teacher and author of Mission Viejo, California, has weathered her share of tragedy. Her first husband, her college sweetheart, died in World War II when his plane was shot down, leaving Elizabeth a widow at twenty-four. She remarried a year later, and during that marriage lost a child at birth.

Still, more than sixty years later, Elizabeth can boast great health, great friends, and pride of accomplishment. Oh, yes, and a finely tuned sense of humor.

My husband died after fifty-two extraordinary years together. After his death I moved to a new community. Again, my humor served me in good stead. I made many new friends and established myself as a comedy writer for a drama group. We put on a major production every year that is highly regarded. Many people have told me that they regard me as their inspiration for old age. To sum it all up, I believe that laughter and an optimistic view of life makes me what I am today.

The word: LOVE
The wisdom: Share it

Our Elder groups seem to have a fondness for "bullet points." These three bullets come from the Heavensviewsages of Delta, Colorado, aged seventy to ninety-three:

FAITH—LOVE—POSITIVE ATTITUDE

Though many individual Elders cite faith as a guiding factor, almost all of the groups write specifically of their belief in God. Perhaps this is generational; the groups, which operate in senior residences, can count among their ranks the very oldest members of the Elder Wisdom Circle, who come from a period in history when religious life played a larger role. In the case of the Heavensviewsages, however, we have put their thoughts in the love category because, in their eyes, that's where faith ultimately leads.

The love of God and His presence in our lives during nearly unbearable sadness and tragedy has taught us that the greatest gift we can give is love. Life is sometimes very hard, but we have learned that with God's help, and a positive outlook on the future, there are better things right around the corner if we can just hold on. This belief has given us the strength we need to push forward and to not look back with pain and regret.

The Rockymountain Owls, aged from late sixties to mid-nineties, also send us a powerful triumvirate. Again, the word *love* seems to dominate.

Faith, family, and love best describe our philosophy.

As we passed through life and were faced with the problems and difficulties that life holds, our faith has helped us to stay the course, while our views of others have softened. We have learned to act with the greatest love for our fellow man, and the love of, and for, our families becomes more precious as the years pass. Love and compassion can and will grow in your heart if God wields the watering can.

Elder Rinchu, seventy-eight, of Albuquerque, New Mexico, has several rules by which she governs her actions. Here is her list. See the end to find out what she has to say about love.

The following have helped me lead a good life:

- *Do not expect any one person to fulfill all of your needs and interests.*
- *Write a daily list of "gratitudes."*
- *When the road you are taking has too many obstacles, try a different one.*
- *Follow your heart.*
- *In the final analysis, you are always alone.*
- *If not now, when?*

- *When unsure of why you are doing something, ask yourself whether you are acting out of love or fear. Most people act out of one or the other.*

The word: MISTAKE
The wisdom: Don't be afraid to make one

Elder Grandma Dee of Grand Rapids, Michigan, and Tucson, Arizona, has held a wide range of jobs in her sixty-four years. She has been a general office clerk, a library clerk, and a teacher; worked on a production line and driven a bookmobile. And she is proud to say that she is still making mistakes. She writes:

If I have wisdom, it was earned by making mistakes. Sometimes by making the mistake over and over until the lesson was learned. I have not learned all lessons.

Elder Ursula, seventy-seven, a native of Munich, Germany, who now shares a home in Tujunga, California, with her astronomer husband, was named Poet Laureate of her community, Sunland-Tujunga, 2006–2008. The poet writes:

Acceptance of the fact that I would make mistakes, because I was human, not divine, came late because my parents protected me from confrontation with the realities of the world, and in that respect, I had to find my own way when I became an adult. I've survived many aspects of life that would have crippled others, and have found lasting love and great respect for the way this Earth of ours functions.

More from Web:

The first rule that I live by is the motto "Semper Avanti" ("Always Forward" for those who didn't take Latin). I have never, and will never, live in the past. I try to learn from my mistakes so I don't repeat them and remember the things that I have done right so I might do them again.

"Don't throw rocks at pigs!"—which is an Ohio boy's way of saying "Think before you act!"—was a lesson I learned early in life when

I actually threw a rock at a herd of wild pigs. It very well could have been my last day on Earth! As I said, I try to learn from my experiences. In this case I graduated summa cum laude!

Elder Laura, sixty-four, a teacher and librarian of Detroit, Michigan, believes in living life as an adventure. That, of course, results in a mistake or two along the way.

I believe mistakes are inevitable and should be used to modify your life. You can and should forgive yourself, but only after you have acknowledged your wrongdoing and taken steps to prevent a reoccurrence. It is by learning that we grow and become better people.

The word: PERSPECTIVE
The wisdom: Keep things in it

For Elder Toni, sixty-three, of Folsom, California, three important words are *live, laugh,* and *love.* Perspective, she believes, is required for all three.

When there have been tough times, I try hard not to lose perspective. If it is not life-threatening to me or anyone in my family, I know I can handle it. With age comes the beauty of seeing the bigger picture. I also think as we get older, our good health and that of our loved ones take a front row. If not, almost everything else is fixable. A favorite expression: "Don't ever confuse tragedy and inconvenience. If my ankle is sprained, it's an inconvenience. If I lose my foot, it's a tragedy."

Elder Jacobus, eighty-one, of Saskatoon, Saskatchewan, was always the "good boy" of the family, the one who always did things right. One might think he turned out that way because his parents pushed him to perfectionism. He says the opposite is true. He was raised, he says, with a healthy perspective on the difference between enjoying accomplishment and becoming an unhappy overachiever.

My father was born in 1889. Although he had only about four years of formal education, I will never forget what he said: "Do your best and don't worry." So simple and yet so profound. If I have done my best, what else can anybody expect?

Elder L. David, seventy-one, of Monterey Park, California, puts the future in perspective by comparing it to his troubled past. He figures no matter how bad it gets, it can't be any worse. L. David writes:

For the first forty-five years, I led a rather easy and successful life. I was a veteran of the Korean Conflict, graduated college with an engineering degree cum laude, had a good job and a seemingly successful marriage with two children. Then, in 1980, everything took a turn for the worse. My marriage of a little over twenty years broke up. While my wife and I were separated, my oldest child, a son, aged seventeen, died as the result of an auto accident, and just for the icing on the cake, a management change where I worked turned a previously comfortable place into a living hell.

By 1991, I had left the job that was so stressful for me, and had developed a fairly successful second career in the world of art sales. It was at this time, however, that I was diagnosed with a rare but extremely dangerous autoimmune system disease. The doctors told my then wife-to-be that I probably wouldn't leave the hospital alive. We had been planning our wedding, and decided to go ahead and send out our wedding announcements. I was out of the hospital in time to attend my own wedding.

All this is to say that I survived a lot, and I came to realize that it's a waste of time to sweat the little stuff.

Elder Ruthie, sixty-four, of Swanton, Ohio, writes:

There is a God and I am not He. (Not an original saying, but after seeing it on a poster I felt it sums it all up.) I don't know how many more years are left to me, or days for that matter, but as I face each one I turn to God and acknowledge that He IS and I am not. That truly puts everything in perspective.

From Grandma Dee:

I compare all pain to childbirth, and it makes anything tolerable.

The word: SELF-ESTEEM
The wisdom: Develop it

Elder Barbara, sixty-four, a glass artist of Greene, New York, believes that self-esteem is paramount.

The most important thing that I've learned is to be myself. I grew up feeling very unloved. When I was five years old and in the hospital in an oxygen tent and no one from my family came to visit me, I decided that there was something wrong with me and that I had to do more for others and become someone nicer so that my parents would love me. I began to pay attention to how others reacted to me rather than to myself and my own needs.

It took many years to learn to be myself. When I got in touch with my real self, I began to develop self-confidence and stopped caring so much what others thought about me.

I used to have nightmares before I went to a class, I would be so scared that no one would like me. Now I just get excited about what I am about to learn.

Elder Kriko starts at the beginning of the alphabet when he cites his guiding tenet, the three A's: Attitude, Action, and Acceptance. But in his response, he has much more to say on the subject of self-esteem.

I believe that every person needs to have appropriate self-esteem. This has nothing to do with pride or ego. A person with positive self-esteem will not allow others to bully him or her, nor will he or she take advantage of the weakness of others. Such people behave in an assertive manner rather than one of aggression or passivity.

The word: SPIRITUALITY
The wisdom: Trust it

Not all of the Elders are members of an organized religion; some don't accept the existence of God at all. Their varying spiritual lives include everything from strict Judeo-Christian observance to exploring Eastern religions to belief in reincarnation. Still, whether traditionally religious or not, most of the Elders seem to find strength in pursuing some type of spiritual understanding.

The word came up when Elder Dawn, seventy-four, of Rockville, Maryland, tried to engage the group she facilitates, the Asbury Friends, in a discussion of their philosophy of life. "As I predicted, they didn't share any personal experiences," says Dawn of her group, most of whom are in their eighties and nineties (one venerable member is 105). "This is a generation that didn't say if they had termites. They lived through two World Wars with rationing, the Depression, and several other wars after that. They are very private people."

But the determined Dawn did manage to coax a little wisdom from these elder Elders. "Probably the prevailing theme with Asbury Friends is one of spirituality," Dawn says. "One lady said that each day is a gift and our challenges are opportunities for growth. Another said that all things work together for good for those who love the Lord. Another said that she finds herself experiencing extended powers when she's doing something worthwhile."

Elder Nancy, seventy-seven, a retired teacher, may live in freewheeling Malibu, California, but attributes much of her spirituality to a strict religious upbringing—and reading a lot of good books.

> My mother, who was interested in Christian Science, instilled in me a strong belief in God's goodness. It gave me a sense that no matter how bad things looked, I was under God's care. The basis came from daily Bible study with verses I had to memorize and be able to discuss as a child. Some of the psalms I learned still come to me in my darkest hours.
>
> In addition to religious studies, my father and mother were great readers. I used to sit on my dad's lap every evening and pick out words from the newspaper he was reading. I think I first started reading when I was three; I never remember being taught.

Writes Elder Aunt Vic, seventy-two, of Eugene, Oregon:

> When the problems of life become seemingly insurmountable, I have learned to just give it all up to the Universe (what some people call God) and let the Universe take care of it. It always does, sometimes in the strangest ways.

Like Nancy, Jacobus gives a lot of credit to his parents:

I grew up in a very conservative Mennonite community in Saskatchewan. I learned to appreciate my parents' simple lifestyle and deep commitment to the Old Colony Mennonite Church. Their daily lives were governed by the Bible, the word of God, which told them to denounce worldly pleasures and live a life of humility, piety, purity, and scrupulous honesty.

Although I never saw my parents touch each other as a gesture of love, I never doubted that they had the deepest love and respect for each other. Although my mother and father never touched me other than to spank me, I knew they loved me.

I lived at home with my parents until I was twenty. During all those years, I saw my father angry only once, and that was when somebody lied to him.

As long as I can remember, I have always prayed because I have believed in a supreme being whom I learned to call God. God is spiritual and real. He is fully aware of me and I can approach Him and talk to Him. He is kind and loving. I am accountable to be likewise kind and loving to my fellow man.

Grandma Dee is not a member of any organized religion, but she relies on a strong sense of personal ethics. She writes:

The world is often cold and impersonal. Often the best helping hand is at the end of your own arm. I do not believe in praying for help or understanding. I'm not concerned about a "God" and what he thinks. I am all I can count on for sure. Sometimes I'm all another can count on, and I try to be there for sure. I can't do everything that needs to be done, but I can do a lot. I care for people, animals, and nature every day.

The word: PERSEVERANCE
The wisdom: Make it happen

Though not all of the Elders use the exact word, a lot of its synonyms—or at least close cousins—can be found throughout their replies. Frank believes in setting a goal. He writes:

A—Always have a goal, B—Believe in yourself, and C—Continue on when all seems bleak and NEVER give up hope. My first experience in goal setting came to me at a very young age. Given the opportunity to advance a grade in elementary school by completing the fifth and sixth grades in one year, I shed many a tear, to the point of wanting to withdraw from the program. My dad, who only finished the fifth grade, made up a set of flash cards and told me, "You CAN do it, but only if you want it strong enough." The rest is history; my graduation came in my sixteenth year.

Elder Helen, sixty-eight, of Sierra Vista, Arizona, also relies on the confidence instilled in her by her father:

I believe that I am a survivor because as a little girl, my father taught me that I could do anything I wanted to do. There was never a difference made between my brother and me because I was a girl and he was a boy.

I had been married, divorced, and had two daughters when I chose to enter the Army Reserve at the age of thirty-four. Just another one of my adventurous pursuits! This was difficult for me because I was the oldest person in Basic Training. The officers (male and female) gave me a hard time because they wanted to find out if I had what it took to succeed.

In addition, I was trained at Fort McClellan, Alabama. I am black, and the nearest town was a racist town. The entire experience was tough, but I did, in fact, succeed.

In all of these life experiences and situations, I had the confidence my father gave me, and I have no regrets.

Elder "Bill," eighty-five, a retired production development engineer for a major health-care product company as well as a member of the Chelsea Elders group of Warren, New Jersey, offers this no-nonsense approach:

My philosophy of life: Don't be concerned with things you cannot do anything about. Apply yourself to things you can effectively pursue and do the very best you can. I had a high school teacher who taught me to provide solutions, never excuses. In fewer words: If it works, use it.

Watchwords

The Elders are good at coming up with words of wisdom—but occasionally, they borrow them. When it comes to relying on the old sayings, saws, and adages, the Elders seem to be saying "If it ain't broke, don't fix it" (well, no one actually used *that* one). Here are a few of the most popular choices:

The Golden Rule (a favorite of Elder "Ginny," ninety-one, of the Chelsea Elders)

And this too shall pass (Grandma-Dan calls it her mantra)

Leave the world a better place (so many of the Elders, in so many different ways)

We're all in this together (Writes Elder Tina, seventy-two, of Greensboro, North Carolina, and Largo, Florida: "Maybe together we can come up with something *better*.")

Quite a few Elders, including Elder Walk-On, seventy-two, of Bethesda, Maryland, say they abide by the Serenity Prayer, written by Reinhold Niebuhr in 1943 for the Union Church of Heath, Massachusetts, and also used by Alcoholics Anonymous and other 12-Step programs:

> *God grant me the serenity*
> *to accept the things I cannot change;*
> *courage to change the things I can;*
> *and wisdom to know the difference.*

And now, back to the original letter:

I love wisdom. I want to be wise. Please can you tell me how I can acquire wisdom. Thanks.

Back when this letter came in, Elder Treefrog, sixty-five, of West Bloomfield, Michigan, took a stab at it. His thoughtful response encompasses many of the points made by the entire group throughout this chapter.

Let me begin by suggesting that we cannot just set out and "acquire wisdom." Wisdom is something that actually very quietly sneaks up and acquires you. It's not like you can go to the grocery store and purchase a bag of wisdom. It's also not something that is passed out along with a high school or college degree. One can have all the knowledge in the world and not be very wise at all.

Personally, I believe that wisdom is the ability of an individual to use their intelligence, knowledge, and experience to put a life into a proper and useful perspective, a perspective that benefits both that individual and all who come in contact with him or her. That might sound complicated, but really, it is not. It simply means that one has the ability to make a difference for the good in his or her own life and the lives of others.

What must you do to become wise? Here's what I suggest:

1. *LISTEN twice as much as you talk. Remember, even the simplest of people can teach us something. Be a "sponge."*
2. *Always look at failure as a wonderful chance to learn. Making mistakes can make you very wise if you learn from them.*
3. *Believe very strongly that the most important thing in life is LOVE. Anger and hate close any path toward becoming wise.*
4. *Know that there are some things in life that will never be understood; accept that.*
5. *Be curious about everything. When we were small children, nothing missed our curiosity. Try to rekindle and keep that curiosity. Love and respect truth in the process.*
6. *Work at developing a good value system and a moral conscience that serves you well. Never compromise them.*
7. *Remember, the path to wisdom never ends; and the person who believes he is wise probably is not even on the path.*

THE LAST WORD

And today's bonus, extra-credit wisdom question is:

In today's fast-paced world, how can anyone manage to keep track of all of these words of wisdom, remember them, and apply them to his or her own life? The operative word is contained in the lone remaining bullet point from WebWisdom. See if you can find it:

Live day to day—have patience.